Cacti and Succulents

THE COMPLETE HANDBOOK OF

Cacti and Succulents

A comprehensive guide to cacti and
succulents in their habitats, to their
care and cultivation in house and
greenhouse and to the genera and
their species.

Clive Innes

 VAN NOSTRAND REINHOLD COMPANY
NEW YORK CINCINNATI TORONTO LONDON MELBOURNE

Library of Congress Cataloging in Publication Data
Innes, Clive.
  The complete handbook of cacti and succulents.
  1. Cactaceae. 2. Succulent plants. 3. Cactus.
I. Title. II. Title: Cacti and succulents.
QK495.C115156 1976   583'. 47   76-2651
ISBN 0-442-23633-6

Contents

Preface

In the world of cacti and succulents the name of Clive Innes is so well known that no introduction is necessary. This is so for many good reasons; his long and tireless work for various societies over so many years combined with his vast knowledge and experience and his superb exhibits at so many Shows of the Royal Horticultural Society which have gained him a quantity of Gold Medals made this inevitable. Everyone knows of his admirable collections at Ashington, which are annually visited by so many thousands of people. Not everyone is aware of how widely he has travelled in search of the plants he loves, or indeed of his immense generosity in distributing rare and uncommon species to eager and grateful recipients. Having spent so long living with these plants it is inevitable that he should have acquired a knowledge which I venture to think is unrivalled in this country today. So who could be more suitable to produce a Complete Handbook of Cacti and Succulents. I make so bold as to say that this is rather a misleading title as it infers a somewhat superficial study of an enormous group of plants. This is far from the truth, for this book deals sensibly and intelligently in very readable prose with every aspect of the subject. Where they are found in nature, how they grow there, the conditions under which they occur will surprise many not too familiar with the group, but makes fascinating and absorbing reading. That they are so widespread, with so many diverse habitats is in itself of the greatest interest.

There are of course today a very large number of, in some cases, expert growers and, in others, of virtual beginners. To them the chapters on how to grow them, the temperatures required, as well as the advice on the various ailments to which they may be subject are of the greatest importance.

This book has been written by a man who has handled them himself and so has a first hand knowledge of how to deal with them. The last part of the book, the Directory, is again of great value and must have involved an immense amount of research. Comprehensive to a degree, anyone seeking information can find it here.

So it is a pleasure to recommend a book by an old friend of many years, which I know will become recognised as the standard textbook on the subject. In these inflationary days it may not appear cheap but it will be used and valued long after the initial cost is forgotten.

Maurice Mason V.M.H.

Introduction

Very few people go through life without a hobby. Many have an instinctive desire to collect – stamps, coins, antiques and so on – and those with a particular feeling for gardening, in its broadest sense, find the collecting together of plants for the sheer pleasure of growing them something which inspires and stimulates the imagination for years on end. Very few groups of plants hold a greater fascination than succulents, and once caught up by the lure of these exotics, seldom is its attraction displaced.

My own interest in succulents began many years ago, and the enthusiasm and allurement has never worn off, or even worn thin. Contrari-wise, succulents have provided endless pleasure and enjoyment, together with a constant absorbing challenge to learn more and more about them and to understand them better. Recalling those earlier days, I remember how great a problem it was to obtain plants in any great variety, and perhaps even more difficult to acquire the right type of book to tell me what I wanted to know, and in a language which I, as a layman, could understand. They were certainly few and far between. In this age we are extremely fortunate in being able to procure many authoritative works relating to cacti and the other succulents generally. Sometimes the botanic terms used can be confusing to the beginner, botanical descriptions are essential but the vocabulary of the botanic world is not exactly that used in every-day language and therefore sometimes difficult to follow. The recognition of a plant – its genus – the specific status – is what most collectors aspire to determine, but would not wish to dissect the plant, the flower, its fruits, its seeds to ascertain the correct nomenclature. Through these pages I shall endeavour to simplify the process, making reference primarily to those aspects most readily appreciated and discernable to the layman, and the beginner.

I would be the last person to question the deliberations and research activities of botanists as I have too many close and respected friends within their ranks. The fact remains however, that the botanic world is seemingly one of change, even turmoil, especially in the realm of nomenclature – the thinking of botanists and horticulturalists do not always run on parallel plains, differing opinions can exist, and undoubtedly one can be complementary to the other. While we have devoted botanists engaging continually in research, and horticulturalists using their skill and imagination to better explain to the world of 'collectors' those things which contribute to their hobby, the fascination of succulents will never fade.

Conditions – geographical and environmental – have been taken seriously into consideration with the division of the chapters. Perhaps it will be found that certain species mentioned are not usually referred to as succulents and this might cause controversy – perhaps this is all to the good. I am nevertheless convinced there is sufficient factual information available which confirms their inclusion, that they should be accepted as succulents, sometimes terrestrial, sometimes epiphytic. Succulent plants have more far-reaching associations than we may generally acknowledge.

What the plant is, to which genus or family it belongs, where it comes from, what it looks like, what peculiarities are of primary importance, the flower colour – these – and other obvious aspects are my main consideration, and I hope I have been successful in meeting this challenge. I hope this book will stimulate even more interest in this vast group of wonderful plants – succulent species of the Cactaceae and many other obvious and sometimes obscure plant families.

C.F.I.

Holly Gate, Ashington, Sussex.

Part 1
Succulents in Habitat

1 General Distribution

The world of succulent plants is one of sheer fascination, unaccountable beauty, extraordinary allurement and distinctive charm. Yet these features, which make succulents not only among the most diverse of all groups of plants but also among the most popular, have come into being mainly through the slow evolutionary processes by which they have adapted to harsh conditions – conditions under which most other plants would perish. It is this that has forced them to take on the curious shapes and modes of growth that give them their great appeal.

In spite of their diversity, all succulents (including cacti) have one thing in common: the ability to store water. All the evolutionary changes they have undergone have been in order to modify themselves to achieve this one end. Yet in fact there are only three parts of plants which can be adapted to storing water – the leaves, the stems and the roots. Succulents are, therefore, loosely grouped together according to whether they are stem succulents, leaf succulents or root succulents. The majority of cacti are typical stem succulents, as are many species of the Asclepiadaceae and Euphorbiaceae. The majority of species of Crassulaceae and Mesembryanthemaceae are typical leaf succulents. Examples of typical root succulents – in which the root system is tuberous and is generally referred to as a 'caudex' – come from a wider range of families including some, perhaps, unexpected ones: the Convolvulaceae, Cucurbitaceae, Euphorbiaceae and others.

This essential peculiarity – the ability to store

It is the sheer diversity of shape, form, size and colour that makes the world of succulent plants one of unending fascination.

water in leaves, stems or roots – brings together a host of plants from all over the world that are generally accepted as succulents. Some are cacti; others look like cacti and are easily mistaken for them because of their similarity of form, yet have no direct relationship with cacti, having merely evolved a similarity of appearance in order to adapt to a similar mode of existence. All, however, have

Euphorbia dregeana – a typical stem succulent.

Succulents from different parts of the world—an Agave from the Mexican highlands, Aloes from central Africa and *Euphorbia obesa* from South Africa—all possessing special adaptations to growing in dry conditions.

thence southwards to the Antarctic: they are found equally in the eastern and western hemispheres. In fact, they are found anywhere where the conditions might be described as those of privation.

To delve in detail into the worldwide distribution of succulent plants would require many volumes—large volumes at that—but a brief yet reasonably precise survey is useful since, by showing how and where plants grow in the wild one can gain a pretty fair idea of how to treat them in cultivation.

It is generally accepted that cacti are indigenous to the New World—as for that matter are many species of other succulent plants. Most of the non-cacti succulents occur in Africa, Asia and Australia; a few are endemic to many European countries. Thus the succulents are an extensively distributed group—ranging through the temperate zones where periods of warmth and cold alternate, periods which are usually associated with summer and winter, but which may also be extreme day and night temperature variations. By contrast, there are the torrid regions of many tropical and sub-tropical countries with their parched landscapes and relatively high temperatures which persist continuously throughout the year, knowing no seasons as such—a perpetual summer with its awful implications of drought and famine.

Europe, including Britain where native Sedums are to be found, is the natural home of several species of the Crassulaceae. Throughout southern France, Spain and Portugal are others of the same family—Sempervivum, Crassula, Aeonium and Greenovia, as well as Asclepiads, represented by Caralluma and Ceropegia, to mention but a few. The Iberian Peninsula, together with the Canary Islands and Madeira, still offer splendid scope for the adventurous plantsman! It is quite usual to find Cacti, Agaves, Aloes and other exotics established and thriving on rock faces in southern Europe and also cultivated in gardens. None of these is native to those regions; they have become naturalized over the years, and thrive in their adopted environment.

To travel through the Americas would provide a continuous presentation of succulents varying from country to country. The USA is rich in species. California, on its borders with Nevada in the region

in common the ability to resist climatic and environmental conditions and changes so extreme that they would destroy any plants that had not made these adaptations. Changes, for example, from midday temperatures well over 100°F, to night temperatures below freezing—changes which regularly occur within successive twenty-four hour periods.

Most people think of succulents, particularly cacti, as plants of the dry, arid, even desert, regions of the world. Though many do indeed come from these regions, the statement is not true of succulents in general. Succulents can be found in almost every part of the world, literally from the Arctic through the northern hemisphere to the Equator, and from of the Clark Mountains, provides Yucca and Agave together with Coryphantha, Mammillaria, the dwarf Corynopuntia and many members of the great Opuntia family. Arizona is the home of the giant Saguaro *Carnegia gigantea* and species of Ferocactus and Mammillaria. In the south of Texas are species of Ancistrocactus, Dolichothele, and Echinomastus, while Utah has its own peculiar Utahia, named for its type locality, a rarity of the Cactaceae.

Moving into the exotic Baja California, still mainly a wild peninsula, even with modern techniques gradually encroaching, with well-provided highways pushing down from the north and up from the south, the desert regions still hold the major attraction. Temperatures vary considerably on the Baja, with warm, comfortable conditions along the Pacific Coast, while bordering the Gulf of California on the east, oppressive heat is characteristic. Excit-

A very fine specimen of *Ferocactus acanthodes* over 2m tall.

A fine group of North American cacti including Ferocactus, Echinocactus and Ariocardus species.

ing plant life abounds from end to end—*Idria columnaris*, the boogum tree sometimes wrongly referred to as the elephant tree, can be found in forests in Lower California, also *Pachycormus*, the true elephant tree, rare species of Echinocereus, Mammillaria, Dudleya, Agave, endemic species from the many off-shore islands, Fouquieria, Opuntia, including the very rare *O. invicta* and Machaerocereus the creeping devil, with its long spiny branches trailing many feet in length.

On the other side of the Gulf of California, in Sonora—on the dry plateau or mountain slopes—cacti and succulents dominate the landscape. Opuntia, the prickly pear—the Cholla—in all its many forms abound, vying with the Agave for

Another illustration of the diversity of succulent body forms—including round, columnar, rosette shapes as well as curious forms such as cristate and digitate cacti.

prominence, both a menace to any unwary traveller. Mexico is the so-called home of cacti—by far the greatest number of species is congregated there, and this becomes increasingly apparent as one travels through the country. Echinocereus, Mammillaria, Coryphantha, Neobesseya, Ferocactus, Lemaireocereus and many other genera are encountered journeying southwards, and several Cereus species, usually referred to as the organ-pipe cactus, adorn the roadside. Alongside the Gulf of California plants usually attributed to Lower California are to be seen: Pachycereus, Echinocereus and Mammillaria. Below Guaymas the coastal strip becomes arid, often devoid of rainfall for months or years on end with only the moisture from the fogs, which descend on the area almost daily, bringing relief from the continual drought. Here are what are really only survivors of persistent hardship—Wilcoxia, Neovansia, Peniocereus, Opuntia and Ferocactus together with Pedilanthus and a few epiphytic Bromeliads. Through Sinaloa to Durango, Mammilopsis can be found on high rock faces, content to accept near freezing conditions at times, as well as many differing forms of Agave, Yucca and Dasylirion. Heading inland towards Coahuila are Ariocarpus, that look so very rock-like that they are indeed well nigh indistinguishable from the real rocks, Echinocereus, Hamatocactus, Thelocactus, Lophophera, Astrophytum—and near to Monterrey the beautiful *Agave victoriae-reginae*, found on the precipitous mountain slopes of the Huasteca Canyon close to Santa Catarina. Around Saltillo, mountains rising to over 6000 ft offer foothold to Echeveria species, together with cacti such as the beautiful white *Mammillaria plumosa*, clinging to minute cracks in the rock faces. Many of the most ornamental and distinctive cacti are found in Mexico. Hidalgo is the home of *Cephalocereus senilis*, where it is found on steep limestone hillsides. Beyond Mexico City species of Heliocereus abound. To the extreme south are new vistas of interest. The moist tropical zones of Chiapas and Tabasco are the beginning of the chain of rain forests which extend southwards into Central America. Here are some of the truly epiphytic cacti—Epiphyllum, Hylocereus and Selenicereus climbing and clambering through the forest trees,

Cephalocereus senilis

Chiapasia, Disocactus, Cryptocereus and other lesser known but indisputedly exotic species.

And on to Central America – to Guatemala with its lush jungle coastlines and high rugged mountains, and while epiphytes are instinctively associated with this still unspoiled countryside, species of Myrtillocactus, Lemaireocereus, Nopalea, Ritterocereus, Acanthocereus and Nyctocereus abound. From the forest areas of Guatemala and Honduras comes *Wilmattea minutiflora*, a monotypic genus of epiphytic cactus. Farther south the land narrows towards Costa Rica and Panama. The climate of Costa Rica is most variable – humid and hot in the lowlands – while the highlands provide a reasonably temperate climate. Rain forests

cover much of the country and here again the emphasis is on epiphytic genera – the monotypic *Eccremocactus bradei*, Cryptocereus, Epiphyllum, Rhipsalis, Selenicereus, Weberocereus and Werckleocereus. Acanthocereus, Pedilanthus, Yucca and Agave grow on the drier mountain slopes.

The tropical zones of South America gradually reveal new and different succulents. In the endless rain forests of Amazonia, very much of which is still unexplored, are numerous Bromeliads and other epiphytes in endless assortment and variety – *Strophocactus wittii* – the strap cactus, very rare indeed and almost unknown in cultivation, while in more northerly coastal regions of South America is Melocactus – the Turk's cap cactus. Further epiphytic species occur in Ecuador and Colombia, as do the more columnar varieties of Borzicactus, Armatocereus and Acanthocereus.

Peru is something different again, with its extremes of humid rain forests and barren Andean mountain slopes–of sullen heat and bitter cold. There are enormous contrasts in this remarkable country. It has been more thoroughly explored in recent years than other parts of South America, leading to the discovery of many new species of cacti–Matucana, Submatucana, Oroya, Arequipa, Islaya, Borzicactus, Espostea, Loxanthocereus and Melocactus–and Opuntia now providing a contrasting genus, Tephrocactus, a miniature group of the Opuntieae.

Chile, though so close to Peru, is different yet again, a long narrow strip of coastal plain and numerous off-shore islands bounded from north to south by the Andes rising to snow-covered heights. Here many genera of cacti flourish, Copiapoa, Arequipa, Browningia, Eulychnia, Neoporteria, Neochilenia, Austrocactus, Erdisia, Horridocactus, Neowerdermannia and Reicheocactus. Of the other succulents only few are indigenous and these include Portulaca, Calandrinia, Ullucus and Kalanchoë. The inland state of Bolivia is the home of Lobivia (an anagram of Bolivia), Bolivicereus, Gymnocalycium, Quiabentia (another unusual member of the Opuntieae), Rebutia, Sulcorebutia and others. Paraguay has many species similar to surrounding countries–Parodia, Notocactus, Monvillea, Echinopsis and the non-cactaceous Chorisia.

The south and east of Brazil provided some of the most popular of all cacti–Zygocactus, Schlumbergera, Epiphyllanthus, Rhipsalis, Lepismium and Pseudozygocactus–to mention just a few of the choicest and, in some instances, the rarest. Farther inland many important discoveries have been made, during the last two decades, of species which have caused excitement and interest to botanists and amateurs alike–Uebelmannia, Discocactus, Melocactus, Gymnocalycium, Notocactus; these, and others, are still a talking point with many enthusiasts and open up a continual and extensive sphere for further research.

On the higher mountain slopes of southern Argentina, almost at snow-line level, is the elusive Opuntia-like Maihuenia, while Patagonia as a whole provides many important members of the Cactaceae. In northern Argentina, where it joins borders with Paraguay, and in Uruguay, are species of Trichocereus, Gymnocalycium, Pfeiffera, Parodia, Chamaecereus, Echinopsis and Oreocereus, with some of the more xerophytic genera of Bromeliaceae–Puya, Bromelia and Abromeitiella.

The West Indian islands–from Curacao and Trinidad in the south to the northerly islands of the Bahamas–provide an ever-fascinating profusion of exotic succulents. The drier mountain slopes of many of these islands abound with Agaves–and it is worth noting that a great number of the islands have Agave species differing from the neighbouring islands, almost a matter of one species, one island. Other succulents of consequence include Jatropha, Pedilanthus, Portulaca, Kalanchoë, Furcraea, Sansevieria, Plumiera – the 'franzipani' – Chorisia, Peperomia and Talinum. In many, if not all, of these islands, the contrasting temperatures between coastal areas and mountain heights, between the leeward and windward coasts, produce varying plant characteristics–Melocactus and Pilocereus appear on the coastal fringe–usually not penetrating farther than 50 to 100 yards from the shores of the Atlantic Ocean and the Caribbean Sea. Cuba is the home of Dendrocereus and Leptocereus. Harrisia, Hylocereus and Selenicereus are found in many of the islands as are Rhipsalis species and Rhodocactus, one of the few cacti with true leaves.

The Galapagos Islands, a sanctuary of protected flora, have as endemics many attractive and sought-after plants–Brachycereus, Jasminocereus and some 'de-luxe' species of Opuntia–all exclusive to these remarkable islands.

The continent of Africa offers the greatest diversity of the 'other' succulents. The Old World still holds a glory all its own when it comes to plant-life, and succulents in particular have a high place of honour. The countries bordering the Mediterranean and the Red Sea–from Morocco through to Somalia, much of which is arid and semi-desert–produce species of Caralluma, Euphorbia, Kalanchoë, and Jatropha, while Somalia is the home of the rare Pseudolithos, the Trematosperma and Pterodiscus. The off-shore and almost inaccessible island of Socotra is another 'Galapagos'–even more so. Only one botanic expedition has been made possible for many years and that was almost an accident. Rarities exist in wild array–Adenium, Caralluma, Echidnopsis, Edithcolea, Dendrosicyos, Dorstenia and Pedalium, to mention but a few.

Many of the desert regions of Arabia have their endemic species of Caralluma and other members of the Asclepiadaceae, especially Euphorbias, shrunken and leafless so as to provide the smallest possible area through which moisture can evaporate. Farther south, in East Africa, are countries of extremes–areas of savannah, of humid mountain slopes and valleys where hosts of succulents of many genera capture the eye: Pelargonium, Stapelia, Huernia, Caralluma, Lithocaulon, Merremia, Turbina, Gerardanthus, Kedostris, Corallocarpus, Momordica. Kenya in particular is the home of many remarkable succulents; Pyrenacantha with its huge swollen trunk, species of Euphorbia, Synadenium, and Dorstenia are but a selection, while many species of the Ascelpiadaceae, Gynura, Stenadenium, Adenium and Adenia, together with Aloe and Sansevieria, are native to Tanzania.

On the west coast a totally different character of succulent is dominant. The West African countries of Nigeria and Ghana have peculiar forms of Euphorbia indigenous to their respective countries, together with Kalanchoë, Aloe, Jatropha, Stephania and Cissus.

It is best to consider South West Africa apart from South Africa–because it covers so vast an area. Much of this terrain remains comparatively unknown botanically–though what is known is decidedly enthralling. An endless array of Aloes and Mesembryanthemums colours the landscape, backed-up by Euphorbias together with Ammocharis and Haemanthus of the Amaryllidaceae; Pachpodium species, Asclepiadaceae represented by Decabelone, Duvalia, Hoodia, Hoodiopsis, Huerniopsis, Piaranthus, Stapelia, Tavaresia and Trichocaulon. Here too is the baobab tree *Adansonia digitalis*, Commiphora, Othonna, Ipomoea, Adromischus, Cotyledon, Kalanchoe, Acan-

thosicyos–a rare cucurbit–together with unusual succulent forms of Pelargonium and Sarcocaulon. One of the world's wonders also comes from South West Africa–Welwitschia–a huge desert plant giving the effect of a gigantic bulbous species, believed by some botanists to be the 'original' flowering plant. It would be possible to go on elaborating the various succulents from this vast countryside–many rarities, Dolichos, Moringa, Ceraria, Cissus and Chamaegigas.

In South Africa each province seems to provide different dominant succulents. Because the seasons are in complete contrast from east to west, there is a never-ending opportunity to enjoy flowering succulents at almost any time. Mesembryanthemaceae or Ficoidaceae or Aizoaceae–whichever naming is most acceptable (they are all the same)– abound throughout most provinces from Cape Province in the south to Natal and Transvaal in the east. Aloes also are an eye-catching feature. In addition, many other succulents endemic to the south–Stapelia, Kinepetalum, Luckhoffia, Pectinaria, Stultitia and the tuberous-rooted Brachystelma–are representative of the Asclepiadaceae, as well as species of the Senecio, Othonna, Kalanchoë also Kedostris and Melothria. The elephant's foot *Testudinaria elephantipes* and other Dioscoreaceae are also from South Africa, and Liliaceae in its many varied forms–Bowiea, Bulbine, Chamaealoe, Drimia, Gasteria, Haworthia–in addition to Aloe already mentioned, help to garnish the picture.

Madagascar 250 miles off the east coast of Africa, is the homeland of some of the most beautiful and awe inspiring of all plant species–and many are succulents. This is a large island, nearly 1,000 miles in length, mountainous in the north, with rain forests towards the east and vast plateaux in the centre. In recent years extensive exploration by diligent botanists has resulted in many new succulents being recorded. Some expeditions were made only just in time, before the area was deliberately cleared for agricultural purposes. Aloes, Kalanchoës, Euphorbias–many having the distinctive quality of being of miniature growth–and Rhipsalis were found, the last being one of the few true cacti found outside the Americas. To elaborate on the flora of Madagascar would be an encyclopædic – a mammoth – task, but a few plants must be mentioned. Pachypodium, Cynanchum, Stapelianthus, Trichocaulon, Adansonia, Senecia, Corallocarpus, Seyrigia, Xerosicyos, Alluaudia, Decaryia, Didierea, Jatropha, Iomatophyllum, Adenia, Peperomia, Uncarina, Cyphostemma – these and many others constitute what is undoubtedly one of the grandest conglomerations of plant life to be found anywhere in the world.

Australia has a number of succulent plants, most of which are rare in cultivation and yet not difficult to rear successfully once obtained. Dischidia, Hoya, Sarcostemma, Adansonia, Bulbine, Xanthorrhoea, Anacampseros, Calandrinia, Portulaca, Myrmecodia and Hymenanthera are representative of the many species within these and other genera, and it is likely that future exploration could provide an ever-increasing list of such exotic succulents.

Many parts of Asia have relatively few succulents. The sub-continent of India has Sansevieria, Ceropegia, Caralluma, Dischidia, Hoya, Arthrocnemum, Kalanchoë and Coleus, while far away to the east the Philippines also provide Dischidia and Hoya. Japan has a few indigenous species related to the Crassulaceae – Meterostachys and Orostachys – and from the regions of the Himalayas and China are still further members of the Crassulaceae, namely Sempervivella and Sinocrassula.

Finally, Malaysia and the other East Indian islands all have romantic vegetation, the monsoons providing tropical forests containing a profusion of exotics. This is one of the principal homes of orchids, but nevertheless succulents do feature prominently. All are epiphytic or semi-epiphytic, or at least have an association with the forest regions. A number of Hoya species, succulent Impatiens, Senecio, Kalanchoë, Coleus, Hydnophytum and Myrmecodia – the ant tuber – all grow here. If for no other reason, this region deserves mention on account of the last two species.

More clarification will be given when individual species and genera, so briefly surveyed in this chapter, are described more fully in the chapters that follow.

2 Epiphytes and Rain-Forest Cacti and Succulents

Epiphytic plants are so distinct in their life style that they really deserve a book to themselves. The peculiarity of using other plants as accessories to their growth and development provides a unique characteristic – yet on the other hand, many of the same species are capable of surviving and indeed prospering in terrestrial conditions. They prove an endless fascination to the connoisseur – not only the succulents, but also in the orchids, bromeliads and ariods.

Epiphytes should not be confused with parasites. There is an important difference. While parasites derive sustenance from the host plant, and can not exist in any other way, epiphytes simply use the host as a method of 'anchoring' themselves. They take no nourishment at all from the live tissues of the host plant; the only advantage they gain from their hosts is the humus from the decaying leaves of the tree, which may accumulate round the root system of the epiphyte.

The association of epiphytic plants with rain forests is not accidental, since only in rain forests is there sufficiently high atmospheric humidity to support their mode of growth, although a number of species are to be found in more arid conditions and might better be termed 'xerophytes'. To adequately define a rain forest and to explain the environmental conditions which exist in one would demand consideration of a great number of highly complex interrelationships. Suffice it to say that these densely wooded, vine-entangled forests – dripping moisture long after the tropical rain shower has passed, where at times a subtle quietness pervades and animal and bird life momentarily appears to be non-existent (though there are occasions when the shrill sounds from birds and insects become almost intolerable) are where some of the most beautiful exotic plants grow.

In the rest of this chapter we shall take a closer look at epiphytic and rain forest cacti and succulents, considering the cacti first, placing them into their botanical divisions and providing sufficient description to make recognition possible. Hence some botanic details, such as fruit and seed, may be omitted if other aspects are sufficient to make identification fairly simple. It is not intended to refer to every species unless peculiarities justify it.

Epiphytic cacti are grouped into three divisions – Hylocereaneae, Epiphyllanae and Rhipsalidinae – a classification created by Dr Britton and Dr Rose, pioneer botanists in the realm of cacti. Some slight adjustments and amendments have been proposed by later botanists; in fact the question of further changes is currently undergoing considerable investigation. However, for an easily appreciated presentation of the kinship of differing species, the Britton and Rose classification is used here, and any pertinent findings by other botanists are duly noted.

Agavaceae
The genus *Sansevieria* provides the only epiphytes in this family. The species described is decidedly epiphytic: some others are indifferently epiphytic or terrestrial.

Sanservieria grandis from Somali with large broad obovate leaves, deep green with reddish margins and having numerous thick rhizomes. Flower in dense raceme, whitish, followed by greenish, turning black, berries.

Species have been found in tropical East Africa

in recent years – all epiphytic but still awaiting descriptions.

Araceae

Are well known as exotic plants, particularly the genus *Philodendron*. Due to the presence of aerial roots many might be considered epiphytic, but only those are noted which are totally epiphytal and succulent – and this only represents a small selection from a great number.

Philodendron cannaefolium Mart.
Very succulent stems with deep green ovate leaves and red margins. A Brazilian species with creamy-white spathe and yellow spadix.

Philodendron fragrantissimum Kunth.
Has large arrow-shaped leaves with many depressed veins. A beautiful and rare species with purplish-white spathe having an elusive fragrance. From eastern Venezuela and Guyana.

Philodendron laciniosum Schott. (syn. *P. pedatum*)
From northern Brazil and Guyana, epiphytic on trees or rocks. A climbing species, large leaves with 3 to 5 broad lobes and pronounced midrib. Spathe greenish-white and cream spadix.

The naming of plants may need some explanation to those unfamiliar with the international formulae. A plant name consists of three parts: 1) the name of the genus eg: *Acanthocereus*, 2) the specific name eg: *pentagonus*, and 3) the name of the person who gave the plant that name; this normally appears in an abbreviated form, and a full list of authors will be found at the end of the book. In the case of *Acanthocereus pentagonus* this name was given to the plant by Br. and R. The currently correct name for this plant is therefore *Acanthocereus pentagonus* Br. & R. This is the currently accepted name of the plant. This plant, however, was originally known under another name and this gives rise to confusion. The plant was originally named by Linnaeus and his initial therefore precedes the initial of the current author. The full name therefore becomes *Acanthocereus pentagonus* (L.) Br. & R. The name which Linnaeus gave the plant appears as a synonym – in this case, *Cactus pentagonus* (L.). The entry therefore appears as: *Acanthocereus pentagonus* (L.) Br. and R. (Syn *Cactus pentagonus* LL.)

In general, the book is so organized that the genera are arranged within their sub-tribes and tribes. Occasionally it has been necessary to depart from this arrangement and in these cases the sub-tribes is given in brackets, following the generic, specific and author's name eg: *Opuntia quimilo* Sch. (Platyopuntia).

Philodendron rudgeanum Schott. syn. Ariod 78 (syn. *P. cannifolium*) with beautiful lanceolate leaves, deeply channeled and having white spathe with yellow spadix. A showy species from Guyana.

Philodendron saxicola K. Krause
A beautiful species with leathery sword-shaped leaves. Usually saxicolous, but sometimes epiphytic on trees. A rare and unusual plant.

Philodendron teretipes Sprague
Has elongated sword-like leaves with many prominent veins, glossy-green with red margins. Colombia.

Philodendron wittianum Engl. from the Amazon rain forests above Manaus. Has oblong leaves similar to a Musa and about 50 cm in length. A creeping epiphyte with pale green spathe and cream spadix.

Asclepiadaceae

Includes the genus *Hoya* most of which are climbers frequenting forest regions. The majority are succulents but only few have epiphytic habit. This genus embraces a great number of species – often referred to as the 'Wax Flower' – and with only minor exceptions the flowers give rise to this description.

Hoya engleriana Hoss.
A pendent species with thin stems, climbing or creeping. Leaves very small, elliptical, upper surface convex, dark green. Flowers in umbels usually 4 together, white with purplish centre. From Thailand.

Hoya linearis Wall
The most noteworthy epiphyte of this genus, has thin, almost thread-like leaves on pendent stems with scented whitish small flowers. Himalayas.

DISCHIDIA are also of the family Asclepiadaceae, and include some remarkable plants of unusual growth and habit. Most species are true epiphytes.

Dischidia pectinoides H. H. W. Pears.
Thin trailing stems, rooting freely. Leaves opposite, oval-lanceolate and tapering to the tip, thick, urn-leaves like a mussel with many nerves and an opening at the base into which grows a root. The whole plant is grey-green. Small flowers at leaf axils, purplish-red. Philippines.

Dischidia platyphylla H. H. W. Pears.

A climbing vine with many thin branches. Leaves opposite, greyish-green, somewhat rounded or kidney-shaped. Flowers small, pitcher-shaped 4 mm diameter, pale buff. Philippines.

Dischidia rafflesiana Wall.

With thin twining stems having opposite leaves starting small and rounded, later becoming large pitcher-like, hollow, fleshy-green outside, purplish inside, often frequented by ants in habitat. Flowers yellowish in umbels. From Malaysia and Australia.

There are over 40 species recorded all having very similar peculiarities; others of particular importance include *D. merillii* Becc. and *D. collyris*.

Epiphytic succulents are by no means encompassed in this chapter – the story as we know it is still not fully told. Even more exciting is the fact that the rain forests of tropical and sub-tropical regions, and even more temperate climates, have still not been totally explored, and therefore it is conceivable that many more species have yet to be discovered and introduced into cultivation.

Crassulaceae

Has representative epiphytes.

Echeveria rosea (Bak.) Lindl. is apparently the only true epiphyte of the genus Echeveria. Frequents forest trees in eastern and central Mexico. Has very closely set spike of pinkish-red flowers.

Kalanchoë gracilipes (Bak.) Baill. also from Central Madagascar with obovate elongated leaves, a true epiphytic creeper – very rare in cultivation.

Kalanchoë porphyrocalyx (Bak.) Baill. from Central Madagascar with fleshy crenated but small leaves and developing aerial roots. Flowers usually pink but yellow flowering species have been observed.

Kalanchoë uniflora (Stapf.) Hamet, from forest areas of Ambre, Madagascar, with small fleshy leaves, crenate near the apex and having small reddish 'urn-shaped' flowers.

Epiphyllanae

Mostly epiphytic cacti, the majority of genera consist of nocturnal flowering species while other genera are composed of totally diurnal flowering varieties. Associated with rain forest regions, growing on trees or saxicolous on rock faces in the shade of trees, where the crevices have become receptacles for soil rich in humus. The majority are spineless, but there are noteworthy exceptions.

This group has been under consideration by botanists for a long time, and indeed there are several schools of thought generally conflicting one with the other. In recent years several species have been transferred from one genus to another within the Epiphyllanae, as also have a few species from the Rhipsalidinae been transferred to genera within this group. Furthermore, some genera have been merged with other genera.

It would appear that many appreciate the well-known nomenclature, and to avoid confusion each species will receive explicit mention, giving, where appropriate, the current findings of a number of botanists. Embraces some of the most fascinating of all Cactaceae; all species have truly exotic flowers, including those which have made acceptable houseplants for many generations. It is also interesting to note some hybrid genera where one or both parents are included in this sub-tribe.

DISOCACTUS Lindl.

A much branching epiphytic group, having flattened stems and branches, sometimes terete. Flowers diurnal. Indigenous to Central America. Of easy culture, and providing a most desirable flowering plant.

Disocactus alatus (Swartz) Kimn.

A true epiphytic species with lanceolate stems having crenate margins. Small yellowish-cream flowers with slender style and 5 stigma lobes. From mountainous regions of Jamaica. Long known as *Pseudorhipsalis alata* (Swartz) Br. & R.

Disocactus biformis Lindl.

Long branched species with fleshy, flattened stems with slightly serrate margins. Long slender flower, magenta with purple style and 4 white stigma lobes. From Guatemala and Honduras.

Disocactus eichlamii (Wein) Br. & R.

Tends to branch from the base with wider and more serrated stems than *D. biformis*. Flowers bright red, about 4 cm long. Style protrudes with 5 stigma lobes. From Guatemala.

Disocactus himantocladus (Roll.-Goss.) Kimn.
Stems flat and elongated, branching freely with small creamy pink flower with white style and 4 stigma lobes. Endemic to Costa Rica. Known as *Pseudorhipsalis himantoclada* (Roll.-Goss.) Br. & R. until transferred to Disocactus.

Disocactus macranthus (Alex.) Kimn. & Hutchis.
An attractive, easy-flowered epiphytic species. Long strap-like stems with slightly crenate margins. The flower is sweetly scented, yellowish-cream and floriferous, usually in winter months. Widely known as *Pseudorhipsalis macrantha* Alex. until transferred to the genus Disocactus. From high altitudes in Chiapas, Mexico, and possibly also in Guatemala.

Disocactus nelsonii

Disocactus nelsonii (Br. & R.) Lindinger.
From high altitudes in south Chiapas and Guatemala. Many-branched elongated species with flattened stems, margins obtusely crenate. Flower purplish pink on tube up to 3 cm long, and short-lived. Rare in cultivation. This once constituted a monotypic genus, *Chiapasia*, now merged with Disocactus. Stigma yellow.

Disocactus nelsonii v. *hondurensis* Kimn.
A distinctive variety of the species, branching from the base and with larger flowers. Stigma purple. From Honduras.

Disocactus quezaltecus (Standl. & Steyerm.) Kimn. from Guatemala. Originally *Bonifazia quezalteca*.

Disocactus acuminatus (Cuf.) Kimn. from Costa Rica and Guatemala. Earlier known as *Pseudorhipsalis acuminata*. Both are recognized species and are possibly distinctive–but bear certain pronounced similarities to others.

Disocactus ramulosus (Salm-Dyck) Kimn.
A much-branching species with thin, flattened stems, terete at base. New growth commences reddish and gradually changes to green. Stems crenate with small lobes. Has small open flower, pinkish cream. Widely distributed species–Guatemala, Costa Rica and some West Indian islands. Originally *Rhipsalis ramulosa* until incorporated within the genus Disocactus.

ECCREMOCACTUS Br. & R.
A monotypic genus of considerable interest and having unique characteristics. Epiphytic with pendent habit. The low branches are flat and thick. From the dense forest regions of Costa Rica, usually at low altitudes.

Eccremocactus bradei Br. & R.
Light dull green branches with regular slightly crenate margins. Flower pinkish-white or creamy-white, nocturnal. Short tube only about 1 cm long. A rare species in cultivation, most easily recognized by the very broad, thick, strap-like stems, often to 30 cm long and pendent habit.

NOPALXOCHIA Br. & R.
Very closely related to Epiphyllum, with which it is often confused. The genus was originally erected for *Nopalxochia phyllanthoides* (D.C.) Br. & R. and subsequently three other species have been included. All epithytic with reddish or pink flowers. All species from Mexico, although escapes have naturalized in northern parts of South America.

Nopalxochia ackermannii Haw.
For a long period this was considered a hybrid, but in recent years collections have been made in south Mexico as wild plants, and therefore the species now appears to be recognized. This certainly differs considerably from the hybrid varieties named *Epiphyllum ackermannii*, in particular as far as stem growth is concerned. Stems, usually flattened and thin with slightly crenate margins, sometimes 3 or 4 angled; branches freely, mostly from the base.

Nopalxochia phyllanthoides × '*Deutsche Kaiserin*'

Flowers crimson, diurnal. Style rose-pink, short, and white stigma lobes.

Nopalxochia conzattianum MacDoug.

With firm strong branches, thick with pronounced crenations along the margins and areoles. Flower is bright red with short tube. Style red with purplish stigma lobes about 5/6. From about 6,000 ft in rain forest in the Mixe district, Mexico. Still a great rarity for which a genus *Pseudonopalxochia* Backeb. was created, but now considered invalid.

Nopalxochia macdougallii (Alex.) Marsh.

Elongated flattened stems, thickish with pronounced crenations and areoles. Generally of pendent habit, branching from the base. Flower lilac-rose, medium-sized with stoutish style and up to 6–9 short stigmas about 5 mm long. From near Cerro Hueitepec, Chiapas, southern Mexico. A day-flowering species, still rare in cultivation. When discovered it was considered to have differing characteristics to Nopalxochia, and the genus *Lobiera* Alex. was created, and was known as *Lobiera macdougallii* Alex.

Nopalxochia phyllanthoides (D.C.) Br. & R.

Branches freely, terete at base, but generally flattened and thin above. Stems bright green with crenate margins. Flowers are shades of pink about 2/3 cm wide on short tube 2 cm long. Long slender style with 5/7 stigma lobes. A very decorative house-plant of easy culture. A hybrid of this species, *Nopalxochia* (sometimes *Epiphyllum*) × '*Deutsche Kaiserin*', has proved one of the most exceptional examples of remarkable hybridizing, resulting in an outstanding plant which has been popular for many generations.

WITTIA Schum.

Epiphytic plants growing from trees and rockfaces. Have elongated branches, flattened with pronounced midnerve. Margins undulating. Flowers very small with a very small insignificant tube. Almost unknown in cultivation.

25

Wittia amazonica Schum.

Flattened branches, coarsely crenated. Flower small, 2/3 cm long, magenta, almost cylindrical on very short tube. From north-eastern Peru near to the Brazil frontier.

Wittia panamensis Br. & R.

Very flattened branches, elongated, dark green with low crenations. Flower purple or magenta with protruding style and stamens. From near Chepo in Panama, and distributed in northerly South American countries.

EPIPHYLLANTHUS Berger.

A rare and unusual genus consisting of three species, although one is in doubt, and if it does exist is likely to be only a varietal form of another. Have small segments like Zygocactus and Schlumbergera, but they have the resemblance of Opuntia pads in miniature. From high altitudes, growing usually in shade of rocks, generally semi-erect but inclined to become pendent. Flower zygomorphic. Currently it is proposed that this genus should be merged with Zygocactus into Schlumbergera. There is undoubtedly a kinship, especially with Zygocactus, but segregation would still seem to be preferable.

Epiphyllanthus candidus (Löfg.) Br. & R.

Not a great deal is known of this species, said also to originate from Mt Itatiaya at very high altitudes with spiny, terete joints and white flowers. Not known in cultivation and could be a variant of one of the other two species.

Epiphyllanthus obovatus (Engelm.) Br. & R.

Sometimes better known as *Epiphyllanthus opuntioides* (Löfgren & Dusen) Moran, in Gentes Herb. viii, 328/345 (1953) which should stand. A much-branched miniature plant, with small opuntia-like segments, dark green and fleshy. Flower purple and lilac, zygomorphic. Found at high altitudes on Mt Itatiaya, Brazil, where the distribution appears to be very limited. This sometimes is referred to as *Zygocactus opuntioides*. Rare in cultivation.

Epiphyllanthus obtusangulus (Berg.)

Synonymous with *Epiphyllanthus microsphaericus* (Engel.). More slender branch segments than the preceding, generally more elongated, somewhat spiny. Flower zygomorphic, purple and lilac-rose.

Very rare in cultivation. From Mt Itatiaya, Brazil.

EPIPHYLLOPSIS A. Bgr.

An obscure genus pertaining to Schlumbergera, but is not in general use. Further supposed generic differences within the Schlumbergera-Zygocactus-Epiphyllanthus complex would only add to the confusion which already exists. Due to the popularity of so-called Epiphyllums, or orchid cacti, it is much simpler to stick to the validated generic naming now in use. Many of these exotic flowering cultivars have no known parentage within the genus Epiphyllum, but have been wrongly attributed, due to the apparent epiphytic habit of some of the parent plants.

The following are some of the more notable such hybrids.

X APOROPHYLLUM

Parents: Aporocactus x Epiphyllum(?) or x Heliochia or x Heliphyllum.

Many interesting cultivars are now available with the appearance of Aporocactus and the exotic flowers associated with present-day Epiphyllum cultivars.

X EPIXOCHIA Rowl.

Parents: Epiphyllum x Nopalxochia

x *Epixochia amarantina* Rowl. is the type product. Several other well-known cultivars are obviously of the same parentage.

X HELIAPORUS Rowl.

Parents: Heliocereus x Aporocactus

x *Heliaporus smithii* (Pfeiff.) Rowley (synonym: *Aporocactus mallisonii*) is the popular and well-known type product.

X HELIOCHIA Rowl.

Parents: Heliocereus x Nopalxochia

x *Heliochia vandesii* Rowl. (syn. *Epiphyllum* x *Jenkinsonii*) and many others have this origin. One of the earliest recorded of British cactus hybrids.

X HELIOSELENIUS Rowl. in L.C.

Parents: Heliocereus x Selenicereus

x *Helioselenius maynardii* (resembling Selenicereus

in many respects but with large red exotic flower) is product.

x HELIPHYLLUM Rowl.
Parents: Heliocereus x Epiphyllum
x Heliphyllum are well represented among the Epiphyllum hybrids–flower colours range from white to purplish-red–type x *Heliphyllum charltonii* Rowl.

x SELENIPHYLLUM Rowl.
Parents: Selenicereus x Epiphyllum
x *Seleniphyllum Cooperi* (syn. *Epiphyllum cooperi*, *Epiphyllum crenatum* v. *kimnachii*) and others of the white or cream flowering cultivars are products of these parents.

For many years the name *Phyllocactus* was used for these plants, and more recently Rowley has proposed *Epicactus* as being more appropriate. This would appear very suitable as all cultivars involved have Epiphytic cacti as one or both parents – which excludes the assumption that all are indeed products of Epiphyllum crosses.

EPIPHYLLUM (Herm.) Haw. non Pfeiff.
Mostly epiphytic with thin flattened stems, occasionally 3-winged. The areoles are very small, and while soft spines are seen at seedling stage, they rapidly disappear as mature growth develops, and to all intents and purposes the stems are spineless. All have large or very large flowers, usually white or cream, perfumed and mainly nocturnal flowering. Indigenous to many parts of Central and South America, Mexico and the West Indian islands. Some species have been used for hybridizing, resulting in an extraordinary array of numerous beautiful cultivars.

Epiphyllum anguliger (Lem.) Don.
Another rick-rack species. Much branched with bright green stems and marginal lobes which are generally more pointed than *E. darrahii*. Scented white flower on stout tube–style and stigma lobes white. A popular species endemic to Mexico. Another species, *Epiphyllum gertrudianus*, seems to be very similar to both *E. anguliger* and *E. darrahii* and might be an intermediate form.

Epiphyllum cartagense (Web.) Br. & R.
A very distinct species from Costa Rica. A true epiphyte with short, sometimes elongated stems, bright green in colour and slightly toothed or crenate margins. Flower white with reddish tube. Style pale pink or whitish and bright yellow stigma lobes. Still uncommon in cultivation.

Epiphyllum caudatum Br. & R.
Has elongated lanceolate stems, tapering towards the tip and the stalk. Develops into a many branched plant, the older stems becoming terete. Leaf margins undulating without spines. Has white flowers about 7 cm long. Little is known of this species from authoritative sources, and many pertinent characteristics of this species have not been recorded. Endemic of Mexico from the region surrounding Oaxaca.

Epiphyllum chrysocardium Alex.
One of the most outstanding discoveries of recent years from the northern region of Chiapas, Mexico, in tropical rain forests. So wide is the stem and so deeply crenated, it was at first thought to be a 'tree fern'. Stem to 30 cm wide and deep-set lobes about 15 cm long which gradually taper towards the tip. Very large flower, pure white with rich golden filaments; this feature provides the name, which translated means 'Heart of Gold'. A unique and very desirable species requiring more care than most of this genus. At one time included temporarily in the genus *Marniera* (Backeb) created for this and *E. macropterum*.

Epiphyllum crenatum (Lindley) G. Don.
A very popular and well-known species from Honduras and Guatemala. Has been used extensively in cross-pollinating with species of other genera to develop many beautiful Epiphyllum cultivars. Has thick glaucous branches, stiff, strong and erect, with fairly deep crenations along the margins. Flowers are diurnal, creamy white and about 15 cm wide. Sweetly scented, lasting many days.

This genus has been considered fairly extensively on account of the problems which still exist in nomenclature. Other species recorded, *Epiphyllum ruestii*, *Epiphyllum gigas*, and *E. costaricense*, are of obscure origin and are much in doubt, and therefore not mentioned.

Epiphyllum darrahii (Schum.) Br. & R.

One of four rick-rack stemmed species. The marginal lobes are generally rounded, usually obtuse. Flower creamy-white on long tube, very fragrant. Very long style, pure white and 8 stigma lobes. Endemic to Mexico.

Epiphyllum grandilobum (Web.) Br. & R.

Many-branched plant with broad stems and deeply lobed margins. This large-growing species is still rare in cultivation and has not proved of easy flowering. Flower is large, white and nocturnal. These develop on a curved tube, are about 26cm wide, funnel-shaped. Style protruding beyond stamens, with many yellowish stigma lobes. Indigenous to Costa Rica.

Epiphyllum guatemalense Br. & R.

Strong-growing species with flat, bright green, fairly wide and soft stems with rounded crenations. Very large flower, white, up to 24 cm diameter. The yellow style has 12/13 deep yellow stigma lobes. Indigenous to Guatemala. This might also be a variety of *E. phyllanthus*; Kimnach proposes this: *Epiphyllum phyllanthus v. guatemalense* (Br. & R.) Kimn. In cultivation a most floriferous species.

Epiphyllum hookeri Haw.

Long thin light green stems with pronounced crenations on the margins. Flower white up to 15 cm wide, nocturnal. Long style about 16 cm long, magenta or purplish, perhaps shaded orange at base and apex. About 14 yellow stigma lobes. Doubt exists as to whether this species, together with *E. stenopetalum* and *E. strictum*, are synonymous. However, Kimnach does not recognize these other two species, and gives varietal status to *Epiphyllum hookeri*, viz: *Epiphyllum phyllanthus v. hookeri* (Haw.) Kimn. Indigenous to Trinidad and Tobago, Guyana, Venezuela.

Epiphyllum lepidocarpum (Web.) Br. & R.

One of the most rare species of this genus with thickish and rather narrow stems having slight crenations along the margins. Medium-sized white flower with white style and yellow stigma lobes. Nocturnal. From isolated area near Cartago, Costa Rica.

Epiphyllum macropterum (Lem.) Br. & R.

A species of doubtful authenticity – possibly synonymous with *E. thomasianum* and with *E.*

thomasianum v. *costaricense* (which would not appear to justify varietal status). In keeping with the synonyms, it is widely distributed throughout Costa Rica, Guatemala and S. Mexico.

Epiphyllum oxypetalum (De Cand.) Haw.

Possibly synonymous with *E. latrifons*. Recorded from Mexico and Guatemala where it is indigenous, and also escapes in Brazil and Venezuela. A much branched plant with flattened thin stems, tapering towards the apex, and wavy margins. Nocturnal flowering with long curved tube (hence this species sometimes called the 'Dutchman's pipe'). Flower white and cream. Style thick and long, about 20 cm and stigma lobes cream. A very popular plant of easy culture.

Epiphyllum phyllanthus (L.) Haw.

Widely distributed in many parts of Central and South America – Brazil, Peru, Bolivia, Panama, Guyana, Trinidad and Tobago. Has elongated stems, usually flattened, light green with a very definite purplish margin. Flower up to 30 cm long, slender and scented, white in colour. Slender tube and long slender rose-pink style and about 10 white lobes. Nocturnal flowering.

Epiphyllum phyllanthus v. *boliviense* (Web.) Backeb.

Differs from the species in the wider stronger stem, and flowers much larger and inclined to be luminous. Beautiful scent. Endemic to Bolivia.

Epiphyllum phyllanthus v. *colombiense* (Web.) Backeb.

Smaller flower than the species – to about 10 cm long – short tube with pinkish style having 5/7 white lobes. From Colombia, Ecuador, Costa Rica and Panama.

Epiphyllum phyllanthus v. *rubrocoronatum* Kimn. C. & S. J.

Long slender branches, flower similar to species but with larger style which is pinkish-orange below and deep red or purplish above and has 10/13 orange lobes. Endemic to Panama, Colombia and Ecuador.

Epiphyllum pittieri (Web.) Br. & R.

Stems are flattened and thin, the margins coarsely toothed. Flower white and small, up to 15 cm long and only 9 cm wide. Shortish style about 12 cm with about 13 cream coloured lobes. Beautifully scented, with perfume resembling that of hyacinths. Considered by Kimnach to be a variety of *Epiphyllum phyllanthus* and recorded by him as *Epiphyllum phyllanthus* v. *pittieri* (Web.) Kimn. C. & S. J.

Epiphyllum pumilum (Vpl.) Br. & R.

A branched species, very long stems becoming terete with elongated flattened branches, some tapering towards the apex, others rounded. Has only small flowers about 5 cm, white and fragrant. Style slender to 7 cm long – white.

Epiphyllum stenopetalum (Forst.) Br. & R.

Many characteristics similar to the foregoing – flower, style and stigma lobes apparently identical. Distribution given as Oaxaca, Mexico. This species is in doubt.

Epiphyllum strictum (Lem.,) Br. & R.

Seemingly distinctive on account of its very stiff upright green stems, elongated and having slightly serrated margins. White flower on long slender tube, with rose or red style, and yellow stigma lobes. Very easy in cultivation, grows rapidly and is most floriferous. Distribution: Guatemala, Panama and southern Mexico.

Epiphyllum thomasianum (K. Schum.) Br. & R.

Having stem characteristics similar to those of *E. oxypetalum*. Flower from curved tube, large whitish-cream, up to 24 cm wide. Fragrant and nocturnal. Style up to 30 cm long and 17 stigma lobes, cream or yellow. From Mexico, Guatemala and Nicaragua where it is widely distributed.

SCHLUMBERGERA Lem.

Similar in many respects to Zygocactus – but nevertheless having some very decided differences – differences which, if the botanist is not prepared to accept, are apparent to the amateur who seeks for guidance in better understanding of plants. Has joints or segments, flat and oval-shaped, slightly serrated margins, but no teeth. The flowers are regular, or nearly so, not zygomorphic. These two characteristics are sufficient to make identification possible, but even so there are other characters which lend even greater force to the validity of two separate genera.

Schlumbergera gaertneri (Regel) Br. & R.

The well recognized 'Easter Cactus'. Flattened and rather fleshy joints, with slightly crenated margins. Stem is bright green, and often the margins have a purplish effect. Flower develops at the apex of the segments, brick red to scarlet. Almost regular flower form. A varietal form is recorded, *Schlumbergera gaertneri* v. *makoyana*, the difference being that longish bristles develop on the joints. In view of the species also having this habit, there seems no reason to recognize the variety.

Hybrids of Schlumbergera have been produced, mostly due to the skill of Graeser, the best known being *Schlumbergera* × *Graeseri* and *S.* × *Elektra*. These also appear as × Rhipsalidopsis, *Rhipsalidopsis rosea* being one of the parents.

Schlumbergera russelliana (Gardner) Br. & R.

The type species. An epiphyte growing on trees or sometimes on rocks in rich humus, having a semi-erect habit, but sometimes pendent. Joints are flat and thin, somewhat elongated and narrow. Flower reddish. Originating from the Organ Mountains, Brazil, but now almost extinct in habitat. Only few plants are to be found in cultivation, and this proves to be rather a difficult plant to maintain. One of the parents of the well-known Christmas Cactus which takes its stem characteristic from this parent.

ZYGOCACTUS Schum.

Recently proposals have been put forward to merge this genus with that of *Schlumbergera*. These proposals merit no recognition as there are so many peculiarities with species of each genus which deserve generic segregation, and nothing but confusion would result from merging. Stems flattened, divided into short joints or segments with pronounced teeth on either side and each new segment growing from the apex of the earlier one. Plants branch freely. Flowers zygomorphic or irregular and these develop from the terminal of the segment. All known species are from Brazil.

Zygocactus delicatus Br. & R.

A white flowering form of *Z. truncatus* – also known as *Z. truncatus* v. *delicatus* Backeb. & Knuth (1935). From the Organ Mountains in Brazil. Flower petals open pure white with a rich magenta style. One of the choicest of epiphytic cacti, and still very rare in cultivation.

Many beautiful cultivars of Zygocactus are now available; the parentage is not always known as

Zygocactus delicatus

many of the earlier forms that were developed resulted from very haphazard cross-pollinating, or at least no records were kept. In more recent years new cultivars have become popular thanks to the outstanding efforts of plantsmen who kept details for the benefit of posterity. Those most frequently seen have been developed by Graeser and Koniger. Particulars of some of these cultivars are given elsewhere.

Zygocactus truncatus (Haw.) Schum.

With sharply serrated dark green segments – the teeth are very apparent. Flower zygomorphic to about 7 cm long, reddish magenta with white filaments and purplish style. From the Organ Mountains in eastern Brazil. This is one of the parents of the typical Christmas Cactus. The species is rare in cultivation.

Hylocereaneae

Consists principally of vine-like climbing or clambering, sometimes trailing plants. Differing forms of stem growth occur – rounded, angled, rick-rack, and flattened. These features do not determine the genus into which a species is placed. With few exceptions, the stem joints have aerial roots which enable the plant to cling and climb. All have mostly large or very large flowers, usually white or cream, rarely pink, red or multicoloured. The fruit develops in the form of a largish berry, sometimes spiny sometimes not.

APOROCACTUS Lem.

The popular 'Rat's Tail Cactus' consisting of slender-stemmed creeping plants, sometimes vine-like and invariably pendent, regardless of the fact aerial roots do develop on some stems. All known species are reputedly of Mexican origin, but escapes have become established in parts of Central and South America. Some species have been cross-pollinated with species of other genera, Epiphyllum in particular, thereby providing most interesting, useful and floriferous cultivars with Aporocactus-like stems, and flowers resembling Epiphyllum. Referred to as × *Aporophyllum*.

Aporocactus flagelliformis (L.) Lem.

The best known of this genus. It would appear certain that the original home of the species was Mexico, although suggestions have been made that it might be native of South America. This seems unlikely as it is very well known in south Mexico, but escapes may have become established in parts of South America. The soft, spiny and pendent branches have 10 to 12 ribs, very inconspicuous being closely covered by many soft spines from areoles set about 6 mm apart. The flowers are diurnal, crimson and zygomorphic, lasting for up to 4 days.

Aporocactus flagriformis (Zucc.) Lem.

From Oaxaca in south Mexico. A creeping species, branching freely with occasional aerial roots from slender stems. Ribs 10 or 11 with smaller areoles and fewer spines than *A. flagelliformis*. This gives the effect of a more open and less densely covered stem – one of the main obvious differences between the two species when not in flower. Flower is dark crimson, up to 10 cm long and broader than the preceding.

Aporocactus leptophis (De Cand.) Br. & R.

An epiphytic species from Oaxaca, south Mexico, and having more slender stems than others of the genus with 7 or 8 ribs. Areoles not so closely set, but with many stiff spines. Has reddish flower with suggestion of lilac shading. A rare plant in cultivation.

Other species recorded include *Aporocactus conzatti* and *Aporocactus martianus*. *Aporocactus mallisonii* is a cultivar derived from *Aporocactus flagelliformis* × *Heliocereus* (possibly *H. speciosus*), and sometimes known as × *Heliaporus smithii* Rowley. The Aporocactus–Heliocereus complex has still to be better appreciated. There is possibly a greater kinship between the two genera than has, as yet, been determined. While *Heliocereus* are not included with the Hylocereaneae, one species deserves mention here on account of its epiphytic habit.

Heliocereus heterodoxus Standl. & Steyerm.

Discovered in Guatemala, but possibly indigenous to Mexico in Chiapas. A clambering species with 3-angled stems, slender with slight prominences. Large flower with reddish colourings, 4/5 cm wide. Still rare and almost unknown in cultivation.

It is also likely there is a greater affinity between Aporocactus and Selenicereus than at present understood. Plant material collected on the island of St Vincent, West Indies, where local records suggest an endemic Selenicereus species, provided evidence of growth reminiscent of Selenicereus, but having the habit, flower and tube similar to Aporocactus. The flower opened white and was much smaller than any Aporocactus species. This has been referred to as *Pseudo-selenicereus*.

CRYPTOCEREUS Alex.

A genus created for what is undoubtedly one of the most fascinating discoveries of recent years, and to which, since, has been transferred another species. At first considered to be one of the Epiphyllanae on account of the stem being similar to certain Epiphyllum species. Develops long branches and has many aerial roots. The rick-rack stem forms a unique characteristic of the genus which includes two species.

Cryptocereus anthonyanus Alex.

A true epiphyte from southern Mexico–in the regions of Chiapas and reputedly also in Costa Rica. Originally discovered growing on the roof of a native's hut, and some time elapsed before the actual habitat was determined. An outstanding exotic flower of brick-red sepals and yellow throat. Nocturnal flowering and only slightly scented. The elongated stems develop many aerial roots which enable it to trail or hang pendent from trees. A desirable species of easy culture.

One other species is recorded, *Cryptocereus imitans*

(Kimn. and Hutch.) Backeb. Said to be endemic to Costa Rica. Has the same rick-rack stem growth, but bears white flowers.

DEAMIA Br. & R.

A monotypic genus, sometimes called the 'tortoise cactus' on account of its sometimes curious method of growth. Found throughout south Mexico and Central America to Colombia. Only in recent years has it become generally known in cultivation.

Deamia testudo (Karw.) Br. & R.

Other names have been associated with this species, and more recently that of *Deamia diabolica*–all are considered synonymous with the species. The stems can be most varied in length with 3/4 or even 6 ribs with narrow margins armed with many spines, mostly on areoles set close together. This is very apparent in young growth. In habitat it is most usual for it to clamber over rock faces or up trees where it proves to be very much an epiphyte, often losing its original root system completely. The large creamy-white flower is up to 20 cm or more long. An exotic diurnal species.

HYLOCEREUS (Berger) Br. & R.

Of wide distribution from western Mexico through to Panama, many of the West Indian Islands and northerly countries of South America. All are climbing plants, usually with 3-angled stems, the areoles bearing few, sometimes many, shortish spines, some species totally spineless. Flowers large, mostly scented, usually white, rarely red. Night flowering. Some species have striking similarities and would cause bewilderment to the amateur, hence those detailed have obvious and very apparent differences.

Hylocereus calcaratus (Web.) Br. & R.

From the forest regions around Port Limon in Costa Rica. A unique species with fresh green and near spineless 3-angled stems and exceptionally prominent marginal lobes. A climbing plant of considerable attraction. Large creamy-white, perfumed flowers on matured specimens. Has long stout scaly tube. It is worthy of note that the flower was not described until very recent years. This is difficult to understand as there seems to be no difficulty in flowering cultivated plants.

Hylocereus calcaratus

Hylocereus ocamponis (Salm-Dyck) Br. & R.
A Mexican species, but escapes do occur in Central and northerly South American countries. While new growth commences green, the stems very quickly change to greyish-blue, and it is this peculiarity which makes it distinctive. Invariably 3-angled with hard horny margins. A fast-growing climber with very elongated stems and having short spines. Aerial roots develop at the joints and along the stems. Very large cream flowers up to 30 cm wide, scented. Night flowering. Must not be confused with *H. broxensis* which it resembles in stem colour and growth, but the flowers are very different.

Hylocereus stenopterus (Web.) Br. & R.
From the Vallee de Tuis in Costa Rica. A much less robust species with dull greenish stems, 3-angled with small but pronounced areoles. Apparently of much slower growth than most of the other species. Has the distinction of having reddish flowers, only shared by one other of this genus, *H. extensus* – a small flower only to 12cm long. Nocturnal. Reported rare in habitat and most certainly rare in cultivation.

Hylocereus undatus (Haworth) Br. & R.
Very similar to *H. triangularis* and *H. tricostatus* and might well be synonymous. One of the best-known and most easily cultivated species indigenous to many tropical and sub-tropical areas.

Possibly originated from the West Indies, but now widely cultivated even in southern France and Spain. Stems usually 3-angled, green with hard horny margins on mature growth and very small spines. A clambering, almost untidy plant with its long stems and branches forming masses like a hedge, for which purpose it is used in some places. Flowers very large and scented, cream in colour and nocturnal. Grown extensively in China and other Far Eastern countries where it is known as the 'Moon Flower'.

MEDIOCACTUS Br. & R.
Tree growing plants having much the same character as Hylocereus. Long slender branches usually 3-angled, with short spines and many aerial roots. Considered to be a genus midway between Hylocereus and Selenicereus and having a resemblance to both genera. Fairly widely distributed in South America – Peru, Colombia, Bolivia, Brazil and Argentina. All species are rare in cultivation.

Mediocactus coccineus (Salm-Dyck) Br. & R.
The type species of this genus. Originates from Brazil, but also found in northern Argentina. A climber, sometimes clambering, having dark green stems, usually 3-angled, with knobby projections below the areoles and very small spines. Large flowers, white and funnel-shaped. Night flowering. The specific name would suggest red flowers, but this is possibly more appropriate to the fruits.

Mediocactus megalanthus (Schum.) Br. & R.
A rare epiphyte from Peru, originally discovered in Loreto, but now reported elsewhere in Peru and Bolivia. Forms masses of stems which tend to hang pendent rather than climb. Stems are 3-angled with undulating margins and brownish spines. Flowers are considered to be among the largest of the Cactaceae – up to 38 cm long – white, scented and night flowering.

Other species are recorded, but their identity is much in doubt. *Mediocactus hassleri* is of interest, having the appearance of Selenicereus with rounded stems, but there is doubt about its authenticity.

SELENICEREUS (A. Bgr.) Br. & R.
A genus of clambering vines, usually developing

Ferocactus acanthodes

Epiphytes

ABOVE *Pseudo-selenicereus* 'St Vincent'

ABOVE *Pseudozygocactus sp.*

BELOW *Eccremocactus bradei*

BELOW *Epiphyllanthus obovatus*

roundish stems, if only with age. Has distinct rib and spine characteristics which gives guidance in determining the species. Very widely distributed in parts of east, west and south Mexico and some of the West Indian islands. In general they are very easy in cultivation. Stem cuttings of some species are used extensively for grafting purposes, especially to develop Zygocactus and Schlumbergera 'standards'.

Selenicereus grandiflorus (L.) Br. & R.

From Jamaica, Cuba and possibly Haiti. Commonly referred to as 'The Queen of the Night', due to its outstandingly large white flower and nocturnal habit. One of the finest but not the largest flower of this genus, being about 20/22 cm wide. Stems which are dark green or bluish-green have between 5 and 8 ribs with small acicular brownish spines, occasionally up to 1 cm long. A prolific and rampant grower and undoubtedly the best known of this genus. Rooted cuttings of about 20/24 cm long make excellent grafting stock.

Selenicereus hamatus (Scheidw.) Br. & R.

Sometimes referred to as *S. rostratus* with which it is synonymous. Indigenous to east Mexico, but also reported from south Mexico. The stems are bright fresh green in colour, 3 or 4-angled and having very prominent lobes or projections at intervals along the margins. Spines usually absent, especially on young growth, but they may develop on very matured growth which will, with age, gradually become rounded. Large white nocturnal flowers, but only on matured plants. In cultivation, flowers are rarely seen.

Selenicereus pteranthus (Link & Otto) Br. & R.

Synonymous with *S. nycticalus*. Species of Mexican origin with large dark green or bluish-green stems with 4/6 ribs and a few short blackish spines. A fast and rampant grower, having the largest of all flowers of this genus, up to 30 cm long, white and beautifully scented.

A great deal of exploratory work has yet to be undertaken before there is a thorough understanding of this genus. It would seem there are a great number of species and varietal forms if the stem peculiarities are accepted as a method of identification. With the changes that take place as the plants mature, and the apparent differences bet-

ween habitat and cultivated plants of the same species, many doubts still remain. Those detailed leave no cause for questioning as to their identity.

Selenicereus wercklei (Web.) Br. & R.

Has a striking resemblance to certain Rhipsalis species. Large red flowers about 15 cm long, but this is rarely seen even in habitat. A true epiphyte, branching with long slender stems, scarcely discernible ribs and no spines. Aerial roots appear along the length of the stems. Endemic to Costa Rica, near Miravalles.

STROPHOCACTUS Br. & R.

A monotypic genus of great interest – and still considered one of the most novel of all cactus species. While it is said to be widely distributed in the swampy forests of the Amazon, this unique plant comes from the area of Manaos, where frequent inundations take place; it is, notwithstanding, rarely encountered in collections around the world.

Strophocactus wittii (Schum.) Br. & R.

This remarkable species with flattened climbing stems achieved by almost continual aerial roots on the midnerve of the branch, and having numerous closely arranged areoles with resultant numerous spines, is an important example of the 'unusual' in the realm of cacti. Sometimes called the 'Strapcactus' on account of its strap-like stems. This epiphyte has white flowers, with red sepals, about 25 cm long. Tube elongated. Night flowering. Records suggest this could possibly be the link between the Epiphyllum and the Selenicereus.

WEBEROCEREUS Br. & R., Contr. U.S. Nat. Herb.

Slender-stemmed epiphytic cacti comprising only 4 species having many aerial roots to encourage both climbing and pendent habit. All species are from Costa Rica where they grow in dense rain forests, and in the Province of Colon in Panama frequenting tree thickets. Have certain resemblances to Rhipsalis, only the flower, while not as exotic as so many of the Hylocereanae, is larger and generally more colourful than those of Rhipsalis.

Weberocereus biolleyi (Web.) Br. & R.

Originally considered a species of Rhipsalis, due to the almost round or only slightly angled stems, spineless and with aerial roots. Found in the area of

Port Limon in Costa Rica growing from the branches of forest trees. Nocturnal flowering. Small flowers, pinkish, up to 5 cm long. This interesting plant remains one of the lesser-known species in cultivation.

Weberocereus trichophorus Johns. & Kimn.

A forest species from Costa Rica, from the area of Peralta in the Province of Limon. Rampant growth with 6/7-angled stems with spines and many blackish hairs at the areoles. Has many aerial roots and is nocturnal flowering with smallish bloom to 6 cm long and pink in colour. Very attractive species.

Weberocereus tunilla (Web.) Br. & R.

Another Costa Rican species from south-west of Cartago. Has slender 4-angled greyish-green stems, occasionally flattened – sometimes with 3 or 5 angles and up to 12 stiff spines at each areole. Of climbing habit with only few aerial roots. The funnelform flower is up to 7 cm long, rose-pink or purplish-pink with short tube. Night flowering. Uncommon in cultivation.

One other species is recorded, *Weberocereus panamensis,* with usually triangular stems and white flower.

WILMATTEA Br. & R.

A monotypic genus. At one time incorporated with Hylocereus but due to certain flower differences a distinct genus was created.

Wilmattea minutiflora Br. & R.

Native of Guatemala and Honduras. A true epiphyte with long slender stems, bright green in colour with few very small insignificant spines from pronounced areoles. Branches freely. A very small flower, white with pinkish markings, fragrant. The tube is almost unnoticeable. Night flowering. A desirable and easily grown species, but still quite rare in cultivation.

WERCKLEOCEREUS Br. & R.

A genus freely distributed throughout Costa Rica and Guatemala in rain forest areas. The stem form resembles that of the Hylocereus, but flowers are considerably smaller with very short tubes. All known species are epiphytes, usually climbers with aerial roots.

Werckleocereus glaber (Eichl.) Br. & R.

Slender, usually 3-angled stems, bright green and glaucous, the margins having pronounced projections from which the areole is born. Spines are few and small. The flower seems to appear at the apex of the stem or at the upper areoles. White in colour, about 10 cm long, tube having many brownish spines. Night flowering. Fruit becomes brick-red. Widely distributed in Guatemala.

Werckleocereus tonduzii (Web.) Br. & R.

From the area of El Copey in Costa Rica where its distribution is seemingly restricted. Has 3/4-angled stems, developing a bushy habit. Branches are deep green in colour and have straight margins with small areoles at regular intervals, and aerial roots. In habitat the stems have short spines about 3 mm long, but these are not usually observed with cultivated plants. Flower white and generally free-flowering, with short tube having dark spines and wool. A rare species.

Moraceae

Includes the genus *Ficus* in which there are a number of interesting species which commence as epiphytes and subsequently grow into shrubs or trees. Most of these are unknown in cultivation, but two are worthy of mention.

Ficus decaisnei Steud, (Syn. *F. philippinensis*) – a climbing epiphyte from the Philippines – with long elliptical fleshy leaves, becoming bushy with maturity.

Other species are recorded of this large genus which commence epiphytal, then throw down their roots and become sizeable trees or shrubs. It might well be asked of such species, 'When does an epiphyte cease to be epiphytic?'

Ficus villosa Blume – from Malaysia – a creeping species with ovate dark green leaves and brown hairy margins. Yellow fruits are developed in clusters.

Piperaceae

Includes the genus *Peperomia* Ruiz. & Pav. This is a remarkably large genus with a number being true epiphytes.

Peperomia fosteri from the Amazon Valley in Brazil is an attractive red-stemmed creeping species with thick leaves, short and elliptical.

Peperomia prostrata Hort. Williams, ex Gard. With small circular leaves, bluish-grey or brown in colour with distinct silvery markings–very attractive, but rare. Colombia.

Peperomia rotundifolia Dahlst. (Syn: *P. nummularifolia*) from many of the West Indian islands where it totally inhabits trees. Very small, almost round leaves, fleshy and waxy on thread-like stems.

Many other species could also be included, *Peperomia pellucida*, *Peperomia nivalis* and *Peperomia trinervula* are but a selection.

Very widely distributed family of plants and the majority are succulents, if not epiphytes.

Rhipsalidinae

Comprise a remarkable group of cacti, all epiphytic or saxicolous, with many forms and peculiarities, comparatively small flowers and many with the potential of having changeable characteristics within the species, particularly with the genus Rhipsalis. The majority are spineless, but with noteworthy exceptions. Flowers are regular and fruits small and berry-like with very small seeds.

RHIPSALIS are a most varied group–many divers forms, some thread-like, others with flattened branches–angled, twisted, indented ribs–and while these give some indication, it is still most difficult to determine some species from others. Flowers are small, usually white, cream or pinkish, and produced freely along the length of the stems.

Many different Rhipsalis names appear in various authoritative works, and it is apparent that a great number must be synonyms. While it is not intended to try and give an adequate description of each species, it is proposed, however, to deal with each sub-genus and list the species included with but sparse data.

1. Sub-genus EURHIPSALIS. K. Schum. Species with cylindrical stems, mostly smooth, some developing a shrubby habit, others having long pencil-like branching tendency. The similarities, especially within this sub-genus, provide many problems for the botanist and amateur.

Rhipsalis burchellii Br. & R.
Much-branched, slender and pendent–branching dichotomous. Flower white. Brazil near Sao Paulo.

Rhipsalis campos-portoana Löfg.
Long pendent branches with small clusters of short branches at the terminal ends. Flower white. Brazil–Serra de Itatiaya. A rare species.

Rhipsalis capilliformis Web.
Thread-like branches hang pendent. A graceful species. Flower creamy-white and numerous. Brazil near Sao Paulo.

Rhipsalis cassutha Gaert.
Very variable species–generally long stems and pendent. Young growth has white bristles at areoles. Flower creamy-white. Widely distributed in Mexico, South and Central America, West Indies, Madagascar, Ceylon and Africa.

Rhipsalis cassuthopsis Backeb.
Also known as *Rhipsalis cassythoides*. Closely akin to *Rhipsalis cassutha* but generally with more slender stems and branching freely. Flowers white and rather small even for Rhipsalis. Brazil.

Rhipsalis cereuscula Haw.
Elongated cylindrical stems with clusters of small branches. Flower white to creamy-pink. Brazil, also in Uruguay.

Rhipsalis clavata Web.
Pendent elongated branches, narrowly clavate. Very distinctive. Flower white. Brazil.

Rhipsalis cribrata (Lem.) Rümpl.
Slender stems, much branched, elongated with short terminal branches in whorls. Flower creamy-white. Brazil, near Sao Paulo, Rio de Janeiro and Minas Geraes.

Rhipsalis handrosoma Lindberg.
For many years a species difficult to locate–often confused with *Lepismium grandiflorum* but stems are less robust and brighter green in colour. Free flowering with creamy-pinkish flowers. From the Organ Mountains, Brazil–a rarity in cultivation.

Rhipsalis heteroclada Br. & R.
Much-branched, stiff stems with purple shading on tips and areoles. Flower white. Brazil.

Rhipsalis lindbergiana Sch.
Elongated stems, pendent, prolific growth. Areoles

with hairs. Flower pinkish-white. Brazil–Rio de Janeiro. *R. densiareolata* and *R. erythrocarpa* are possibly synonymous.

Rhipsalis loefgrenii Br. & R.

With long slender dull green or purplish-green stems with many aerial roots with small areoles and large bract. White flowers with purple fruits. A rare but interesting species, little known in cultivation. Brazil.

Rhipsalis memembryanthemoides Haw.

Stems cylindrical and shrubby. Flower white or pinkish. Brazil.

Rhipsalis minutiflora K. Sch.

A very thin slender-stemmed species, similar to *R. cassutha* but with fewer areoles and no bristles. Flowers freely with relatively minute flowers, whitish-pink. Brazil.

Many other species and varieties have been recorded, most of which are undoubtedly synonyms although a different habitat is cited. It would seem that the pencil-shape stemmed Rhipsalis can have varying growths within the species–even within a plant–and this has encouraged confusion and possibly accounts for the lack of interest in the group generally. They are among the easiest of all cacti to grow and flower, and can be adapted readily to house culture.

Rhipsalis penduliflora N. E. Br.

Long slender stems, rarely branching, dull green with inconspicuous bristles especially on young growth. Free-flowering with pinkish-white flowers particularly from upper areoles of stems. Brazil.

Rhipsalis prismatica Rumpl.

Elongated branches with upper branches much shorter and often angled. Flower white. Brazil.

Rhipsalis pulchra Löfgr.

Long slender stems of bright green, much branched usually in whorls. Distinct minute red areoles. Has a reddish flower and ovary. An interesting species from the Organ Mountains, Brazil.

Rhipsalis shaferi Br. & R.

Stiff erect stems, later pendent–with purplish tips and sometimes at areoles. Lower branches often with bristles, upper branches without. Flower white or greenish-white. Paraguay, Brazil and Argentina.

Rhipsalis simmleri Beauv.

Pendent and much branched. Lower branches

smooth, upper angled, short and slightly hairy. Flower white and pink. Costa Rica.

Rhipsalis teres (Vell.) Steud.

Stems strong, blotched red when mature. Much-branched and semi-erect, areoles pinkish, particulary when young. Flower creamy yellow. Brazil, eastern states.

Rhipsalis virgata Web.

Elongated stems, first ascending, then pendent. Terminal and upper branches shorter. Areoles small and few hairs. Flowers from sides of stem, white. Brazil near Sao Paulo.

2. Sub-genus GONIORHIPSALIS K. Sch. consists of species with angular stem growths. Usually the joints are unarmed, sometimes with 3 wings, rarely flattened or 4, 5 or 6 winged. Stems with short or longish joints.

Rhipsalis cereoides Backeb. & Voll.

Stems invariably three angled, joints short, occasionally elongated. Margins firm and precise. A species of considerable interest with whitish flowers. Brazil.

Rhipsalis heptagona Rauh & Backeb.

A fascinating species still rare in cultivation. Stems very distinctly ribbed with 5 to 7 somewhat irregular ribs. Peru.

Rhipsalis micrantha (HBK) De Candolle,

A clambering bushy species with flattened or 3 to 4-angled stems, light green with pronounced crenations along the margins. Small areoles, but reluctant flowerer. Flowers white or cream and fruit usually pure white. Ecuador and northern Peru.

Rhipsalis pentaptera Pfeiff.

Stems and branches deep green, stiff with usually 6 distinct ribs, areoles with small white bristles and bracts. Very free flowering on more pendent branches, flower creamy-pink with white fruit. From Uruguay and southern Brazil.

Rhipsalis sulcata Web.

Stems 5-angled, elongated and wide with few areoles. Branches freely with few flowers, pinkish-white, but large for Rhipsalis species. Origin uncertain, but possibly Peru or Ecuador.

Rhipsalis tonduzii Web.

A free-growing bushy species, usually elongated

stems and branches with pronounced 3 to 5-angles, occasionally flattened on young growth. Stems grey-green with closely set areoles with small whitish flowers and white fruits. Costa Rica. *R. mercklei* Berg. is possibly a variety or synonymous.

Rhipsalis triangularis Werd.

A species very similar to *R. cereoides* with more elongated triangular stems, slightly crenated. White flowers. Brazil.

3. Sub-genus OPHIORHIPSALIS. K. Schum. Species with mainly cylindrical stems, having pronounced areoles with adpressed bristles. Usually elongated stems with only sparse branching. A very distinctive group.

Rhipsalis aculeata Web.

Fresh green slender stems with closely set areoles, having much wool and many white bristles. Flower creamy-white or pinkish and purplish-black fruit. A rare species from northern Argentina.

Rhipsalis coralloides Rauh.

An interesting species from Madagascar with rounded stems, fairly robust and branching freely. Pinkish-cream flowers towards the apex of the stems. *R. saxicola* Graf is similar and might be synonymous.

Rhipsalis fasciculata (Willd.) Haw.

One of the most floriferous of Rhipsalis with many interesting characteristics. Widely distributed, being found in Brazil, also Madagascar—and it is likely that *R. pilosa* and *R. madagascarensis* are synonyms. Another Madagascan species has been recorded, *R. horrida*, and while this has certain peculiarities, nevertheless it would appear this also is synonymous. Stems somewhat cylindrical, and branching freely—has many areoles with numerous hairs or bristles. Flower quite large, white with pinkish stamens. An outstanding but rare species.

Rhipsalis leucorhaphis K. Sch.

A very much-branched species with many aerial roots. Stems usually terete, but ribs are apparent when plant not in growth. Areoles subtended by small bract—bristles occur on young growth. Flowers white with red fruits. Paraguay and northern Argentina.

Rhipsalis lumbricoides (Lem.) Lem.

Slender angled stems, terete when growing, elon-gated and rooting freely. A much-branched species with white bristles at areoles. Flower white and fruit white. Uruguay, Argentina and Paraguay. An unusual species not often met with in cultivation.

4. Sub-genus PHYLLORHIPSALIS K. Sch. provides yet another remarkable group of this variable genus. All with leaf-like joints, crenated margins, often developing from 'stalk-like' branches. Some species originally included in this sub-tribe have been transferred to *Disocactus*.

Rhipsalis angustissima Web.

A rare species from Costa Rica with narrow elongated flattened branches, tapering at the apex. Widely serrate margins, dark green becoming reddish-green. Main stems terete. A unique species, often wrongly considered synonymous with *R. coriacea* Polak. and *R. leiophloea* Gris. Flowers whitish-pink and white fruits.

Rhipsalis boliviana (Britt.) Lauterb.

Stems somewhat angled at the base with yellowish bristles at the areoles. Branches elongated and flattened, narrow with broad crenations—reddish-green having similar appearance as *Lepismium cruciforme* v. *anceps*. Flowers whitish yellow and white fruit. From the rain forests of Bolivia.

Rhipsalis crispata (Haw.) Pfeiff.

Stems terete below. Branches freely with shortish pale fresh green joints, flattened and crenate. Flower creamy-white, rather small and white fruits. *R. goebeliana* (Hort.) Backeb. would appear to be a synonym.

Rhipsalis crispimarginata Löfgr.

Pendent species with terete stems below and many branched with oblong or roundish joints, bright green with undulating and crenate margins. Flowers creamy-white and white fruits. The obvious 'twisted' undulated margins make identification possible. Endemic to Rio de Janeiro, Brazil.

Rhipsalis cuneata Br. & R.

Elongated stems and branches, thin and flattened, joints cuneate at base. Leaf-like margins are deeply crenate. Has white flowers. Little known in cultivation. Bolivia.

Rhipsalis elliptica Lindb. in Martius Fl. Bras.

Very similar to the foregoing, but with more obvious elliptic joints and only slightly crenate margins. Joints usually reddish. Of pendent habit, and free flowering. Yellow flowers and reddish fruits.

R. chloroptera Web. and *R. elliptica* v. *helicoidea* are so similar in every respect they should be considered synonymous. Endemic to state of Sao Paolo, Brazil, and possibly widely distributed in neighbouring states.

Rhipsalis gonacarpa Web.

A rare species having much the same appearance as *R. rhombea*, but with more lanceolate joints, dark green becoming purplish. Usually flattened, but sometimes 3-angled and crenate, undulating margins. Flower white and narrow blackish fruits. From the region of Sao Paulo, Brazil.

Rhipsalis houlletiana Lem.

A very popular free-flowering species, generally with terete stems below and thin, flat and leaf-like above, about 2 to 4 cm broad, pale fresh green, pronounced crenations with largish creamy flowers, bell shaped. Fruits dark red. Widely distributed in southern Brazil.

Rhipsalis jamaicensis Britt. & Harr.

Of pendent habit with thin angular stems and elongated dull green joints about 2 to 3 cm broad. Margins slightly crenate. Flowers yellowish-cream, sometimes greenish, fruits white. Rare in cultivation and liable to be confused with certain Rhipsalis species transferred to Disocactus. *R. coriacea* Polak. and *R. purpusii* Weing. are too similar to justify distinct status and should be considered synonymous.

Doubt also exists in respect to *R. leiophloea* Gris. and while this has certain similarities to *R. jamaicensis*, it is closer to *R. ramulosa* (now *Disocactus ramulosa*) and is possibly synonymous.

Rhipsalis linearis K. Sch.

Stems pale green, flattened, rarely 3-angled. Has bushy, prostrate habit branching freely. The leaf-like joints are slightly serrated. Flowers white and white fruits. Southern Brazil, Paraguay, northern Argentina and Uruguay.

Rhipsalis lorentziana Gris.

A species known by name only in cultivation, very rare and interesting. A forest plant from north-west Argentina and parts of southern Bolivia. Base of stems terete, branches flattened and thin about 2 cm broad, rarely 3-angled, elongated with serrate margins. Flower large and white and purple fruits.

There are many 'names' of Rhipsalis which may, or may not, justify recognition – a great deal of research has yet to be undertaken before definite conclusions can be reached. This is another family where new species or varieties are frequently being discovered in the rain forests of South America.

Rhipsalis oblonga Löfgr.

Main stems terete at base becoming flattened above. Branches freely with narrow oblong-shaped joints, deep green, sometimes purplish, margins crenate. Very free-flowering, pinkish white with white fruits. Species of easy culture from Ilha Grande, Brazil.

Rhipsalis pachyptera Pfeiff.

Robust stems, often terete below, with many large wide elongated or rounded joints, thick, deep green or purplish-green with margins crenate. A really spectacular species often developing many buds at one areole. Flower creamy-yellow and white fruits. Widely distributed in southern Brazil.

Rhipsalis platycarpa (Zucc.) Pfeiff.

A much-branched species. Joints flattened and broad, somewhat elongated, with broad crenate margins – dark green, sometimes purplish. Flowers usually from the upper areoles, whitish-yellow or greenish and greenish fruits. From the Organ Mountains, Brazil.

Rhipsalis rhombea (S.-D.) Pfeiff.

A popular and well-known species almost resembling Zygocactus (or Schlumbergera) in appearance. Stems terete or slightly angled with flattened branches and joints about 2 cm broad, dark green or purplish, pronounced crenate margins. Flowers freely at areoles, small, creamy-white with red fruits. Southern Brazil.

Rhipsalis robusta Lem. non Lindb.

A much-branched species with large rounded flattened or 3-winged joints, hard, slightly crenate, reddish-green with pronounced midnerve. A distinct species with some similarities in appearance to *R. pachyptera*. Flower whitish, and white fruits. Brazil and possibly Peru.

Rhipsalis roseana Berg.

With fleshy flattened joints and stems with distinct crenations, whitish areoles along the crenate margins, giving the effect of notches. Flowers small, creamy-yellow. An attractive species, little known in cultivation. Colombia, parts of Ecuador and northern Peru.

Rhipsalis russellii Br. & R.
Erect-growing species with many branches. Joints flattened and rounded, crenate, dark green with purplish margins, sometimes the whole joint becomes reddish-green. Flowers very small, often with many at one areole. Fruit purple.

Rhipsalis warmingiana K. Sch.
Stems elongated and strap-like, often flattened, but usually 3-angled with crenate margins. Large flowers, bell shaped, white and deep red or black fruits. A well-known species from Brazil, of easy culture.

LEPISMIUM PFEIFF.
Is closely related to Rhipsalis, differing only because the ovary is sunken in the stem margin or are considered 'transitional' species. There is doubt as to whether this feature justifies segregation, the more so on account of the several Rhipsalis species which have been transferred by Backeberg to Lepismium for only meagre reasons.

1. Sub-genus CALAMORHIPSALIS K. Sch. contains those species formally included in Rhipsalis and includes several species of distinction.

Lepismium dissimile Lindb.
An unusual species of distinction. Free branching with hairy stems and close-set areoles. At first erect, then pendent with many aerial roots. Branches can become 4 or 5-angled with areoles alternating. Pinkish flowers and reddish fruits. This species is possibly synonymous with *L. pacheo-leonii* (Löfgr.) Backeb. While there is recorded a varietal form, *L. dissimile* v. *setulosa*, it would appear to have precisely the same characteristics as the species. Endemic to Brazil.

There are other species included in this sub-tribe of doubtful authenticity which do not merit recognition – *L. chrysanthum* (Löfgr.) Backeb. and *L. rigidum* (Löfgr.) Backeb.

Lepismium epiphyllanthoides (Backeb.) Backeb.
Having stems terete at base, but branches in whorls, stout, but short with indentations similar to certain growth on some Epiphyllanthus species. Very rare in cultivation; has yellowish-creamy flowers.

Lepismium floccosum (S.-D.) Backeb.
Long slender stems, with many branches, of pendent growth. Areoles with white tufts of wool and largish flowers, white or creamy-yellow. Fruit pinkish-white. Brazil.

Lepismium gibberulum (Web.) Backeb.
Has thickish stems and branches, pale green or yellowish green developing in whorls. Areoles almost indiscernible. Flowers pale pink and white fruits. Endemic to Organ Mountains, Brazil.

Lepismium grandiflorum (Haw.) Backeb.
Stems usually erect, smooth and terete. Young branches commence with deep green hairy growth, but gradually become smooth and reddish about the areoles. Very free flowering with largish creamy-pinkish blooms and pinkish-purple fruits. Brazil. An outstanding species.

Lepismium megalanthum (Löfgr.) Backeb.
Similar to *L. grandiflorum*, dark green stems and branches and with large flowers up to 3 or 4cm diameter. Fruit pinkish-white.

Lepismium neves-armondii (K. Sch.) Backeb.
Elongated stems with branches in whorls. Flowers in profusion, whitish with slight orange coloration in the throat. Fruits whitish-yellow. Brazil, in state of Rio de Janeiro.

Lepismium pittieri (Br. & R.) Backeb.
A distinctive and rare species from Venezuela, usually with cylindrical branches, but sometimes flattened. Develops bushy habit. Flower greenish-yellow and white fruits.

Lepismium pulvinigerum (Lindb.) Backeb.
A robust-growing species, at first erect but becoming pendent with very long branches. Branches olive-green with purple markings around the areoles. Flowers creamy-white, fruits red. Central Brazil. There is no great difference between this and *L. grandiflorum* – they may be synonymous or a variety.

Lepismium puniceo-discus (Lindb.) Backeb.
Very slender pendent branches, pale green. Large flowers, creamy-white with pronounced orange-coloured stamens. Fruit deep yellow at maturity. Brazil.

Lepismium tucumanensis (Web.) Backeb.
Much-branched species of pendent habit, often in whorls. Young growth generally terete with reddish areoles, but older growth becomes angular and turns from bright green to dull or yellowish-green. Flowers pinkish-white, fruits deep pink or red. From Tucuman, Argentina, also Bolivia and Paraguay.

2. Sub-genus EPALLAGOGONIUM K. Sch. consists of one species of distinctive character. One of the most outstanding plants of the Rhipsalidinae.
Lepismium paradoxum S.D.
Large-growing species with link-like stems and branches developing in whorls. With many aerial roots from the glossy-green joints. Flower is white and fruit white. From the state of Sao Paulo, Brazil.

3. Sub-genus EULEPISMIUM Knuth & Backeb. includes the 'original' species before the Backeberg transference. All are epiphytic or saxicolous with usually 3-angled stems, sometimes flattened, tufts of woolly white hairs at the areoles and purple fruits.
Lepismium cruciforme (Vel.) Miqu.
Usually saxicolous, rooting freely along the branches. Generally 3 or 4-angled, sometimes flattened branches, purplish-green or reddish, elongated with margins slightly undulate. Areoles sunken in margins. Flower white and fruit purple or red.
Varieties of the species are on record, but in most instances the similarities are so apparent that even varietal status is not justified.
Lepismium cruciforme v. *anceps* (Web.) Backeb. would appear to be distinct as branches are invariably flattened. Flower pink with purple fruits.
All species and varieties are endemic to Brazil, and possibly also Peru.
Lepismium cruciforme v. *cavernosum* (Lindb.) Backeb. has stouter branches and more green. Flower white with purple fruits.
Lepis cruciforme v. *myosurus* (S.-D.) Backeb. has shorter and narrower stems than the species. Flower generally pink.
Lepismium cruciforme v. *vollii* (Backeb.) Backeb.

appears to have no differences at all to the species.

1. Sub-genus TRIGONORHIPSALIS Berg. consists of one species only.
Lepismium trigonum (Pfieff.) Backeb.
Distinctly 3-angled joints which make this species distinctive. Stems broad and very branched with prominent areoles, sometimes woolly. Stems are olive or dull green, except on young growth which commences bright green. Large pinkish-white flowers and red fruits. From the state of Sao Paulo, Brazil.
The Rhipsalis-Lepismium complex presents a fascinating study. Many differing opinions will always be expressed as many mis-named species have been distributed throughout the world. One fact emerges that there are too many similarities to keep the two genera apart; while the 'sunken ovary' of the Lepismiums presents a distinguishing feature, this should not serve as reason for division.

ACANTHORHIPSALIS (SCH.) Br. & R.
Mostly epiphytic on forest trees, stems flattened and sometimes to 4-angled, mostly short, occasionally elongated. Crenate margins with spiny areoles. Flowers mostly orange or reddish-orange. Indigenous of Bolivia, Argentina and Peru.
Acanthorhipsalis crenata (Br.) Br. & R.
Very flat branches and narrow stems, much crenated. Largish areoles with wool and spines. Flower reddish, small. Little known of this species in cultivation and might well prove to be synonymous with *Acanthorhipsalis paranganiensis* Card. From high altitudes near Yungus, Bolivia.
Acanthorhipsalis incahuasina Card.
Another Bolivian species, little known in cultivation. Long flattened or 3 winged branches, less spiny than others of the genus. Flower purported to be reddish-orange.
Acanthorhipsalis micrantha (Vaup.) Br. & R.
Stems flat or 3 winged, branching freely. Flowers small, pale orange. From south-eastern Peru at high altitudes. Rare in cultivation.
Acanthorhipsalis monocantha (Gris.) Br. & R.
Similar to the preceding but with more robust habit, sometimes semi-erect, then pendent stems, often to 4 winged with spiny areoles. Flower rich

orange (records of Br. & R. and Borg are incorrect in stating this has a white flower). A decorative species of easy culture. Northern Argentina.

Acanthorhipsalis paranganiensis Card.

A flattened or 3-angled branched species, stems become elongated and only semi-pendent. Strongly crenate with small spines at areoles. Flower reddish, small. Discovered in Parangani, Ayopaya, Bolivia, at 2,400 m. A rare species, but of easy culture.

ERYTHRORHIPSALIS Berg.

Epiphytic with slender and rounded stems and branches, firstly erect, then becoming pendent. Well distributed areoles bearing many bristles. Terminal, regular flowers. Monotypic genus, very closely allied to Rhipsalis.

Erythrorhipsalis pilocarpa (Löfg.) Berg.

Stems dark greyish-green to purplish. Mostly elongated branches with terminal branches in whorls. Becomes pendent with maturity. Flowers pinkish-cream, scented. Of easy culture. Brazil.

HATIORA Br. & R.

A much-branched slender bushy cacti–spineless with numerous small joints. Closely related to Rhipsalis, indigenous to Brazil.

Hatiora bambusoides (Web.) Br. & R.

With clavate joints, somewhat elongated to 4 cms long. Flower similar to the preceding, orange and flowering from the terminals. Sometimes confused with *Hatiora salicornioides*, but the shape of joints is a very ready method of identification.

Hatiora cylindrica Br. & R.

A more robust species with cylindrical joints up to 3 cms long. Light green with reddish markings. Flower light orange, or yellowish-orange, larger than the two other species. Rare in cultivation.

Hatiora salicornioides (Haw.) Br. & R.

With club-shaped small branches, dark green. An epiphyte on forest trees. Flowers yellowish-orange, small to about 10 mm long.

PFEIFFERA S. D.

Long angled branches, with many spines, usually with pendent habit. Epiphytic. Whether this genus is rightfully placed is still uncertain, but seems to be allied to Rhipsalidinae. Northern Argentina.

Pfeiffera ianthothele (Mon.) Web.

Elongated stems, bright green, usually 3/5 ribs with many spines. Of pendent habit. Flowers yellowish-cream from small ovary. Has distinctive fruits, similar to a miniature gooseberry, purplish-pink, and many black seeds.

Other species of this genus are now recorded– *Pfeiffera stricta*, *Pfeiffera gracilis* and *Pfeiffera taragensis*. It would appear that the first two named are synonymous and probably also with *P. teragensis* which can be considered a distinct species.

RHIPSALIDOPSIS Br. & R.

Shrubby species, usually erect, but becoming somewhat pendent with maturity. Has joints or segments, somewhat flattish but with 3, sometimes to 5 angles. Considerable doubt exists as to whether this should be retained within the Rhipsalidinae as it would appear closer to Epiphyllanae–in fact some species of Schlumbergera have been considered for transfer to Rhipsalidopsis.

Rhipsalidopsis rosea (Lag.) Br. & R.

A popular species from the state of Parana in southern Brazil. Flowers rose-pink, flowering in late spring. This has been one of the parents of a number of popular hybrids with Schlumbergera species, and flowers of lilac, orange and magenta have been produced.

Many plant families are involved when considering the epiphytic species of the 'other' succulents.

There is no intention of making reference to orchids, although many hundreds of species are indeed succulents. Bromeliads will be excluded, primarily as they are more correctly termed 'xerophytes', not succulents. Species of the vast Aroid family might be considered, but really only relatively few justify inclusion in this study. Hence the three major epiphytic plant families are not the principal consideration, but rather the more obscure and perhaps lesser-known plants, whose origins are the rain forests where they grow completely as epiphytes. Many families have the isolated species within the genus which are epiphytic–and all such species are of tremendous interest and appeal. It might be concluded that a vine, even a succulent one whose habitat is in forest areas, is epiphytic. This is not so. Unless the true definition of an epiphyte can be supported by the habit of a particular species in the wild, then it must be excluded.

Two of the most fascinating epiphytic species are to be found in the family, *Rubiaceae*.

Myrmecodia echinata Miq. is a smallish shrub-like plant with a large caudex which is rough and spiny. This is referred to as the 'ant plant'; the caudex has many hollows which serve as nests for stinging ants–and the caudex can be as much as 16 cm diameter. Fleshy stems arise from the caudex and have somewhat obovate fleshy leaves and small white tubular flowers. Followed later by red berries. Grows on trees in Malaysia and Singapore. There are other species of this genus with the same habit, *Myrmecodia platyrea* Becc. from New Guinea with a flatter caudex, and *Myrmecodia anatonii* Becc., an Australian species. All are rare in cultivation and seemingly can only be successfully reared as true epiphytes.

Hydnophytum formicarium Jacq. is another of these peculiar caudiciform succulents likewise inhabited by ants, but having a smooth caudex up to 12 cms diameter. Has many branches with fleshy, oval leaves, small white flowers and red berries. Also from Malaysia.

3 The Succulents of North America

The North American continent contains an abundance of cacti and other succulent species – in most instances very different and distinctive from those of the South American countries.

For the purpose of these descriptions, consideration is being given to plants from a vast area. While species are to be found in some parts of Canada and more northerly States of U.S.A., those from southern California through to southern Texas are of greater interest and importance. Mexico as a whole is rich in cacti and other succulents – over half the known genera coming from that country. The vast variety of environmental conditions which are found in Mexico no doubt account for the widely varying forms of plant-life which exist there – often localizing a species, yet on the other hand encouraging a diversity of varietal forms of a single species. Environment does change the appearance, but not necessarily the species, of a plant. Much of south Mexico, together with parts of the Central American states, are rain forest areas and have been dealt with elsewhere. The same applies to the West Indian islands. There are, however, many non-epiphytic species found in these areas which are detailed in this chapter.

Most genera of the Cactaceae centred in the North American Continent have been mentioned, but relatively few species. With all that is known about Mexico, and its flora, much is still to be learned. In recent years there has been constant and diligent explorative work, undertaken by many prominent field botanists – Glass and Foster, Moran, Lau and others – whose efforts have been directed towards establishing a better understanding of existing known species, endeavouring always to ascertain the utterly correct data for posterity.

At the same time they have been instrumental in discovering many hitherto unknown plants.

The 'other' succulents of this vast area provide another stimulating study. Many have their counterparts in other parts of the world. Once again only very brief reference is made, but as far as possible those species detailed are to some degree, at least, representative of many others within the genus.

Several plant families are included among the succulent flora, some more so than others. With certain genera all species are native to North America or the West Indies and frequent much the same areas and accept the same environmental conditions as cacti – in fact in habitat often the cactus and the non-cactus plants seem to have a peculiar affinity. Some years ago when I was having explained to me the peculiar habits of cacti and how best to locate them in the wild, I was told by a wonderful 'old-timer' who had a familiar knowledge of the plant-life of Mexico: 'Find the agaves and you'll find the cactus' – a remark which has never been forgotten, and utterly true!

Agavaceae
Consisting of rosette plants of several genera.

AGAVES occur throughout many parts of N. America and West Indies and include well over 200 species and varieties from miniatures to giant tree-like plants. The genus is divided into three sub-genera, *Manfreda*, *Littaea* and *Agave*, and into many sub-series.
Agave americana L.
One of the best known, having been naturalized in

Agave americana v. *mediopicta* forma *alba*

many parts of Europe, even Britain in more protected areas. Seemingly of Mexican origin. Stemless rosettes producing offsets, greyish-green leaves, sometimes to 3 m high. Inflorescence to 8 m high with many branches and flowers to 9 cm long. There are also most attractive varieties: *A. americana* v. *medio-picta* Trel. variegated form with yellow stripe down centre of leaves; *A. americana* v. *mediopicta* forma *alba* Hort. which has white centre stripe; *A. americana* v. *striata* Trel. with many cream or yellowish stripes in leaf centres; *A. americana* v. *marginata* Trel. yellow margins to greenish leaves.

Agave attenuata Salm-Dyck.
Plants to 1 m high, 'soft' leaves without spines or prickles, sometimes developing a trunk. Leaves up to 30 forming a rosette, smooth pale green. Inflorescence to 3 m or more high with dense raceme

of greenish-white flowers about 6 cm long. From Hidalgo, Mexico.

Agave bracteosa S. Wats.
A stemless species from near Monterrey, Nuevo Leon, Mexico, growing to about 40 cm high with peculiarity of the lower leaves recurving, upper leaves ascending abruptly with recurved tips. Leaves pale green, no spines but margins minutely denticulate. Inflorescence to 2 m high, flowers in dense spike about 3 mm long, creamy yellow.

Agave filifera Salm-Dyck.
Stemless species from Hidalgo and San Luis Potosi, Mexico, with rosette to 50 cm high. Leaves to about 25 cm long, darkish green with white markings and numerous white threads along the margins and a long brown grooved spine 10 mm long at tip. Inflorescence to over 2 m high with yellowish-green flowers, 2 together. This is one of the most

Agave gracilipes

Agave gracilipes—possibly a sub-species.

attractive of the genus with a number of varietal forms: *A. filifera* v. *compacta* J. Versch. a small rosette with short and broad leaves; *A. filifera* v. *filamentosa* (S-D.) Baker, which is larger than the type and with much narrower leaves.

Agave gracilipes Trel.

Stemless rosette of greyish-white smooth elongated leaves, stiff and tapering forming a hollow on the upper surface, terminal spine brownish, straight or flexuose. Margins with about 15 spines about 20 mm apart, narrow-triangular, brownish. Inflorescence to 5 m high with ascending branches and yellow flowers about 30 mm long on stalks. Native to western Texas, Siera Blanca and Rock Creek, U.S.A.

Agave karatto Mill.

One of the best representatives of the West Indian species – many others from different islands could possibly be varieties, so little difference can be noted in either leaf structure or inflorescence. Undoubtedly *A. dussiana* Trel. and *A. grenadina* Trel. are synonymous. The species is stemless with lanceolate leaves about 150 cm long, hollowed on the upper surface. The wide green shining leaves have a black terminal spine somewhat recurved. Margins with narrow triangular reddish spines. Inflorescence to 6 m high with spreading branches and bright yellow flowers.

Agave maculosa (Rose) Hook.

Species with rather tuberous root from southern Texas. Loose rosette of soft leaves up to 30 cm long, greyish-green with many brown markings, margins with small teeth. Inflorescence to 1 m high or more with greenish-white sweet-scented flowers.

Agave parrasana Berg.

One of the most beautiful species with compact rosette. Leaves about 35 cm long, obovate, thick, fleshy and somewhat concave on upper surface, dull green with bluish-grey pruinose tapering to a brown terminal spine about 2 cm long. Margins dentate, upper portion armed with stout curved reddish spines. Inflorescence to 3 m high with ascending branches and yellow flowers. From near Parras, Coahuila, Mexico.

Agave parviflora Torr.

Widely distributed in Sonora, Chihuahua, Mexico and Arizona. A smallish attractive rosette with stiff narrow elongated dark green leaves having many white markings, margins with short white threads. Inflorescence to over 1 m high with flowers 2 or 4 together. Tends to offset freely after flowering. Certain other species have similar characteristics, *A. toumeyana* Trel. from S. Arizona which has leaves up to 25 cm long and v. *bella* Breit. which is more like *A. parviflora* but, if anything, even more compact and beautiful. *A. schidigera* Lem. from Michoacan, Mexico, has also characteristics in keeping, with leaves to 30 cm long uniformly spreading. A really beautiful hybrid between *A. filifera* and *A. schidigera* is a rarity of particular charm, known as *A.* × '*Leopoldii*' Hort.

Agave pumila de Smet

Possibly the smallest species of the genus being only about 5 cm in diameter and 3 cm high. Beautiful rosette extremely compact, leaves about 8, fleshy, greyish-green, the underside being some-

Agave pumila

Agave echinoides

An Agave species of unknown origin and so far unidentified.

what rounded tapering abruptly to a short white spine. White margins with small teeth. Distribution uncertain but believed to originate from Mexico. *Agave stricta* Salm-Dyck.

One of the most attractive plants with long tapering narrow leaves, erect and slightly incurved forming a dense spreading rosette. Leaves about 35 cm long, thick at base and tapering to terminal spine, surface with parallel ribs or keels on both sides, greyish-green. Inflorescence to 2 m high with flowers in dense spike, white about 20 mm long. Native of Mexico in the state of Puebla. There are other species very similar, *A. striata* Zucc. with longer leaves and less dense rosette from Hidalgo, Mexico. *A. echinoides* Jac. a rare species of Mexican origin with thick rosette of leaves about 15 cm long, narrowly ribbed with roughened margins and terminal spine about 3 mm.

Other species of this family include widely diverse plants, differing considerably in structure, habit and environment.

49

Agave victoriae-reginae

Agave utahensis Engelm.

An erect compact grey-green rosette with stiff tapering leaves and pronounced terminal spine. Widely distributed throughout parts of Utah, California, Arizona, where it grows on desert and mountainous areas at from 1,000 to 2,500 m altitude. Leaves to 17 cm long and 2·5 cm wide, concave on upper side, convex below. Margins sinuate with teeth 10 mm apart, hooked, triangular 2 mm long. Inflorescence 2·5 m high with yellow flowers 25 mm long. Several varieties of the species are recognized; *A. utahensis* v. *nevadensis* Engelm., an erect rosette with very long terminal spine to over 8 cm long, endemic to Clark Mountains, California, and Ivanpah Mtns. Nevada. *A. utahensis* v. *eborispina* (Hester) Breit. with light green leaves, ivory-white spine to 20 cm long, also from Nevada. *A. utahensis* v. *kaibabensis* (McKelvey) Breit. is a very large rosette to over 1 m diameter, greyish-brown and long terminal spine with well-separated marginal teeth which curve backwards or forwards, from Arizona.

Agave victoriae-reginae T. Moore

One of the most outstanding plants in the succulent world! From near Santa Catarina, Monterrey, Nuevo Leon, and in certain other restricted areas

ABOVE *Encephalocarpus strobiliformis*

ABOVE *Lophocereus schotti*

BELOW *Thelocactus conothele* v. *aurantiacus*

BELOW *Mammillopsis senilis*

ABOVE *Mammillaria microcarpa*

ABOVE *Calibanus hookeri*

BELOW *Opuntia pycnantha* v. *cristata*

BELOW *Obregonia denegrii*

of Coahuila and Durango. Rosette usually simple with leaves 15 cm long, long and narrow, with a blunted tip, thick, about 5 cm wide, slightly curved inwards, concave on upper side and convex on lower surface with keel towards the tip; keel and margins with white bands and markings; terminal spine about 2 mm long, often with two minute spines. Inflorescence to 4 m high dense with creamy flowers usually 3 together. Several forms are recognised: *A. victoriae-reginae* forma *nickelsii* (Hort. ex Godd.) Trel. which used to be known as *A. fernandi-regis* Berg. has fewer leaves, more open rosette and leaves acute from base to apex; *A. victoriae-reginae* forma *ornata* Breit. is of smaller growth with brilliant white markings.

Beaucarnea recurvata (Lem.) Lem.
(syn. *Nolina recurvata* Lem.) A tree-like plant from south-east Mexico about 6 m high with pronounced globose base. Leaves elongated, thin and tapering and recurved about 1 m long with smooth edges. Flowers inconspicuous, white.

Others of similar character, *B. bigelovii* Bak. from Sonora and *B. longifolia* Bak. from southern Mexico are also tree-like species. *B. gracilis* Lem. is a somewhat smaller plant, but still tree-like, with straight leaves about 50 cm long and 6 mm broad, grey with rough edges, endemic to south central Mexico.

Beschorneria tubiflora Kunth.
Leaves up to 30 cm long and 2 cm broad, roughened on both sides, rosulate, fleshy greenish-grey. Inflorescence 1 m high with violet red bracts and reddish-green tubular flowers. *B. bracteata* Jacobi has a very succulent rosette, thin fleshy leaves about 35 cm long, glaucous green with rough margins. Inflorescence 2 m high with arching raceme, reddish bracts with yellowish-red flowers. Another species, *B. yuccoides* Hook. f. consists of rosette of about 20 leaves, 50 cm long and 5 cm wide, greyish-green, rough on margins and on under-side. Inflorescence about 1·5 m high, stem coral red and large reddish bracts and bright green flowers. All are from Mexico.

Calibanus hookeri Trel.
Native of Jaumava in Tamaulipas, Mexico, where it is found in hilly country hardly distinguishable from surrounding grasslands. Caudex generally

Calibanus hookeri—showing the typically grass-like leaves and the thick, corky swollen caudex.

underground, large globose about 30 cm diameter with thick corky bark. Branching from crown with many long grass-like leaves about 15 cm long. Branched inflorescence with numerous inconspicuous pinkish, somewhat purplish flowers.

Dasylirion longissimum Lem.
Large rosette on stem up to 2 m high with numerous elongated tapering leaves to over 1·5 m long and only 6 mm wide, upper surface somewhat convex and angled on lower surface. Inflorescence to 2 m high with whitish bell-shaped flowers. All species have much the same habit. *D. glaucophyllum* Hook.

with bluish-grey leaves, slightly convex and prominent rib off-centre, margins with small hook-spines in both directions and whitish or greenish-white flowers. *D. acrotrichum* Zucc. with short thick stem topped by dense rosette of 1m long leaves and yellow spiny margins, flowers white. The three species mentioned are from eastern Mexico.

Furcraea bedinghausii C. Koch
Very large succulent species forming large trunk topped by rosette of 30 or more elongated, leathery fleshy bluish-grey leaves about 1m long and 6cm wide, with rough minutely dentate margins. Inflorescence to nearly 5m high with drooping branches and flowers in loose panicles. Native of central Mexico. *F. cubensis* Vent. A Cuban species, has shorter stem with elongated sword-like leaves, rounded on lower surface and keeled, rough with marginal teeth almost straight about 3mm long. Tall inflorescence to 5m and pure white flowers.

Anacardiaceae

Has only one succulent genus but includes several well-known non-succulents – *Mangifera indica*, the mango tree, *Harpephyllum caffrum*, the Kaffir plum, *Anacardium occidentale*, the cashew-nut tree, *Rhus vernix*, the poison ivy and *Schinus molle*, the peppercorn tree, and it was into this latter genus that Pachycormus was originally placed.

Pachycormus discolor (Benth.) Coville
A native of Baja California and off-shore islands. Commonly known as the 'Elephant Tree' – an ideal plant for cultivation as a natural bonsai. A short, dwarfed swollen trunk with papery bark and branching quite freely with somewhat slender elongated branches and small leaves, deciduous. Flowers small, reddish or yellowish. During rest season the branches can be trimmed to encourage compact shape. An uncommon plant in cultivation.

Apocynaceae

Includes a number of genera, species of which are succulent. Mostly represented in Africa and Madagascar; only one genus has species in North America and West Indies.

Plumiera acuminata Ait.
A species distributed throughout much of Mexico, Central America and West Indies. The typical 'Franzipani tree'. A succulent tree with fleshy stems and branches, which exude a latex-like substance. Large green leaves which fall in rest season. Flowers very beautiful, dark cream with yellow centre.

Plumiera acuminata v. *purpurea* Ruiz. et Pav.
Similar in most respects to the species, apparently native to several of the West Indian islands, having beautiful reddish-purple flowers. Another variety is *P. acuminata* v. *alba* L. from the Windward Islands and Leeward Islands having slender succulent stem and narrow leaves, long and tapering.

Begoniaceae

Includes the genus *Begonia*, species of which are to be found in many parts of the tropical and subtropical world. Only one North American species is generally considered succulent, which again emphasizes the problem of deciding the *exact* definition of a 'succulent'. The species recognized has fleshy stems; others with similar stems or with fleshy (succulent) leaves have thus far been omitted. These include *Begonia caroliniaefolia* (Mexico) with fleshy glossy green leaflets, quilted with toothed margins; *Begonia conchaefolia* (Costa Rica) having cupped, peltate and fleshy glossy green leaves; *Begonia dayii* (Mexico) succulent leaves with many chocolate brown markings; *Begonia hidalgensis* (Mexico) with deep green fleshy leaves, somewhat kidney-shaped; *Begonia kenworthyi* (Mexico) ivy-shaped bluish-grey fleshy leaves and stems.

Begonia incana Lindl.
A Mexican plant from high altitudes, about 5,000m at Tierra Caliente, erect becoming shrubby, with succulent stems and large fleshy shield-shaped leaves covered with whitish scurf. Flowers pinkish-white.

Bombacaceae

Includes many genera of tree-like plants, only two of which have representative succulent species.

Bombax ellipticum H.B. et K.
A Mexican tree-succulent recorded from many parts of the north, central and more southerly areas usually in limestone rocks. Has greenish caudex-like stem with greyish-brown bark and large green deciduous leaves. Flowers have purplish petals surrounding delicate soft pinkish stamens about 6 cm long tipped with yellow anthers. Another species, *B. palmeri* Wats. is recorded as having a reddish caudex, but in all other aspects very similar to *B. ellipicum* – they may be synonymous.
Chorisia species are reported from West Indian islands; these may be escapes from South America; in any event, while their existence can be substantiated, no descriptive data is available.

Bromeliaceae
Possibly not true succulents, but due to their xerophytic characteristics many genera have been recorded as such, one such genus being native of North America.
Hechtia argentea Bak.
Stemless rosettes with dark glossy green leaves about 35 cm long covered with silvery whitish scurf on both surfaces and prominent sawtoothed margins. Long inflorescence with many greenish-white inconspicuous flowers. A number of other species, all Mexican, are of interest. *H. glomerata* Zucc. fleshy, dark green leaves with whitish scales on the lower surface and the upper surface often pale reddish-brown variegated, toothed margins and whitish flowers. *H. ghiesbreghtii* Lem. recurved leaves covered with silvery scales on both sides, the upper surface having brownish markings. *H. marnier-lapostellei* is a dwarf species with short tapering silvery-grey leaves; *H. tillandsioides* has elongated waxy green leaves, somewhat curling and very much resembling a *Tillandsia*.

Burseraceae
The 'incense-tree' family includes a few succulent species, some tree-like, others of comparatively short growth, frequently with an obese stem.
Bursera microphylla (Rose) A. Grey
Fairly widely distributed from the Colorado Desert to many parts of Sonora, Mexico. Commonly known as the 'elephant-trunk tree'. A tall tree succulent tree to 10 m high with thickish stem and branches consisting of soft wood with milky sap, thin yellow papery bark which is easily shed. Fernlike leaves which seem to be deciduous. Other species include *B. fagarioides* with small insignificant heart-shaped leaves and small reddish flowers; *B. hindsiana* similar to the other species and having reddish papery bark.

Cactaceae
Cacti are divided into three Tribes, each having distinctive characteristics. These can be simply defined as follows:

Tribe 1. Cereoideae
Areoles have no glochids and flowers borne on definite tube.
   All three tribes are represented among the North American cacti.

Tribe 2. Opuntioideae
Generally leafless, some with leaves similar to Pereskia, but usually elongated and very fleshy. *The areoles have glochids* and often produce very small leaf-like growths. Stems much branched with simple or multiple joints.

Tribe 3. Pereskioideae
Having leaves like normal plants, no glochids and flowers borne on stalks.

Tribe 1. Cereoideae
Contains the majority of the genera of the Cactaceae. The plant form takes many guises, tall and columnar, sometimes with shorter erect stems. A host of species come within the category of being barrel-shaped or globular and while many of these can reach large dimensions, others are extremely small, even miniature. All have one thing in common – their areoles do not have glochids. The flowers are almost entirely borne on a definite tube – some of which are nocturnal, others diurnal flowering. The fruit usually takes the form of a berry.

New classifications have taken place with Sub-tribe *Cereanae* resulting in a number of generic titles becoming obsolete and new ones emerging. Hence many species with long-standing familiar names are now embraced by another or new genus.

SUB-TRIBE CACTANAE

Melocactus broadwayii Br. & B.

A West Indian species from the Windward Islands and Tobago. Very shallow rooted with somewhat flattened base, pale green up to 15cm long, 14cm broad at the base and narrowing towards the cephalium. Ribs 14 to 18 with areoles regularly set about 1cm apart, 8–10 radial spines and usually one central, all yellowish-brown. Cephalium about 6cm diameter and eventually to 3 or even 5cm high consisting of densely set soft brown bristles and whitish wool. Flowers small, purplish. This is one of the many recorded species from these parts of the West Indies – termed the 'Turks Cap' cactus on account of its cephalium. *M. intortus* (Mill.) Br. & R. is very similar in most respects, but invariably with a longer cephalium more rounded at the top having lilac-pink flowers.

Melocactus matanzanus Leon.

One of the choicest species, always small and producing its cephalium after about 6 years. Stem fresh green, 10cm high and 8cm broad with wide shallow ribs. Areoles with short reddish spines.

Melocactus sp. This species is newly introduced and has not yet been named.

Cephalium bright orange composed of dense bristles and white wool. Flowers deep pink. This is one of the several species endemic to Cuba; most are rare in cultivation and would appear, in most cases, to be somewhat smaller in growth than those from other parts. *M. acunai* Leon, with wide somewhat acute ribs, armed with long spreading rigid spines. *M. harlowii* Br. & R. with light green body with narrow low ribs, closely set areoles with up to 16 spines, spreading and some curved. *M. guitartii* is the rarest of these Cuban species, about 10cm broad and 12cm high, densely armed with long spreading and protruding spines.

This is one of the earliest groups of cacti introduced into Europe; for many years they had the generic title of *Cactus* (e.g. *Cactus broadwayii* etc.) until the existing title of Melocactus was established finally in 1827.

SUB-TRIBE. CEREANEA

Acanthocereus pentagonus (L.) Br. & R.

(syn. *Cactus pentagonus* L.) Type species. A long clambering plant, rooting at tips and forming further growths and colonizing. Stems 3–5 angled with regular areoles along the margins and many short acicular spines. Large flower up to 20cm long, white with spreading petals. Tube covered with brownish felt. Very widely distributed throughout some of the southerly states of U.S.A., the eastern coast of Mexico through to Guatemala, also some West Indian islands. Also known in parts of northerly South America. Other species are recorded from Mexico, *A. subinermis* Br. & R. and *A. occidentalis* Br. & R. having much the same characteristics as the type species.

Anisocereus gaumeri (Br. & R.) Backeb.

An erect slender plant with usually 3, sometimes 4-angles, very winged. Areoles small and far apart with many slender brownish spines. Flower greenish-yellow to 5cm long, tube with leafy scales. Fruit very large, deep red and with small bristles. From southern Mexico.

Anisocereus lepidanthus (Eichl.) Backeb.

(syn. *Cereus lepidanthus* Eichl.) Type species. A little-known species from Guatemala. An erect plant, rarely branched, having 7 to 9 low ribs. Areoles very small with many central and radial spines. Flowers up to 8 cm long, whitish. Flower tube and ovary with thin scales.

Backebergia chrysomallus (Lem.) Backeb. (syn. *Pilocereus chrysomallus* Lem.) Type species. Sometimes called *B. militaris.* A very large columnar species with many branches up to 18 m high.

Backebergia chrysomallus showing the well developed cephallus.

Branches with many ribs, up to 14, dull greyish-green. Mature growths develop a brown cephalium eventually covering the whole apex which becomes larger as the plant grows taller. Flowers from the cephalium, about 3 cm long, creamy-white. A plant of exceptional attraction – cuttings of flowering stems will root easily and the cephalium will continue to grow. Endemic to more southerly parts of Mexico around Oaxaca and Puebla.

Bergerocactus emoryi (Engelm.) Br. & R. (syn. *Cereus emoryi* Engelm.) Type species. A sprawling species with bright green cylindrical stems and branches having many ribs and completely covered with long golden-yellow spines, often with over 30 to an areole. Flowers creamy-white with very spiny fruits. Distributed in more southerly areas of California and into north-westerly parts of Baja, California, in coastal regions.

Carnegia gigantea (Engelm.) Br. & R. (syn. *Cereus giganteus* Engelm.) Type species. One of the most spectacular plants of the cactaceae – the giant Saguaro of Arizona. This species also occurs near Kino Bay, Sonora. A huge columnar cactus, stout, with many ribs and areoles felted and spiny. For many years the plant remains simple, then branches with thick ascending growths – can become up to 25 m tall. Flowers up to 12 cm long, white, short tube with small but broad scales. Fruits red. Woodpeckers make their nests within the body of the plant; when deserted they are occupied by other forms of bird-life.

Cephalocereus hoppenstedtii (syn. *Haseltonia hoppenstedtii* (Web.) Backeb.) Type species. A doubtful genus, probably better called *P. hoppenstedtii.* A very attractive rare plant, tall slender and erect to 10 m high. Has many ribs, often up to 20, with areoles close together and the whole body covered with whitish spines. In maturity the terminals develop a pseudocephalium. Flower whitish, bell-shaped. From southern Mexico.

Cephalocereus senilis (Haw.) Pfeiff. (syn. *Cactus senilis* Haw.) Type species. A well-known and attractive plant from the limestone hills of eastern Hidalgo, Mexico. A tall-growing cactus up to 14 m high, columnar, with numerous ribs and densely covered with white bristles and thick long whitish wool. Has become known as the 'Old Man Cactus'. Pseudocephalium develops when the stems are about 6 m tall. Flower rose-pink about 5 cm long, tube with few scales. This species has the distinctive quality of having a similar attractive appearance from seedling stage through to maturity.

Many species of Cephalocereus have now been transferred to other genera, and what was at one time a large genus is now reduced to only few species.

Dendrocereus nudiflorus (Engelm.) Br. & R. (syn. *Cereus nudiflorus* Engelm.) Type species. A very rare species from Cuba, West Indies, scarcely known in cultivation. A tree-like plant up to 10 m high with woody trunk and many terminal branches. Branches dull green with 3 to 5 ribs, very pronounced and areoles with many spines. Mature growth is stout and sturdy, while young immature branches tend to be weak and small jointed. Flower whitish. A monotypic genus.

Escontria chiotilla (Web.) Rose (syn. *Cereus chiotilla* Web.) Type species. A monotypic genus. A tall-growing plant up to 7m high. The main stem is usually short with numerous weak branches, having 7 or 8 acute ribs. Areoles very close together with many short, somewhat flattened spines and one very much longer. Flower creamy-yellow, the tube and ovary with many overlapping scales. Endemic to southern Mexico.

Harrisia gracilis (Mill.) Britton
(syn. *Cereus gracilis* Mill.) Type species. A tall-growing and much-branched species from Jamaica, dark green with up to 11 ribs, somewhat rounded with shallow depressions between. Areoles far apart with many white spines tipped black. Flowers large white with brownish-green scaly tube. Better known as *H. repandus*. Somewhat rare in cultivation.

Heliocereus elegantissimus Br. & R.
An interesting clambering plant with decumbent habit. Branches light green, usually 3 or 4-angled, the ribs being strongly undulate. Areoles are well apart, large, brownish-yellow felted. Spines very short in two series, the radials acicular, white and bristly, the inner ones very stiff. Flowers deep scarlet to about 15cm diameter. A distinctive variety is recorded, *H. elegantissimus v. stenopetalum* Bravo, which has many similarities to the species, but with a greater number of ribs, up to 7 and flowers somewhat zygomorphic, smaller than the species and with very narrow petals. It would seem also that the colour is different, this being given as purplish-red. Both are from the same area of Mexico, on the highway between Durango and Mazatlan, at an altitude of between 2,000 and 2,500m.

Heliocereus speciosus (Cav.) Br. & R.
(syn. *Cactus speciosus* (Cav.) Type species. A deservedly popular species from central to southern Mexico. A semi-erect plant with up to 5 ribs, somewhat undulating and large felted areoles with numerous yellowish spines. Flowers rich scarlet to 16cm long. This species has been used extensively in cross-pollinating with *Epiphyllum* to produce some of the most exotic 'Epicactus' forms e.g. × *Heliophyllum* Rowl.).

Lemaireocereus aragonii
(syn. *Marshallocereus aragonii* (Web.) Backeb.) Type species. Originates from westerly regions of

Costa Rica and represents one of the few columnar types of cacti in that country. A tall-growing plant having many terminal branches with 6 to 8 large rounded ribs. Brown felted areoles with about 10 greyish spines, the centrals to 3cm long. Flowers yellowish-white to 8cm long.

Lemaireocereus beneckei
(syn. *Hertrichocereus beneckei* (Ehrenb.) Backeb.) Type species. A shrubby species, erect and much branched up to 5m high. Branches greyish-green with 8 ribs strongly tuberculate. Small black-felted areoles with up to 5 brown acicular spines. Flowers small, brownish-white diurnal. From the area around Guerrero, central Mexico. This is a monotypic species which perhaps is warranted on account of its pecular tuberculate ribs and small flower.

Leimaireocereus dumortieri
(syn. *Isolatocereus dumortieri* (Scheidw.) Backeb.) Type species. A tall erect plant up to 15m, branching freely. Main stems usually woody with age, branches dark bluish-green with 6 ribs or even more, many areoles, grey-felted with numerous spines, yellowish. Flower small about 5cm long, diurnal, whitish. Fruits small, oblong and spineless. From central Mexico.

Lemaireocereus hollianus (Web.) Br. & R.
(syn. *Cereus hollianus* Web.) Type species. An imposing species from Puebla, Mexico, with erect habit up to 5m high. Stems dark green with up to 12 acute ribs. Areoles with many reddish spines becoming greyish. Flowers white, about 10cm long from the upper areoles, fruits very large, red with many spines and bristles.

Lemaireocereus marginatus
(syn. *Marginatocereus marginatus* (De Cand.) Backeb.) Type species. Tall erect stems, rarely branching, to 7m high. Stems dark dull green with 5 or 6 acute ribs and white cushioned areoles which form an almost continuous line on the ridges. Spines small. Flower funnel-shaped, very compact about 4cm long from ovary to tip and globular fruits about 4cm diameter covered with wool and spines. Fairly widely distributed in central Mexico.

Lemaireocereus stellatus
(syn. *Stenocereus stellata* (Pfeiff.) Backeb.) Type species. Columnar plant branching freely from the

base, pale bluish-green with up to 12 low obtuse ribs. Areoles with many radial and central spines, centrals often 6 cm long. Flowers towards the apex, diurnal, small, bell-shaped, reddish about 4 cm long. Ovary with small scales and bristly spines, rather woolly. Red spiny globular fruits about 3 cm diameter. From more southerly regions of Mexico.

Lemaireocereus thurberi (Engelm.) Br. & R.
A widely distributed species from S. Arizona to Sonora and Baja California. A stout much branched plant forming huge clusters to 7 m high. Branches dark brownish-green with many low ribs, often 15 or more. Large circular brown felted areoles with numerous spines up to 5 cm long. Flowers large, whitish, fruits spiny. A popular species in cultivation.

Leptocereus assurgens (C. Wright) Br. & R.
(syn. *Cereus assurgens* C. Wright.) Type species. A clambering, untidy plant up to 3 m high with many branches. Usually 4-angled having areoles with brown acicular spines up to 8 cm long. Flowers white and fruits with clusters of short spines. A rare plant in cultivation from north-western coast of Cuba on limestone rock.

Leptocereus leonii Br. & R.
A tree-like species with decided rounded trunk up to 5 m high. Branches freely, slender, elongated and having 6 to 8 ribs, bright green. Ribs are crenate with the areoles at the depressions having up to 12 yellowish spines. Flower pinkish-white. From Sierra de Anafe, Cuba. Rare in cultivation.

Lophocereus schottii (Engelm.) Br. & R.
(syn. *Cereus schotti* Engelm.) Type species. A columnar spreading plant forming clusters usually branching from the base. Stems dull to fresh green with 5 to 7 ribs. Non-flowering areoles with greyish-brown felt and few short spines. Flowering areoles with numerous bristles at terminal areas of stems, these thickening and almost forming a cephalium. Flowers white to 4 cm long. Large fruits about 3 cm diameter. There are varieties with only trifling differences to the species.

Machaerocereus eruca (Brand.) Br. & R.
(syn. *Cereus eruca* Brand.) Type species. Commonly called the 'Creeping Devil' on account of its lengthy crawling branches reaching to sometimes 15 m in length. From Lower California including Magdalena Island. Of prostrate growth with large thick very spiny branches. Ribs about 12, large areoles having about 20 spines of unequal length to 3 cm long. Flowers yellowish-cream, 12 cm long on long tube which has scales on the lower part. Large spiny berry-like fruits.

One other species is recognized, *M. gummosus* (Engelm.) Br. & R. which generally has more compact and erect growth with less vicious spines, also native to Lower California and off-shore islands.

Myrtillocactus geometrizans (Mart.) Cons.
(syn. *Cereus geometrizans* Mart.) Type species. A well-known Mexican species from the regions of San Luis Potosi to Oaxaca, having edible fruits which when dried resemble raisins. Young seedlings are frequently used for grafting stock. Popular in collections. A tree-like plant with short blue-green trunk and many branches above. Ribs 5 or 6, very pronounced, areoles well apart with strong blackish spines, the central spine usually being more elongated. Flowers small from the upper part of the areole, creamy-yellow. Fruits bluish.

Neoabbottia paniculata (Lamarck) Br. & R.
(syn. *Cactus paniculata* Lamarck.) Type species. The only representative of this obscure genus. Rarely met with in cultivation. Apparently quite widely distributed in Haiti and Cuba and has a striking resemblance to certain species of Leptocereus and Dendrocereus all from the same areas. A tree-like plant often to 10 m high. Branches from the top, the branches being 4 ribbed and strongly winged with somewhat crenate margins. Many brownish-grey spines at well spaced areoles. Cephaliums develop on terminal ends. Flowers nocturnal, white, short and tubular.

Neobuxbaumia euphorbioides
(syn. *Rooksbya euphorbioides* (Haw.) Backeb.) Type species. An obscure species rarely encountered in cultivation. A tall columnar plant to about 5 m high. Stems with 8 acute ribs, somewhat crenate and very closely set areoles, white felted and with few small spines. Flowers diurnal, reddish. Native of Mexico around Tamaulipas.

Neobuxbaumia tetetzo (Web.) Backeb.
(syn. *Pilocereus tetetzo* Web.) Type species. Origin-

Pachycereus pringlei in habitat. The author is dwarfed by this giant plant.

ally included with Pilocereus, with which it could well be re-united or with Pachycereus. An erect columnar species with greyish-green stems and many rounded ribs, areoles well armed with many spines. Flowers somewhat small, rather cylindrical and not widely opening. From the limestone slopes of Mt Guiengola, near Oaxaca, Mexico.

Neodawsonia apicicephalium (Dawson) Backeb.
(syn. *Cephalocereus apicicephalium* Dawson.) Type species. An erect columnar plant, rounded stems with numerous ribs having closely set areoles and many short spines. Mature growth develops pronounced woolly rings around the stems due to the annual displacement of the terminal cephalium from which the nocturnal pink flowers emerge. A rare and desirable species from Cerro Guiengola, near Tehuantepec, Oaxaca, Mexico.

Nyctocereus serpentinus (Lag. & Rodr.) Br. & R.
(syn. *Cereus serpentinus* D.C.) Type species. An erect then spreading plant, forming clumps, creeping and hanging to sometimes 3 m long. Stems slender-pale green. Ribs 10 or 12, low and rounded with closely set areoles, somewhat felted with about 12 white bristle-like spines. Flowers usually from the upper areoles, whitish, about 16 cm long, tube with bristles and areoles on ovary. Has very large seeds. Possibly from eastern Mexico, but it has been so much cultivated throughout Mexico that its actual habitat is in doubt. Sometimes called the 'Snake Cactus'.

Pachycereus pringlei (S. Watson) Br. & R.
(syn. *Cereus pringlei* S. Watson) Type species. One of the largest species of columnar cacti, frequently to 12 m tall. Usually with short trunk, then branching freely with ascending stems. Ribs up to 15 somewhat obtuse, very large areoles, brown felted with many spines. Young branches are almost bluishgrey with only few spines, but become more green and more heavily spined with growth. Flowering areoles very large. Flower tube and ovary covered with small scales and brownish hairs, flower whitish about 8 cm long. Widely distributed throughout western Sonora and parts of Lower California and offshore islands in the Gulf of California.

Peniocereus greggii (Engelm.) Br. & R.
(syn. *Cereus greggii* Engelm.) Type species. A plant of considerable interest. When not in flower it is totally unimpressive, but in full bloom creates a wonderful effect. Root system very fleshy, frequently having enormous tubers. Stems slender, 4–6 angles, somewhat crenulate ribs and areoles with very small black acicular spines. Stems are greyish, looking almost like twigs. Flowers towards the terminal ends on slender tube, set with small scales, petals pure white about 12 cm diameter, opening at night but remaining in flower for much of the following day. Native to parts of Arizona, Texas and New Mexico and also northern Sonora.

Other species of this genus are recorded, *P. marianus* from Topolobampo, Sinaloa, *P. johnstonii* native to Baja California, and also *P. diguetii* (*Neovansia diguetii*) from south of Guaymas and also reported from Topolobampo in Sinaloa, seemingly always in close proximity to coastal areas. All have the same characteristics of large tuberous roots and slender straggling twiggy stems with beautiful flowers.

Rathbunia alamosensis

Pilosocereus leucocephalus (Roul.) K. Schum.
Type species. A genus which has been sunk and resurrected, this species was recently included with Cephalocereus, then Pilosocereus.

An erect plant to 5 m high, many branches from towards the base and ascending. Branches dull green with 12 low ribs, areoles with about 10 acicular spines. Flowering areoles develop on one side of the branch terminals and form a pseudo-cephalium of long white hairs often to 10 cm long from which the flowers protrude. From eastern parts of Sonora and Chihuahua, Mexico.

Many other beautiful species of this genus are available; *P. palmeri* Rose from Victoria, eastern Mexico is a well-known species which develops an extraordinarily beautiful cephalium of thick white wool. Other species are native of South America.

Polaskia chichipe (Goss.) Backeb.
(syn. *Cereus chichipe* Goss.) Type species. A tree-like plant up to 5 m high. Usually with short trunk and branching freely at the top. Branches greenish-grey with undulate, acute ribs, 9 to 12, areoles with 6–7 greyish spines and one longer central. Flowers small, greenish-yellow, diurnal. Spiny reddish fruit, globose, about 2 cm diameter.

Rathbunia alamosensis (Coulter) Br. & R.
syn. *Rathbunia sonorensis (Cereus sonorensis)* which is the type species. A large sprawling plant forming clusters with stems to 3 m in length. Occasionally somewhat erect in growth, columnar with 5 to 8 ribs, obtuse. Areoles with many straight and spreading spines, greyish. Flowers scarlet to 10 cm long, tube and ovary with few spines and tufts of felt. Globular red fruits about 4 cm diameter. Distributed in many parts of Sinaloa and southern Sonora, especially in the area around Alamos.

Wilcoxia poselgeri (Lemaire) Br. & R.
(syn. *Echinocereus poselgeri* Lemaire.) Type species. Root system extremely tuberous. Stems elongated and slender with about 10 insignificant ribs, greyish-green. Areoles small with minute slightly adpressed spines, one central spine rather longer.

Flowers purplish-pink with brilliant green style, 5 cm long. Tube and ovary with small spines and whitish hairs. A popular species endemic to S. Texas, parts of Sonora and Coahuila.

Not all genera within this tribe have been considered here. The plants mentioned are typical of the group. The sheet number of synonyms mentioned gives some indication of the progressive study which has taken place over the years to bring about a better classification which tends to make identification easier for non-botanists.

SUB-TRIBE CORYPHANTHANAE

This sub-tribe includes many genera and a great number of individual species and varieties. The inclusion of some genera (and species) is still in doubt. Further exploration and research, particularly in the wild, will no doubt help to validate or exclude some species. Only a very representative selection is here recorded, mentioning especially those more recently introduced.

Ancistrocactus megarhizus (Rose) Br. & R.
(syn. *Echinocactus megarhizus* Rose.) Type species. Plant with long fleshy tap roots. Stems usually solitary, sometimes in clusters, globular to 8 cm high ribs in spirals, divided into dark-green tubercles to 5 cm high. About 20 pectinate, pale, radial spines, spreading, and 4 central spines, the lower ones being stouter and longer and strongly hooked. Flower funnel-shaped, small with short tube from the base of the long tubercles. A rare species from near Victoria, Mexico.

Ancistrocactus uncinatus Gal. (Beus.)
(syn. *Glandulicactus uncinata* (Gal.) Backeb.) Type species. Short-cylindrical plant to about 20 cm high with 13 ribs having strong tubercles undulate. Areoles with many hairs and spines, the central spine and 3 lower radial spines are prominently hooked. Flowers brownish. From western Texas to central Mexico. This was included with the genus *Ferocactus*, then transferred by Backeberg to a new genus created for this and one other species because they had glands in the areole from which a honey-like substance would secrete. These glands were often elongated and gave the effect of stunted spines. The actual status of this plant is still in doubt.

Bartschella schumannii (Hild.) Br. & R.
(syn. *Mammillaria schumannii* Hild.) Type species. There would now appear to be insufficient differences to retain the generic title of *Bartschella* and it is proposed that this species be re-united with Mammillaria.

An uncommon plant, usually clustering to about 6 cm high, somewhat globular to short-oblong with ungrooved large rounded tubercles, axils slightly woolly and no bristles. Radial spines to about 15, spreading, stout, central spines slightly hooked. Flower about 4 cm diameter, short and hidden among the tubercles, dark pink to violet-rose. Distributed in more or less coastal areas from La Paz to Todos Santos, Baja California.

Coryphantha organensis D. Zimm.
With cylindric stems, clustering freely, yellowish-green with pronounced tubercles. Areoles with numerous spines, radials about 35, stiff, straight, whitish; centrals about 12, straight, stout, yellowish. Flowers pale pink. Endemic to the area of the Organ Mountains, New Mexico, U.S.A.

Cochemia halei (Brandeg.) Walton
(syn. *Mammillaria halei* Brandeg.) Type species. Current opinion veers towards the uniting of this species and other of the Cochemiea with Mammillaria. Usually clustering stems, very erect to 30 cm long and to 7 cm diameter. Tubercles very short, axils woolly. Radial spines to 20, about 10 mm long, 3 or 4 centrals about 25 mm long– all straight. Flowers towards the centre, 5 cm long yellowish with scarlet lobes. An attractive plant from the offshore islands of Baja California, particularly Magdalena Island. Other species within this genus include *C. setispina* (Coulte) Walton, *C. pondii* (Greene) Walton and *C. poselgeri* (Hild.) Br. & R. all having many similar characteristics and all originating from Baja California.

Coryphantha pulleineana (Backeb.) Glass
(syn. *Neolloydia pulleineanus* Backeb.) With elongated growth and very long fleshy tuberous roots. Pronounced tubercles with many radial and central spines, centrals being much longer, straight, brownish-black. Flower yellow or golden yellow from near the apex. From San Luis Potosi, Mexico.

Coryphantha scheeri (Kuntze) L. Benson
A rather elongated plant to 15 cm long and 9 cm

diameter at base, solitary, sometimes clustering, pronounced tubercles and densely spined. Radial spines 1 to 5, slightly hooked or curved, spreading irregularly 2·5 cm long, centrals thickish, about 2·5 cm long, light brown with red tips, spreading. Flower to 7 cm diameter, yellowish with reddish markings. Two varietal forms are recorded, *C. sheeri* v. *valida* (Engelm.) L. Benson and *C. scheeri* v. *robustispina* (Schott) L. Benson – all from high elevations in Chihuahuan Desert, S.E. Arizona, Texas, and to parts of Chihuahua in Mexico.

Coryphantha sneedii (Br. & R.) Berg. v. *leei* (Rose) L. Benson

This variety is synonymous with *Escobaria leei* Rose ex. Boed. A choice miniature growing species from limestone rock ledges in Rattlesnake Canyon, New Mexico. Rarely solitary, generally clusters freely, densely covered with small whitish spines. Flowers pinkish-white.

Coryphantha sulcolanata Lem.

(syn. *Mammillaria sulcolanata* Lem.) Type species, a somewhat sub-globose plant, usually clustering about 5 cm high and 6 cm diameter. Tubercles 5-angled at base, conical above with wool in axils of young plants. About 10 radial spines of unequal length up to 16 mm long, brownish with black tips. Large flower about 4 cm long, pinkish. From Hidalgo, Mexico.

Dolichothele longimamma (De Cand.) Br. & R.

(syn. *Mammillaria longimamma* De Cand.) Type species. A clustering species, pale fresh green with prominent elongated tubercles. Spines from areoles at tip of tubercles, radials up to 12 acicular, spreading, central spines 1 to 3 protruding horizontally, all yellowish, centrals with blackish tips. Flowers to 6 cm long, bright yellow. Native of parts of central Mexico.

There are three or four other species or varieties of this genus, each having great similarity with one another, with only rare exceptions. The present trend would seem for this genus to be merged with Mammillaria.

Escobaria tuberculosa (Engelm.) Br. & R.

(syn. *Mammillaria tuberculosa* Engelm.) Type species. The validity of the nomenclature now stated is much in doubt. This species has been reduced to varietal status of Coryphantha, viz.

Coryphantha strobiliformis v. *strobiliformis* (Poselger.) L. Benson, the other variety being *C. strobiliformis* v. *orcuttii* (Rose) L. Benson. Plants usually clustering, cylindrical to about 18 cm high, tubercles regularly arranged in spirals, with numerous radial spines, up to 30, acicular, several centrals, usually tipped brown or blackish and one protruding horizontally. Flowers pale pink, about 2·5 cm diameter lasting several days. This plant is found at fairly high altitudes in limestone soil, and is native to Arizona, New Mexico and Chihuahua, Mexico.

Escobaria chaffeyi Br. & R.

An interesting species, cylindrical to 12 cm long and 6 cm diameter with many short light green tubercles having a narrow groove above. Radial spines numerous, stiff and bristly, together with several shorter centrals, pure white but tipped brown, which almost envelop the body of the plant. Flowers about 15 mm long, cream or pale. pink. Native of Zacatecas, Mexico.

Krainzia longiflora (Br. & R.) Backeb.

(syn. *Neomammillaria longiflora* Br. & R.) Type species. A choice species from Puerto Coneto, Durango, Mexico. Usually solitary, sometimes clustering, stems about 3 cm in diameter, smallish tubercles, closely set and almost hidden by spines, radials about 30, acicular to 12 mm long, yellowish, spreading; centrals 4, reddish brown, one much longer and hooked at the tip. Flowers borne freely at the crown, about 2 cm long, pink with slightly purplish throat.

This species together with *Krainzia guelzowiana* Werd. also from Durango and having large rich reddish-purple flowers, are likely to be transferred to the genus *Mammillaria* with which there is a close relationship.

Mammillaria – this genus constitutes one of the largest of the Cactaceae. Considerable interest is centred around these species, and while existing grouping appears to be poorly founded, constant investigation and study is undertaken to ensure the best system of classification. In recent years several new discoveries have been made which have increased its already popular appeal, and it is in this field of exploration that there lies the most successful research.

Mammillaria gracilis – one of the rarer members of this popular genus.

Mammillaria candida Scheidw.

A most attractive and popular species from San Luis Potosi, Mexico. Usually considered a solitary plant, but occasionally caespitose. Plant body, to 8cm diameter or more, covered completely by white spines, globose. Areoles with scant white wool and numerous radial spines, 50 or more, slender, spreading, white; centrals to 12, stiff, whitish with 1 protruding. Flower funnel-shaped, pinkish with brownish markings. There are supposedly varietal forms; *M. candida rosea* which tends to have pinkish tips to the spines particularly towards the crown of the plant; and *M. candida* v. *caespitosa*, so named

due to its consistently caespitose habit and other minor differences. Whether or not these varieties are valid is much in doubt as it would seem the species itself has such variations.

Mammillaria fittkaui Glass & Foster

Species from rocks near north shore of Lake Chapala, Jalisco, Mexico. Stem cylindric 4–5 cm diameter, clustering. Tubercles in spirals, terete with rounded apex. Areoles with little wool having 7–9 radial spines, acicular, white about 5 mm long; centrals 4, yellowish brown, 3 hardly distinguishable from the radials, protruding horizontally, slightly longer and hooked. Flower about 1 cm diameter, whitish-pink and slightly darker midrib.

Mammillaria garessii Cowper

From S.W. of Matachic, Chihuahua, Mexico, in rock crevices. A solitary or clustering species to 8 cm long and to 5 cm diameter, having dullish grey-green tubercles up to 8 mm long. Areoles with wool and up to 22 radial spines, whitish, spreading, somewhat adpressed, acicular and interlacing; usually only 1 central, stiff, reddish-brown, acicular, hooked and protruding at sharp angle. Flower whitish-pink.

Mammillaria glassii Foster

Discovered in Nuevo Leon near the village of Dieciocho de Marzo, Mexico. A clustering species, globose to 3 cm diameter, tubercles in 8–13 spirals, pale green 7 mm long, axils with thin whitish bristles. Radial spines 50–60 about 10–15 mm long, fine, white ascending and interlaced; 6–8 sub-central spines spreading and mingling with radials; 1 central, brownish, hooked about 5 mm long protruding horizontally. Flowers forming ring around crown, somewhat funnel-shaped, pale pink.

Mammillaria goldii Glass & Foster

A miniature species from north of Nacozari, Sonora, Mexico, at over 1,000 m elevation. Small stem, simple, rarely caespitose to 25 mm diameter, sub-globose. Tubercles in spirals, 5–7 mm long, dark green sometimes pinkish at base. Areoles with up to 45 radial spines, pectinate, thin, white and interlacing. Flower funnel-shaped to 35 mm diameter, lilac-pink.

Mammillaria mainae K. Brandeg.

An uncommon plant found between Nogales and Hermosillo, Sonora, usually in the shade of shrub. Stem globose, somewhat flattened to 8 cm diameter, frequently clustering. Tubercles pale green to dark green having about 10 radial spines, yellowish with brown tips, widely spreading; central spines few, stout, hooked at tip. Flowers from upper part of plant, about 2 cm long with open throat, pinkish-white.

Mammillaria microcarpa Engelm.

A well-known species of wide distribution from Texas to Arizona and to Sonora, Mexico. Stem globose, often forming clusters to 8 cm high, tubercles smallish greyish-green with up to 30 radial spines, white with blackish tips, rigid and

Mammillaria microcarpa

spreading to 12 mm long; centrals 1–3, brownish to 18 mm long, hooked. Flowers from near the crown about 2·5 cm long, somewhat funnel-shaped, purplish with sometimes whitish edges.

Mammillaria nivosa Link

An interesting and unusual West Indian species distributed in the Virgin Islands. A clustering species to 12 cm or more diameter with long tubercles about 10 mm long with white wool in axils. Spines about 14, acicular up to 1·5 mm long, golden yellow. Flowers creamy white. An uncommon and rare species, its spines give the effect of almost a golden yellow plant.

Mammillaria pottsii Scheer

An elongated species of wide distribution from Texas, Chihuahua, Coahuila, etc. Stems cylindric to 15 cm long, usually forming clusters from base and stem. Tubercles almost hidden by spines, radials about 30 white, short spreading; centrals 6–12, stout and longer than radials, greyish with brown tips; axils with wool. Flowers from below the crown, small about 1 cm long, magenta or purplish.

Mammillaria pringlei K. Brandeg.

Native of San Luis Potosi, Mexico. A rather large species, generally solitary, globose to 16 cm high and 8 cm diameter with dull greenish tubercles, conic, the axils woolly. Radial spines to 20 spreading;

A well-displayed collection of Mammillaria species

Mammillaria plumosa is a clump forming species often found in enthusiasts collections.

central spines about 7, much stouter and longer than radials and very much recurved all deep yellow. Flowers about 10 mm long, red.

It would be difficult to select only few for mention, so many have a popular appeal due to pleasing appearance and flowers. *M. zeilmanniana* Boed. is grown mainly as a pot plant in certain parts of Europe and is most attractive with its masses of purplish flowers. *M. spinosissima* Lem. has a variety of spine colours, densely covering the plant body and with rings of flowers, pink to reddish, around the crown. *M. hahniana* Werd. is another deservedly popular plant, densely covered with white spines and long flexible bristles and producing a ring of carmine flowers near to the apex. This is a specialist genus which has inspired enthusiasm and research by laymen as well as botanists. In Britain the Mammillaria Society with its regular publications is doing valuable work on the subject.

Mammillaria santaclarensis Cowper

Native of Santa Clara Canyon west of Ciudad Juarez to Chihuahua Highway. Somewhat cylindrical stem up to 16 cm long with soft green tubular tubercles becoming conical at the base. Radial spines about 30 on mature plants, acicular, stiff and straight to 12 mm long, yellowish white, about 10 spreading and adpressed towards the base of the plant; centrals 1–4 strongly hooked, acicular, stout, reddish-brown and protruding horizontally. Flower 1·25 cm long, pale pink with darker midrib.

Mamillopsis senilis (Lodd.) Weber

(syn. *Mammillaria senilis* Lodd.) Type species. A most attractive plant, even without flower, but more so when in full bloom. Native of mountainous regions of Chihuahua and Durango at elevations of 2,000 m or more, often in almost bare rock crevices and enduring very low temperatures. Stems to about 8 or 9 cm high, sometimes longer and to 6 cm diameter, rarely simple, more generally clustering freely. Tubercles about 4 mm long with numerous pure white spines to 2 cm long. Flowers about 6 cm long and almost the same diameter, red or orange-red. A really spectacular species currently being considered for merging with Mammillaria. With so many of these choicer monotypic genera or those with only few species, invariably having

characteristics which recommend them forcibly to the layman, and their very generic titles encouraging popularity, botanists tend to sink them into insignificance by merging with already large genera. While unnecessary splitting is to be deplored, too many well-known and respected genera are liable to be faded out of memory by 'lumping' or merging – and all too often new research produces either the resurrection of a genus or the creation of a new one.

Neobesseya asperispina (Boed.) Boed.

This is the sole representative of the genus from Mexico, from valleys in the mountains south of Saltillo, also in the state of Nuevo Leon. A rather small plant, darkish green with pronounced tubercles with few spines about 12, somewhat spreading and greenish-yellow flowers with deeper midrib and ciliate margins.

Neobesseya is a rather obscure genus belonging somewhere between Neolloydia and Coryphantha. *N. arizonica* Hester has now been transferred to Coryphantha. A Cuban species, originally described by Britton and Rose as *Coryphantha cubensis*, and transferred by Backeberg to *Neolloydia*, would possibly fit better into *Neobesseya* than either of the other two genera. Such is the scope for research.

Neobesseya missouriensis (Sweet) Br. & R.

(syn. *Mammillaria missouriensis* Sweet.) Type species. From mountains in Missouri, North Dakota, Colorado, Oklahoma and possibly elsewhere in the more southerly states of U.S.A. Plants usually solitary, frequently clustering. Stem globose about 5 cm diameter with tubercles somewhat spiralled, 10–15 mm long. Invariably all spines are radial, occasionally 1 central, up to 20 in all, grey, acicular, pubescent. Flowers yellow, somewhat insignificant but fragrant.

Neolloydia ceratites (Quehl.) Br. & R.

A Mexican species usually solitary but also forming clusters. Stem to 10 cm long with somewhat 4-angled tubercles spirally arranged. Radial spines about 20, white and more or less spreading about 1·5 cm long; centrals 5 or 6 slightly longer with blackish tips. Flower large, purple.

Neolloydia conoidea (De Cand.) Br. & R.

(syn. *Mammillaria conoidea* De Cand.) Type species. A clustering species, sometimes solitary with tubercles in spiral rows, somewhat obtuse with woolly axils. Spines numerous almost completely obscuring the plant. Radial spines whitish, 25 or more, spreading 10 mm long; central spines longer to 3 cm long, blackish. Large flowers, purple. Native of northern Mexico.

Neolloydia grandiflora (Otto) Berg.

One of the most outstanding of this genus from Tamaulipas, Mexico. Usually solitary, cylindrical to 12 cm or more high, brownish-green, small tubercles with whitish wool in the axils; radial spines about 25, yellowish-brown, spreading horizontally and few centrals, sometimes absent, blackish. Large beautiful reddish-purple flowers from crown of plant.

Neolloydia matehualensis Backeb.

A rare plant from south of Matehuala in San Luis Potosi, Mexico. Stems bluish-grey somewhat elongated with soft tubercles and many radial but few central spines and large pinkish-purple flowers.

Neolloydia warnockii L. Benson

A little known species from Chihuahuan Desert and parts of Texas, where it grows on limestone hills at 900 to 1,200 m altitudes. Stems solitary to 11 cm long and 7 cm diameter with long tubercles and elliptic areoles. Radial spines about 14, brownish, spreading irregularly at low angles; centrals about 4, some straight and 1 protruding horizontally. Flowers about 2·5 cm diameter, pinkish.

Other species of these genus include *N. mariposensis* (Hester) L. Benson, from near the town of Mariposa, Texas; *N. intertexta* (Engelm.) L. Benson, from widely distributed regions of Arizona, Texas and northern Mexico; *N. erectocentra* (Coulter) L. Benson, for long known as *Echinomastus erectocentrus* Br. & R. from the Arizona Desert. This genus adds emphasis to the problems of nomenclature which exist today and for the non-botanist it would be so easy to accumulate plants under various names only to find they are all the same!

Normanbokea pseudopectinata (Backeb.) Klad. & Buxb.

(syn. *Pelecyphora pseudopectinata* Backeb.) Plant body usually simple with closely set very small 4-angled tubercles and minute pectinate slender whitish spines, arranged comb-like. Flowers from apex of plant, pinkish-white to yellowish-white. A northern Mexican species.

Normanbokea valdeziana (Moeller) Klad. & Buxb.

(syn. *Pelecyphora valdezianus* Moeller.) A very miniature plant, almost completely globular and covered entirely with minute plumose spines. Flowers borne from the apex and range in colour from white to purple. Grows on limestone rockfaces around San Luis Potosi and Nuevo Leon, Mexico.

Oehmea nelsonii (Br. & R.) Buxb.

(syn. *Neomammillaria nelsonii* Br. & R.) Type species. A globose plant to 5 cm diameter with about 15 white acicular radial spines 8 mm long and spreading, several centrals similar to radials but one longer and strongly hooked. Flowers yellowish. This genus has now been merged with *Mammillaria*.

Ortegocactus macdougallii Alex.

One of the most outstanding discoveries of recent years and only now becoming generally known in cultivation. Native of Oaxaca near the village of San Jose Lachiguiri, Mexico, where it was discovered by T. MacDougall growing on limestone rocks. Stem short cylindric to globose, frequently solitary, often clustering with distinctive bluish-grey-green body. Tubercles rhomboidal 12 mm in diameter, spirally arranged. Areoles bearing wool in their upper part, radials about 7 mostly black or black tipped to 10 mm long and 1 central to 5 mm long. Flower about 30 mm long and 25 mm diameter, bright clear yellow on short pale green tube. Just where this genus should be placed is still in doubt – this species has the peculiarity of a woolly ovary and this would seem to provide a reason for complete separation.

Pelecyphora aselliformis Ehrenb.

Type species. Interesting species from San Luis Potosi, Mexico, with cylindric stem, clustering, covered with strongly flattened tubercles providing a 'hard' surface to the plant. Areoles at top of tubercles, long and narrow; radials thick, arranged comb-like, pectinate. Flower from apex at axil of tubercle, purple.

Phellosperma tetrancistra (Engelm.) Br. & R.

(syn. *Mammillaria tetrancistra* Engelm.) Type

Yucca filamentosa

ABOVE *Echinocereus viridiflorus*

ABOVE *Agave victoria-reginae*

BELOW *Yucca gloriosa 'Variegata'*

BELOW *Agave americana 'Medio-variegata'*

species. A globular plant, somewhat cylindric, solitary or caespitose and very spiny. Has large fleshy tap root which branches. Tubercles rounded and elongated with numerous radial spines, acicular, whitish and tipped brown; centrals 1 to 4, brown or blackish and longer than the radials, usually hooked. Flower to 4 cm purplish. This has now been transferred back to *Mammillaria*.

Sclerocactus: This genus would now appear to be totally obsolete; the type species *S. polyancistra* (Engelm. & Bigel.) Br. & R. together with *S. whipplei* (Engelm. & Bigel.) Br. & R. have been transferred to the genus *Pediocactus*.

Solisia pectinata (B. Stein.) Br. & R.
(syn. *Pelecyphora pectinata* B. Stein.) Type species. A rare but well-known plant, native of Tehuacan, Puebla, Mexico. Plants solitary to 3 cm diameter covered entirely by overlapping white spine clusters. Tubercles hatchet-shape, low and small with narrow elongated areoles and numerous slender spines, all radials, white and arranged comb-like, pectinate. Flowers yellowish.

This attractive plant deserves generic status although the current trend would suggest that it will become merged with Mammillaria.

Thelocactus bicolor (Gal.) Br. & R.
One of the best known of the genus widely distributed from S. Texas through to central Mexico. Plants solitary, globose to conical to 12 cm or more high and 7 cm diameter. Ribs about 8 or 10, broad and tubercled. Spines are colourful, reddish, brown or yellowish – radials up to 18 widely spreading 3 cm long, central spines about 4 ascending and protruding, straight to 5 cm long. Flowers about 6 cm long and broad, purplish-pink. An attractive form, *T. bicolor* v. *flavidispinus* Backeb. from Texas, has shorter, fewer spines which are yellow.

Thelocactus conothele (Reg. & Klein) Knuth
From the region around Jaumave, Tamaulipas, Mexico. Plant solitary, about 13 cm or more diameter, light green and somewhat cylindrical in shape, tubercles with 14–16 whitish radial spines spreading; centrals usually 4, one of which extends horizontally. Flowers pinkish-white. Two outstanding varieties are recognized. *T. conothele* v. *argenteus* Glass & Foster has a greater number of spines, which are 'shredding' and of silvery appearance and flowers lilac-pink. *T. conothele* v. *aurantiacus* Glass & Foster also has a greater number of spines than the type plant and somewhat brownish with rich orange-yellow flowers. *T. saussieri* (Weber) Berg. is very similar to the species and possibly synonymous.

Thelocactus hexaedrophorus (Lem.) Br. & R.
(syn. *Echinocactus hexaedrophorus* Lem.) Type species. A globose somewhat flattened plant, dark greyish-green, strongly tubercled, overall to 14 cm diameter. Prominent tubercles, 6-sided arranged in spirals with up to 9 rigid spreading radial spines of unequal length to 18 mm long; and 1 central spine, erect to 3 cm long. Flower 5 cm or more diameter, pinkish-purple. A variety, *T. hexaedrophus* v. *fossulatus* (Scheidw.) Backeb. with bluish ribs divided into thick large tubercles with 4–5 thick spines. Flowers white, flushed pink. The species and the variety are from San Luis Potosi, Mexico.

Thelocactus leucacanthus (Zucc.) Br. & R.
A clustering plant from near Ixmiquilpan, Hidalgo, Mexico. Ribs to 13, often spiralled and obtusely tubercled with up to 20 yellowish-grey radial spines, spreading or recurved of unequal length, some to 4 cm long; central spine blackish-grey to 5 cm long. Flowers bright yellow. A pleasing form, *T. leucacanthus* v. *schmollii* Werd. from N. of Bernal, Queretaro, Mexico, has prominent tubercles on a smallish stem and almost pectinate spines with deep red flowers.

Thelocactus nidulans (Quehl.) Br. & R.
Distributed in many parts of Coahuila, particularly around Saltillo and Parras. Somewhat flattened body to 10 cm high and 20 cm or more diameter, silvery-grey or bluish-grey with many wavy ribs about 20, divided into tubercles with long, shredding silvery white spines. Flowers to 4 cm long, yellowish-white.

Thelocactus rinconensis (Poselg.) Br. & R.
Native of Nuevo Leon near Rinconada, Mexico. A globose somewhat flattened plant about 8 cm high and to 14 cm diameter. Ribs spiralled with strong tubercles. Tubercles angled and flattened with few spines usually 3. Flowers white.

SUB-TRIBE ECHINOCACTANAE
Includes many North American genera containing

species of particular interest to collectors through-out the world.

Ariocarpus agavoides (Cast.) Anderson

(syn. *Neogomesia agavoides* Cast.–a monotypic genus now absorbed into Ariocarpus.) Thick fleshy root. Tubercles only few, spreading, semi-erect, horny–giving the effect of a miniature Agave. Areoles roundish on upper surface of tubercle just below the tip, woolly. Flower deep purplish-pink, funnel-shaped. A unique species from Tamaulipas, Mexico.

Ariocarpus fissuratus (Engelm.) Sch.

(syn. *Roseocactus fissuratus* Sch. A. Bgr.) There is no justification for separating this from other species of Ariocarpus. The genus *Roseocactus* has never been totally accepted in Britain. Has thick turnip-like root. Tubercles triangular and thick, in habitat scarcely showing above the ground. Plant about 15 cm or more diameter, the whole surface fissured and warty and generally almost flat. Areoles

contain many hairs. Flowers from the centre areoles, purplish pink. From W. Texas and northern parts of Coahuila and Zacatecas, Mexico. *A. lloydii* Rose, is closely related to this species, has somewhat rounded surface with generally larger tubercles and is possibly only a variant. Usually referred to as 'Living Rock'.

Ariocarpus retusus Schweidw.

Type species. Widely distributed in Coahuila, Zacatecas and San Luis Potosi in Mexico. Globular plants with somewhat flattened or depressed surface, about 12 cm or more diameter, greyish, with wool at the centre. Tubercles very horny up to 5 cm long, generally 3-angled and tending to overlap one another. Flowers from the axils of the young tubercles at the centre, white. Associated with rocky, stony places and often almost covered by sand leaving only the tips of tubercles visible.

Astrophytum myriostigma Lem.

(syn. *Echinocactus myriostigma* S.-D.) Type species.

Astrophytum myriostigma

A well-loved species, commonly known as the 'Bishop's Cap'. A globular plant usually solitary with few ribs 4 sometimes up to 8, very broad and covered with woolly scales. Areoles along the ridges, sometimes woolly and pronounced. Flower yellow. Native to northern central Mexico. There are a number of varietal forms. *A. myriostigma* v. *strongologonum* is a fat form of the species with more rounded ribs. *A. myriostigma* v. *columnare*, a white columnar plant with somewhat paler flowers. *A. myriostigma* v. *quadricostata* which is typical of the species but with only four ribs, and this has been known to revert to the normal 5. *A. myriostigma* v. *nuda* is similar in every respect only having no whitish scales and presenting a greenish appearance.

Other species include *A. asterias* (Zucc.) Lem., a very distinctive plant, commonly known as the 'Bishop's mitre', a very sought-after species. *A. ornatum* (De Cand.) Web. has a number of forms;

Astrophytum myriostigma v. *columnare*

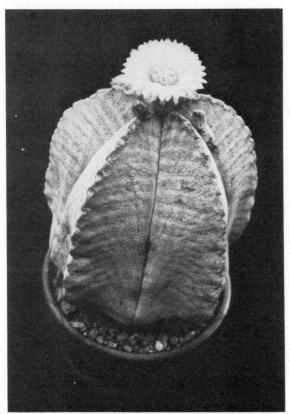

along with *A. capricorne* (Dietr.) Br. & R. and its varieties, these are the only members of this genus which are heavily spined.

Aztekium ritteri (Boed.) Boed.
(syn. *Echinocactus ritteri* Boed.) Type species. A monotypic genus for this one species from Nuevo Leon, Mexico. A small globular plant, sometimes grouping. Having 9 to 11 rather spiral ribs with small glandless areoles having short hairs. The surface has many furrows, and notches at each areole. Spines insignificant. The whole plant gives the effect of being hard and similar to species of Ariocarpus, dark dull green with small white flowers. A rare species in cultivation.

Coloradoa mesae-verdae Boissev & C. Davison
Type species. Has also been included within the genus *Echinocactus* and later *Sclerocactus* by Benson, and it would appear this species has a close kinship to Sclerocactus – hence *Sclerocactus mesae-verdae* (Boissev. ex Hill and Salisb.) L. Benson might be more appropriate. Even later opinion has included it with *Pediocactos*.

A small globular species about 6 cm high and 8 cm broad, ribs 13 to 17 set with areoles having brown or greyish wool. Radial spines 8 to 10 and only rarely a single central. Flowers creamy-yellow with brownish midrib. A rare species from southerly slopes of dry hills, Mesa Verde cliffs in Colorado, and possibly in New Mexico, Utah and Arizona.

Echinocactus platyacanthus Link & Otto
Type species. A nearly globular species, large and bright green with woolly apex. Ribs very acute, about 30 and having brownish, later becoming greyish, spines, the radials 4, short and spreading and 3 or 4 central spreading spines about 3 cm long. Flowers about 3 cm long. Known only from eastern Mexico.

Echinocactus grusonii Hildm.
One of the best known species in cultivation, referred to as the 'Golden Barrel'. Very large globular plant, light green body with many ribs up to nearly 40. Areoles with golden yellow spines up to 5 cm long. Flowers are embedded in deep felt, yellowish, opening in full sunlight. From central Mexico in the region of San Luis Potosi through to Hidalgo.

Echinofossulocactus coptonogonus (Lem.) Lawr.

Echinocactus grusonii

(syn. *Echinocactus coptonogonus* Lem.) Type species. A globular plant, somewhat depressed, to 10 cm high and 8 cm broad having 10 to 14 stout acute ribs. Areoles well apart and 3 to 5 rigid, incurved flattened spines. Flowers white and purplish. Native to the region of San Luis Potosi, Mexico.

Echinofossulocactus multicostatus (Hild.) Br. & R.
A most attractive species, globose with over 100 narrow wavy ribs. Areoles few with 6 to 9 spines, the 3 upper ones being somewhat flexible, elongated and erect, the lower spines being short and spreading. Flowers pinkish-white about 2·5 cm long. From near Rio Nazas in Durango and also Saltillo, Coahuila, Mexico.

Echinofossulocactus pentacanthus (Lem.) Br. & R.
A handsome species, somewhat globose, dark green. Has up to 45 sinuous ribs with only few areoles to each rib. Spine cluster consists of 3 upper, elongated flat spines and 2 lower, more slender and shorter with occasionally a single central. Flowers large, deep purple with white margins. Endemic to the region of San Luis Potosi and Hidalgo, Mexico.

This genus consists of a great number of 'names'. Species are inclined to be so variable so as to cause confusion and duplication. Certainly an attractive and unusual group with the unique characteristic of wavy ribs. This genus is sometimes referred to as *Stenocactus*.

Echinomastus erectrocentrus (Coult.) Br. & R.
(syn. *Echinocactus erectrocentrus* Coult.) Type species. An attractive plant about 10 cm diameter and to 14 cm tall, somewhat ovoid, greyish-green. Many low ribs made up of closely set tubercles bearing about 14 radial spines and 1 or 2 elongated erect centrals, these often being somewhat swollen towards the base. Pinkish flowers to about 5 cm long with green style. From S.W. Arizona, U.S.A.

Echinomastus unguispina (Engelm.) Br. & R.
A unique species completely covered by elongated, somewhat twisted spines almost hiding the entire body of the plant. Globular, sometimes short-cylindrical, to about 12 cm high and 7 cm diameter, pale green with rather obscure low ribs. Spines whitish, the radials about 25 widely spreading and the 4 to 8 central spines being much stouter and

longer, some turning upwards, others downwards and all somewhat curved. Flowers red. A desirable and rare species from states of Chihuahua and Zacatecas, Mexico.

There is apparently a close kinship between Echinomastus and Thelocactus, in the instance of *E. macdowellii* (Rebut) Br. & R. It has now been transferred to Thelocactus.

Encephalocarpus strobiliformis (Werd.) Berg.
(syn. *Ariocarpus strobiliformis* Werd.) Type species. The genus was erected to include only this one species of peculiar characteristics. A small globular plant, sometimes simple, often clustering and forming groups. Tubercles numerous and densely imbricate and with a keel at the back surface, terminating in a point with a small areole on the inner side, with wool and insignificant spines, scale-like, which makes it distinctly different to species of Ariocarpus. Flowers purple with fringed edges and yellow stigma. Endemic to Tamaulipas, Mexico. A rare and desirable species resembling a pine cone, its closest relation would appear to be *Pelecyphora aselliformis*–and these might deservedly be united in one genus.

Epithelantha bokei L. Benson
Stems similar to those of *E. micromeris*. Spines from areoles in 4 or 5 series, generally longer forming a dense covering over the body of the plant. Flowers pale pink. At altitudes of up to 1,200 m on limestone hillsides in Texas.

Plants of this genus are of particular interest to collectors, and while generally well-known in cultivation are still considered uncommon and are much in demand.

Epithelantha micromeris (Engelm.) Weber
(syn. *Mammillaria micromeris* Engelm.) Type species. A very small species, usually clustering, sometimes simple. Almost globular up to about 5 cm in diameter, having small, low-set tubercles arranged in spirals. Spines numerous in 2 or 3 series. Flower from near the apex of the plant, small, pinkish white to light pink. The 'button cactus' from western Texas and parts of northern Mexico.

Ferocactus acanthodes (Lem.) Br. & R.
One of the most attractive of all this genus. Globular becoming cylindrical with age up to 3 m high. With numerous ribs, 27 or more, very acute

and large areoles densely brown felted and numerous spines. The radials somewhat weak and usually spreading, the centrals rather flattened, slender, spreading and tortuously curved, white, pink, yellowish or red – and these mainly contribute to the beauty of the species. Flowers yellow or pale orange about 6 cm long from near the crown of the plant. Endemic to the arid areas of southeastern California, S. Nevada, Arizona, and parts of northern Lower California.

Ferocactus latispinus (Haw.) Br. & R.

Plant globular, somewhat depressed to 4 cm high and about 4 cm in diameter. Usually with 21 ribs, but up to 23, sometimes much less. Large areoles with 6 to 10 pinkish-white radial spines, rather slender and 4 or more stout centrals, brownish or reddish all straight except one which is very flattened and decidely hooked. Flowers purplish. Widely distributed in Mexico and possibly Guatemala.

A number of other species of Ferocactus are of particular note; *F. fordii* (Orcutt) Br. & R. one of the smaller growing plants from Baja California, which has rose-pinkish flowers. *F. schwarzii*, a very rare species from Ranche del Padre, Sinaloa. *F. gatesii* Lindsay which is native of the islands in Los Angeles Bay on the west coast of Baja California, beautifully spined with red flowers. These and many more make this one of the most popular genera of large-growing plants.

Ferocactus wizlizeni (Engelm.) Br. & R.

(syn. *Echinocactus wislizenii* Engelm.) Type species. Globular at first becoming cylindrical with age and reaching a height of 2 m or more. Ribs 25 or more with large elliptical areoles with brownish felt with many thread-like radial spines and several reddish or white central spines, one of them being slightly hooked and much stouter than the others, strongly flattened. Flowers yellow about 6 cm long. A widely distributed species from Texas to Arizona and in parts of Sonora and Sinaloa, Mexico.

Gymnocactus aguirreanus Glass and Foster

Having soft fleshy tuberous root, somewhat globular body to about 5 cm high and 7 cm diameter. Ribs usually divided into soft tubercles. Areoles

Ferocactus acanthodes

Ferocactus acanthodes

Ferocactus latispinus

BELOW *Ferocactus schwarzii* — large plants of this very rare species.

have many reddish spines, with upper and lower radials, up to 20 or more, central spines 2 to 5, at times difficult to distinguish between radials and centrals. Flower small, yellowish. An interesting new discovery from southern Coahuila, Mexico.

The genus was created by Backeberg, an intermediate between Thelocactus and Toumeya. The type species is *G. saueri* (Boed.) Backeb. (syn. *Echinocactus saueri* Boed.). The genus now consists principally of species which were wrongly placed in the Coryphantanae and a number of new species of recent introduction.

Hamatocactus setispinus (Engelm.) Br. & R.
(syn. *Echinocactus setispinus* Engelm.) Type species. A fibrous rooted plant up to 15 cm high, darkish-green. Ribs usually 13, thin, high and undulate on the margins. Twelve to 16 slender spines, central spines 1 to 3 longer than radials and hooked. Large flower to 7 cm long, yellow with red throat. Distributed in southern Texas and northern Mexico. A very popular and easily cultivated plant.

Homalocephala texensis (Hopff.) Br. & R.
(syn. *Echinocactus texensis* Hopff.) Type species. Usually globose, but often very much depressed, almost flattened, to about 30 cm diameter with 13 to 27 ribs, acute but with only few white-felted areoles having about 6 radial spines to 4 cm long, spreading and recurved with long solitary central about 6 cm long. Flowers to 6 cm long, reddish in the lower part, pinkish above. Native of south-east New Mexico, Texas, and parts of northern Mexico. A species which is now becoming exceedingly rare, even in habitat.

Leuchtenbergia principis Hook.
Type species. An unusual, fascinating plant with invariably long tap roots. Plants to 15 cm high, usually solitary but sometimes clustering. The elongated tubercles are the feature of the species, these are erect and up to 12 cm or more long, 3-angled. Spines from the almost truncate tip of the tubercle, thin and papery with several radials and 1 or 2 longer centrals to almost 10 cm length. Flowers golden yellow, lasting several days, scented. From northern Mexico and certain more central areas. Sometimes called the 'Agave Cactus'.

Lophophora williamsii (Lem.) Coulter
(syn. *Echinocactus williamsii* Lem.) Type species.

Spineless globular plants of dull bluish-green colour, having thickened tap-root. Ribs varying from about 7 to 13, not very prominent and few areoles with tufts of thick hairs. Flowers pink. Endemic to parts of central Mexico to southern Texas. Called the 'Mescal button' or 'Peyote'. The narcotic extracted is said to cause hallucinations.

Other species of this genus are very similar to the above; *L. ziegleri* and *L. lewinii* are possibly only variants. All are rare species.

Obregonia denegrii Fric.
Type species. A unique plant, looking somewhat like an artichoke. Discovered in the Valley of Jaumave, Tamaulipas, Mexico, having characteristics peculiar to itself and for which a monotypic genus was created. Stem usually simple, sometimes clustering, about 12 cm diameter, greyish-green, tubercles rather leaf-like, thick and flat above, strongly keeled below, spines and wool almost obsolete. Areoles at tips of tubercles, with few bristles. Flower funnel-shaped, white.

Pediocactus simpsonii (Engelm.) Br. & R.
(syn. *Echinocactus simpsonii* Engelm.) Type species. Plant globular somewhat depressed to about 15 cm diameter and to 12 cm high, with many tubercles, radial spines up to 30 each areole, spreading, creamy-white; central reddish-brown about 8, spreading. Flowers massed in crown of plant and surrounded by brown or whitish wool, pinkish-white to pinkish-magenta. A rare species from Arizona and other more southerly states.

Pediocactus papyracantha (Engel.) L. Benson
(syn. *Toumeya papyracantha* (Engelm.) Br. & R.) Somewhat elongated stem, ovoid or short cylindrical with low spiral tubercles. Areoles with thin papery, flexible white spines, centrals longer than the radials. Flower from the terminal about 2·5 cm long, white with brownish midribs. A rare and uncommon species from grasslands at elevations of over 2,000 m in Arizona and northern New Mexico.

Pediocactus peeblesianus (Croizat) L. Benson
(syn. *Navajoa peeblesiana* Croizat.) From desert hillsides at high altitudes up to 1,600 m or more in Navajoan Desert. A very rare species, stem globose, greyish-green, and in habitat often only the crown of the plant is visible, up to 4 cm diameter and 6 to

7 cm high. Areoles circular with 3 to 7 radial spines and usually 1 central pale grey, flexible and curving slightly upwards. Flower about 2 cm in diameter, yellowish.

This interesting genus has become increasingly enlarged due to extensive research, and in consequence has absorbed certain monotypic genera for long associated with rare and desirable species. The genus also includes *P. bradyi* L. Benson from the Coconino County in Arizona and elsewhere at high elevations with yellowish flowers, *P. knowltonii* L. Benson from near La Boca, Colorado.

Pediocactus polyancistrus (Engelm. & Big.) G. K. Arp

(syn. *Sclerocactus polyancistrus* (Engelm. & Big.) Br. & R.) An oblong stem up to 30 cm long with up to 17 ribs, undulate, areoles with up to 20 spreading acicular white radial spines and several long centrals, some erect and flattened, others rounded and hooked. Flowers magenta, nearly 8 cm diameter. Distributed in some desert areas of California and Nevada and possibly parts of western Arizona.

Other species of *Sclerocactus* have been transferred to *Pediocactus, S. whipplei* (Engelm.) Br. & R., *S. glaucus* (Schum.) L. Benson, *S. pubispinus* (Engelm.) Br. & R. and *S. wrightiae* L. Benson.

Pediocactus paradinei (B. W. Benson) B. W. Benson (syn. *Pilocanthus paradinei* B. W. Benson & Backeb.) From high elevations up to nearly 2,000 m in Navajoan Desert and parts of northern Arizona. An unusual and rare plant, usually solitary, sometimes in pairs or even three together, somewhat globular about 4 cm diameter. Circular areoles with straw-coloured centrals, about 6 hairlike, and up to 20 flexible radial spines, straight or curving. Flower about 2 cm diameter, white with pinkish midrib.

Pediocactus sileri (Engelm.) L. Benson

(syn. *Utahia sileri* (Engel.) Br. & R.) An exceptionally rare plant long cherished as a *Utahia*– and found to be rather difficult in cultivation, but nevertheless much sought after. Ovoid plant, to about 12 cm long and 10 cm diameter with pronounced tubercles having circular areoles and densely spined, 3 to 7 centrals, brownish-black and 10 to 12 radials greyish, spreading. Flower yellowish with reddish markings about 2 to 3 cm

diameter. This unique plant is found in Utah and parts of northern Arizona at altitudes of 1,000–1,500 m.

Strombocactus disciformis (De Cand.) Br. & R.

(syn. *Mammilaria disciformis* De Cand.) Type species. A somewhat flattened semi-globose plant to 5–7 cm diameter. Tubercles thick, imbricate and spineless in maturity. Flower whitish from centre or near centre of plant. The peculiarities of this plant resulted in the erecting of a genus to include just the one species from Mineral del Monte in central Mexico.

Turbinicarpus schmiedickeanus (Boed.) Buxb. & Backeb.

(syn. *Echinocactus schiedickeanus* Boed.) Type species. Diminutive species, globular, about 3–4 cm broad, dark greyish-green having many tubercles. The feature of this plant is the small crown covered with rather long, thick, slightly curved spines. Flowers pale pink with deeper pinkish midrib. Native to San Luis Potosi and Tamaulipas, Mexico.

A number of other species of this genus are of considerable interest, all miniatures and uncommon in cultivation. *T. pseudomacrochele* (Backeb.) Buxb. & Backeb. has dark green body, hair-like spines and large pink flowers. *T. schwarzii* (Shurly) Backeb. with pointed tubercles and heavier spines. *T. polaskii* Backeb. from Matehuala, San Luis Potosi, Mexico, resembles a small Lophophora with few soft curved spines and large pink and white flowers. *T. lophophoroides* (Werd.) Buxb. & Backeb. from near Las Tablas, San Luis Potosi, Mexico, very similar in appearance to Lophophora, grey-green body somewhat larger than that of *T. polaskii,* flowers large and white blushed pink.

SUB-TRIBE ECHINOCEREANAE

Echinocereus includes over 80 species all endemic to North America. The stems vary considerably from one species to another, some cylindrical, others oval or roundish. Many are free branching from the base, others tend to remain solitary. Usually with many ribs and very spiny, rarely spineless or nearly so. All have exceptionally colourful flowers, generally large.

A collection of Echinocereus species showing several in flower.

A further group of Echinocereus species, showing several pectinate forms, some in flower.

A collection of Echinocereus species including *E. delaetii* in the centre.

Echinocereus brandegeei (Coulter) Sch.

An uncommon plant from the low hills bordering the coastline of south Baja California. A clumping species sometimes with very elongated stems. Ribs with many tubercles, and areoles bearing very stout longish spines. Radial spines about 12, acicular and spreading with long rigid centrals usually 4. Flowers purple with whitish wool and spiny areoles on the ovary.

Echinocereus delaetii Gurke

A remarkable species very much resembling a small *Cephalocereus senilis*. Native to a restricted area north of Parras de la Fuente in Coahuila, Mexico. Densely clustering plant almost completely covered with long whitish hairs from the areoles which also have a few reddish stiff spines. Flowers pink, the ovary also being hidden by clusters of long white bristles.

Echinocereus fendleri (Engelm.) Rumpl.

A well-known species from southerly states of U.S.A. and northern Sonora and Chihuahua,

Mexico. Can be extremely variable. Clustering with erect stems from the base with prominent ribs, somewhat undulate. Areoles with up to 10 spreading radial spines and one central. Flowers from the upper part of the stems, large, deep purple.

Echinocereus pulchellus (Mart.) Sch.

A comparatively small growing species from western Puebla and Hidalgo where they are found growing flat to the ground. Stems simple, somewhat cylindrical, greyish-green with about 12 ribs divided into tubercles. Areoles with only 2 or 3 short spines, yellowish and deciduous. Flowers pinky-white about 4 cm diameter. An unpublished *E. aguirrei* is synonymous. This species is very similar to *E. amoenus* (Diet.) Sch. and the two are frequently confused.

Echinocereus russanthus Weniger

A species for long confused with *E. chloranthus*. Found in a restricted area of Brewster County, Texas, U.S.A. Stems cylindrical to over 20 cm long, branching profusely from the base. Ribs about 11 to

18, low, narrow with very indistinct tubercles. Areoles with white wool when young with up to 45 slender bristle-like spines completely covering the body of the plant. Flowers brownish-red, funnel-shaped with long yellowish style.

Echinocereus sciurus (K. Brand.) Br. & R.

A dense clumping species from south of Baja California. Stems slender 20 cm long, ribs about 12 to 15, low and divided into tubercles. Areoles closely set with up to 18 radial spines which are longer than the centrals. Flower bright cerise with greenish filaments and dark green pistil.

Echinocereus stoloniferus Marsh.

An almost unique species on account of its habit of producing stolons from which develop the offsets. Somewhat cylindrical plant with many ribs and areoles with dense whitish spines, closely set together. Flowers yellow. Rather rare in cultivation, from Sonora, Mexico.

Echinocereus viridiflorus Engelm.

The type species of the genus. Small almost globular plants, either simple or clustering with 14 low ribs and elongated areoles. Radial spines about 16 with centrals usually 2 or 3 in a row. Flowers greenish. Native of New Mexico and parts of Texas and Dakota, U.S.A.

Morangaya pensilis (K. Brand.) Rowl.

(syn. *Cereus pensilis* K. Brand.) Type species. This species has always been considered distinctive from other species of the genus *Echinocereus* and a monotypic genus has been erected to include this one species ('Ashingtonia' Vol. 1:4). By some it is considered 'half-way' between Echinocereus and Aporocactus, seemingly having characteristics of both. Native of Lower California in the high mountains of Sierra de la Laguna. Stems erect or semi-erect, sometimes pendent to nearly 3 m long. Ribs 8 to 10 with fairly close set areoles having about 8 radial spines and one central. Flowers orange-red about 6 cm long, rather narrow. Tube and ovary with bristly spines and whitish or brownish wool. Fruit globular about 2 cm diameter.

Tribe 2 Opuntioideae

The best known of cacti – having many 'common' names (e.g. 'Prickly Pear', 'Bunny Ears', 'Teddy Bear Cactus', 'Beavertail Cactus', etc.). Several genera are included, all species bearing the typical glochids, one of the main peculiarities of the tribe. Attempts have been made to merge many of the genera into the genus *Opuntia* and for the original generic title to remain as sub-genera or sections. Some titles were given because of geographical location and for shape of joints. While these aspects are of importance and in themselves provide a guide-line to better understanding, segregation would appear unnecessary, especially if the titles were retained as sectional headings.

One of the largest families, containing several hundreds of species, many very large and tree-like, heavily padded with large spines, others with cylindrical stems – and at the other extreme, charming miniature plants which cluster freely with either roundish or flattened joints. Flowers in many brilliant colours – hence a popular and apt description, 'The Desert Rose'.

OPUNTIA (TOURNE.) MILL.

Includes many sub-genera, sections or series. Most species become tree-like, others remain dwarf or prostrate. Roots are invariably fibrous, but there are a few with tuberous roots frequently resembling a caudex. All N. American species are of easy culture, in fact there are those which have proved almost totally hardy in protected areas of Britain. Only a few can be mentioned, but these are generally representative of many within the same group.

Opuntia arbuscula Engelm (Cylindropuntia)

A bush-forming species with numerous slender cylindrical branches becoming woody. Terminal joints have low indistinct tubercles, sometimes with very small leaf-like growths and long yellowish-brown spines with sheath to 4 cm long. Flower greenish-yellow, somewhat tinged rose. Distributed originally throughout much of Arizona and Sonora, but now becoming more localized.

Opuntia basilaris Engelm. & Bigelow (Platyopuntia)

A popular and still rather rare species, referred to as the 'Beaver Tail Cactus', forms compact clumps to about 25 cm high and spreading. Joints very attractive, obovate, blue-green to purplish with numerous areoles. Flower purplish. There are varietal forms. *O. basilaris* v. *cordata* would appear

Opuntia basilaris v. *cordata*

to be only an even more attractive form than the type material, having a heart-shaped pad. *O. basilaris* v. *treleasii* (Coulter) Toumey is similar to the species but with generally more narrow elongated pads. *O. basilaris* v. *brachyclada* (Griff.) Munz from high elevations is a low-growing rather dwarf plant having miniature pads compared with the species and pinkish-rose flowers. All are from California/Nevada/Arizona border areas.

Opuntia bigelovii Engelm. (Cylindropuntia)
A rare species, referred to as the 'Teddy Bear Cactus' – intensely spined on cylindrical joints having many tubercles and armed with golden yellow spines many from an areole. Flowers yellowish-green. Usually growing in rocky mountainous areas up to nearly 1,000 m in S.W. states of U.S.A., Sonora particularly on the coastal regions of Gulf of California, and Baja California. One of the most beautiful of the genus.

Opuntia bradtiana K. Brandegee. (Grusonia)
A cylindrical-stemmed plant forming thick clusters to 2 m high. Stems pale green with tuberculate ribs and heavily spined, particularly at the apex. The spines often to 20 or more are pale yellow on young growth but becoming white, not sheathed. Flower yellow and fringed. A difficult species to establish in cultivation, especially from cuttings, so while it is common in Coahuila, Mexico, its habitat, it is rarely seen in collections.

Opuntia erinacea v. *ursina* (Weber) Parish (Platyopuntia)
A low-growing plant forming clumps. Plants semi-erect bearing flattened oblong joints with large, somewhat tuberculate areoles and numerous spines, almost pure white and giving the effect of very long hairs up to 14 cm long. These hairs are in fact elongated spines, very flexible and usually from the bases of the lower joints. Flowers generally pink, but sometimes yellow. From northern Arizona areas of the Mojave Desert and the Clark Mountains in California. This is a species of distinctive qualities; the long hairy form has become known in horticulture as *O. erinacea* v. *ursina* forma *senilis*.

Opuntia invicta Brandegee (Corynopuntia)
A rare species from the Baja California, uncommon in cultivation. In habitat it masses into large clusters with club-shaped joints, dark green, strongly tubercled and armed with vicious red spines which become greyish with age. Flowers yellow. In many ways this resembles some species of Echinocereus for which it was mistaken when originally discovered. From Lower California, in central regions around San Juanico.

Opuntia leptocaulis De Cand. (Cylindropuntia)
A well-known species with very slender erect stems forming thickets. The bright green stems branch freely, often at right angles and the new joints tend to be very brittle. Areoles often almost spineless but bearing few minute leaves which quickly fall. Where spines are apparent they are small, yellowish white and very short, usually in small clusters. Flowers greenish-yellow. There are certain species very close, particularly *O. kleiniae* De Cand. with which it is sometimes confused. Varietal forms of *O. leptocaulis* are recorded, *O. leptocaulis* v. *longispina* Engel. deserves mention on account of the very long spines, yellowish-brown. All are endemic to Mexico and certain of the southerly states of U.S.A.

Opuntia pulchella Engelm. (Micropuntia)
An interesting and desirable miniature species with large 'bulbous' caudex-like tuber much of which is usually below ground. Stems develop from the caudex with small joints somewhat elliptical with tubercles and many spines, mostly whitish or greyish-white; such growths come from an areole with glochids and which are ultimately deciduous. Flowers in varying shades of pink to purple.

83

Associated with sandy plains and deserts in Nevada, Arizona and California at about 1,000–1,300 m elevation. The type locality is given as Walker River, Nevada.

Opuntia pycnantha Engelm. (Platyopuntia)
A low-growing species forming clumps with oblong joints having numerous areoles and spines. The yellowish-brown glochids are a feature, being heavily massed in the upper part of the areole, the spines developing from the lower part. The flower is reputed to be yellow, but this cannot be confirmed. An uncommon species rarely seen in cultivation, from the region around Magdalena Bay in the south of Baja California.

Opuntia ramosissima Engelm. (Cylindropuntia)
A distinctive species with greyish stems and branches forming either large or frequently miniature bushes. Stems slender and angled giving the effect of being covered with rough diamond-shaped sections. Often spineless, but sometimes with long yellowish-golden sheathed spines. Flower pink, with a suggestion of being purplish. A rare species from Nevada, Arizona and California borders on low mountain slopes. This is almost a non-succulent, the stems being very woody and becoming more so with age, quickly dehydrating and therefore difficult to cultivate from cuttings.

Opuntia bigelovii in habitat.

Opuntia rubescens S-D. (Consolea)
Representative of a group of Opuntias endemic to West Indies. Backeberg recognizes the genus *Consolea* Lem., erected for those species with erect continuous stems, unjointed and branching from opposite or alternate sides of the main stems, giving the effect of a cross (cruciform). Flowers variable, usually yellow, but sometimes reddish. Two distinctive forms are found, one with quite long spines, the other totally spineless, but this is not considered sufficient reason for giving even varietal status. Endemic to the islands from Antigua to Dominica.

Opuntia versicolor Engelm. (Cylindropuntia)
An erect bush-like species to 3 or 4 m high. Main stems quickly become woody and branching freely with terminal joints in whorls about 20 cm long. Joints cylindrical, somewhat tuberculate, with few areoles having many spines with sheaths. Flowers in many colours, yellow, pink, purplish, reddish or sometimes brown–hence its name. Widely distributed throughout parts of Arizona and northern Mexico. This is another instance where variations within the species do not justify varietal status.

Nopalea cochenillifera (L.) S-D.
Closely related to Opuntia, the most outstanding feature which separates it is the flower with its closely adpressed petals surrounding the numerous stamens and style, the style and filaments being much longer than the petals.

Tall plants with smooth rounded stems and branches and scarcely any spines. Joints very brittle and break away easily, dark glossy green with shaded diamond-shaped tubercles. Flower orange-red with pinkish stamens and greenish stigma lobes which, with the style, protrude beyond the petals. A well-known species, originally cultivated for the production of cochineal, the bug being reared on these plants. Its origin is possibly southern Mexico or Central America–but it has been widely cultivated in some of the more northerly islands of the West Indies.

Pereskiopsis spathulata (Otto) Br. & R.
An erect-growing shrubby plant with few branches. Glaucous stems with thick dark green spatulate leaves to about 5 cm long. Few areoles, woolly and

Rhodocactus grandifolius

having only occasional spines. The brownish glochids appear on the upper portion of the areole. Flower bright red. From south-west Mexico. This species is used extensively for grafting. Other species of Pereskiopsis are recorded, some very similar to the above. *P. velutina* Rose is outstanding on account of the velvet-like soft stems and leaves and yellow flowers.

Other species of the large genus *Opuntia* are dealt with in the chapter on South American plants.

Pterocactus marenae (Pars.) Rowl. (Marenopuntia)
An interesting species with thick tuberous roots and short, elongated, slender cylindrical stems about 14 cm long and branching freely. Stems dark grey-green with many areoles and downward-pointing spines. Flower pure white at the terminal ends of the pencil-like branches. An unusual species having similar appearance to that of the *Wilcoxia*,

from Sonora near to Kino Bay on the Gulf of California.

Tribe 3. Pereskioideae
Includes two definite genera, *Pereskia* and *Rhodocactus*—both having very pronounced leaf growths.

Pereskia aculeata (Plum.) Mill.
A very much-branched vine-like shrub with long elliptical dark green leaves. Very spiney, usually 2 or 3 together. Flowers creamy-yellow produced in clusters. A widely distributed species, particularly in S. Mexico and West Indies.

Rhodocactus grandifolius (Haw.) Knuth
An exceptionally free-growing species with erect thick stems developing tree-like proportions, fleshy, becoming woody with age. Leaves oblong narrowing at the base. Usually 2 or more spines

at the areoles. Flowers particularly attractive, deep lilac-rose, usually in clusters at terminals of branches. Large pear-shaped fruit. This species is widely distributed, particularly in the West Indies.

There is very close affinity between Pereskia and Rhodocactus, and basically it can be presumed the division was made on account of the flower colouring characteristic. 'Rhodo' suggests pinkish-rose-coloured flowers, but some species still remaining within Pereskia also have flowers of this colour, so the 'splitting' seems unjustified, at least, in this respect.

Other species of this tribe are endemic to South America.

Commeliniaceae

Tripogandra warscewicziana (Kumph & Boucke) Woodson

An attractive rosette plant with dark-green fleshy leaves developing from thick succulent stems. Leaves are somewhat recurved, elongated with the base clasping the stem. The long lasting flowers of rich purple are carried on a branched inflorescence in clusters. Endemic of Guatemala.

Compositae

The sunflower family, is represented by two genera of succulents.

Coreopsis gigantea (Kellog) Hall

A fleshy stemmed succulent plant from southern California, erect and stout, surmounted by a thick tuft of feathery leaves and corymbose infloresence. This species is not difficult to grow and will retain its normal characteristics if rested completely in summer with very little water, and then encouraged to grow in cooler weather.

Crassulaceae

Has a number of genera peculiar to North America, invariably having a 'rosette' character.

Diamorpha cymosa (Nutt.) Britt.

A sedum-like plant generally accepted as an annual. Slender stems to about 10 cm high branching from the base with small reddish flowers. From Carolina

to Alabama, U.S.A. There are other species of the genus, all with many similarities.

Dudleya–the genus consists of about 40 species, divided into three sub-genera, Stylophyllum, Dudleya, Hasseanthus. All have rosette growth with persistent dried leaves at the base. Floral stems annual with sessile leaves.

Dudleya edulis (Nutt.) Moran

The type species of the sub-genus *Stylophyllum*. Native of California and Baja California. Each rosette has from 10 to 12 linear cylindric leaves, erect, bluish-green. Flowers white.

Dudleya attenuata subsp. *orcuttii* (Rose) Moran

From the Baja California with fleshy rounded green leaves covered with thick white pruinose. Flowers white, blushed pink.

Dudleya farinosa (Lindl.) Br. & R.

From coastal areas of California. Beautiful rosette about 10 cm diameter on stems often elongated, branching. Leaves green and farinose, sharp pointed and pale yellow flowers.

Dudleya variegata (S. Wats.) Moran

From the area around San Diego, southern California and Baja California. Type species of the sub-genus *Hasseanthus*. With a corm-like rootstock, typical of this sub-genus. Spatulate leaves about 7 cm long and to nearly 4 mm thick forming loose rosette. Floral stem about 20 cm high with yellow flowers.

Dudleya densiflora (Rose) Moran

A beautiful plant from San Gabriel Canyon, Los Angeles, California, with bright bluish-white farinose leaves forming rosettes of about 40 leaves on stems. Leaves almost round about 10 cm long. Flowers pinkish-white.

The genus comprises some of the most attractive succulents of North America. They are generally easy in cultivation, but great care is required when watering as a heavy pressure can remove much of the white farinose from the leaves.

ECHEVERIA comprises one of the largest genera of N. American succulent species, widely distributed throughout Mexico and Central America with also one species in Texas, U.S.A. Freely branched plants, rapidly forming clusters of varying shaped rosettes with smooth margins and generally

ABOVE *Yucca filamentosa 'Variegata'*

ABOVE *Agave parryi*

BELOW *Agave sp. nov.*

BELOW *Agave utahensis* v. *nevadensis*

Pachypodium densiflorum with *Aloe conifera* (courtesy of Professor Rauh)

Aloe aristata

A group of Echeverias flowering freely in cultivation.

with small pronounced tip. Inflorescence with several bracts and bell-shaped flowers on stalks.

Echeveria agavoides Lem.

A fleshy rosette with rigid triangular-shaped pointed leaves, apple green or greyish-green, margins sometimes reddish. Flower stalks 50 cm high with reddish flowers tipped yellow. Sometimes known as *Urbinia agavoides* Rose from San Luis Potosi, Mexico.

Echeveria calycosa Moran

From south of Uruapan, Michoacan, Mexico, with light green, spatulate, rounded leaves forming rather flat loose rosette of up to 25 leaves to about 10 cm diameter or slightly more. Tall floral stem about 20 cm long, flowers yellowish.

Echeveria ciliata Moran

A beautiful species from over 2,000 m elevation at Canada Vetutla, Oaxaca, Mexico. Smooth glabrous leaves with very pronounced ciliate margins giving the effect of a continual feather-edge. A striking dense rosette having a silky appearance with floral stem to about 12 cm long and reddish flowers.

Echeveria crenulata Rose

Large rosette on short thickish stem, rosette of broad obovate leaves, grey pruinose, with reddish undulate margins to 30 cm long. Flower stem up to 100 cm long with yellowish-red flowers. Native of Mexico, near Cuernavaca, Morelos.

Echeveria derenbergii J. A. Purp.

A popular and well-known species from south-west of Sierra de Mixteca, Oaxaca, Mexico. Small globular-shaped rosettes in clusters with many thick silvery bluey-grey-green leaves tipped red. Flowers on short stems, golden yellow or reddish-yellow.

Echeveria gibbiflora De Cand.

From south of Mexico City, a tall growing plant with long glabrous stem sometimes branched-topped with large rosettes of spoon-shaped greyish-blue leaves, tinted pink with reddish margins. Flower stem to 60 cm long with reddish-yellow flowers. There are varieties of this well-known species: *E. gibbiflora* v. *metallica* (Lem.) Bak. with rounded leaves, bronze coloured and intensely pruinose; *E. gibbiflora* v. *crispata* Bak. is similar to species but with wavy margins. One of the most outstanding forms is *E. gibbiflora* v. *carunculata* having blister-like warty protuberances on the upper surface.

Echeveria globulosa Moran

Probably from an altitude of 3,000 m or more near Carrizal, Tlacolula, Oaxaca, Mexico. Compact rosette on short thick stem, clustering freely. Rosettes globose, somewhat depressed having up to 60 leaves bluish-green, spoon-shaped, 2 cm or more long and 4 mm wide with reddish margins. Floral stems to 8 cm long, reddish, flowers yellow.

Echeveria procera Moran

A tall growing species from La Muralla, Cerro Yucunino, Oaxaca, Mexico, at over 3,000 m elevation. Stems to nearly 2 m tall, and to 3 cm thick! Rosettes at terminal ends about 25 cm diameter consisting of up to 30 leaves. Leaves oblong-obovate rounded at tips, to 10 cm long and 10 mm thick. Floral stem to over 1 m tall, with up to 50 flowers to an inflorescence, flowers yellow.

This genus has been the subject of much research by prominent botanists and field collectors. The names of Reid Moran, Eric Walther, Tom McDougall will range alongside those who originally contributed so much to the knowledge of these plants.

GRAPTOPETALUM is closely related to Echeveria forming rosettes either with or without stems. The main difference is centred in the flowers which are star-like, the petals being united up to the centre of the tube, then spreading almost horizontally and the petals having many dots or bands.

Graptopetalum filiferum (S. Wats.) Whitehead

From Chihuahua, Mexico. A stemless miniature species forming clumps with numerous rosettes rarely more than 5 cm diameter having up to 100 small spatulate leaves about 30 mm long and 12 mm wide, light green, rather greyish at times,

margins minute, white papillose tapering and ending in a brown filiform bristle. Inflorescence about 8 cm long with flowers whitish with reddish spots.

Graptopetalum paraguayense (N. E. Br.) E. Walth.

A Mexican plant regardless of its misleading specific name. A well-known species looking very much like an Echeveria with loose rosette of thick, fleshy, brittle leaves recurved on upper surface and keeled beneath, reddish-grey with silvery bloom. Rosette borne on long thick fleshy stem, firstly erect, becoming prostrate. Flowers white on long inflorescence.

Lenophyllum is closely related to Echeveria, all rosette-forming with flowers single or few together at terminal ends of densely leafy stem.

Lenophyllum acutifolium Rose

Large rosette to 10 cm high with sword-like leaves tapering abruptly, upper surface furrowed. Flowers numerous, yellowish. A Californian species.

Lenophyllum pusillum Rose

Small rosette consisting of thick, fleshy, narrow leaves about 16 mm long, keeled on back surface, reddish-green. Flowers solitary, yellow. A Mexican species.

PACHYPHYTUM, related to Echeveria, generally with elongated rosettes, the flowers being the main characteristic. They are hanging, bell-shaped and enclosed in bracts on shortish stalks.

Pachyphytum kimnachii Moran

Native of the region around San Luis Potosi, Mexico, on mossy rocks at 1,800 m altitude. Leaves glaucous, somewhat purplish, elliptic-oblong with rounded margins, to about 8 cm long forming elongated rosette on slender stem. Flower reddish and cream with greenish bracts.

Pachyphytum oviferum J. A. Purpus

A beautiful and popular species called the 'Sugar Almond' plant, from Barranca Bagre, San Luis Potosi, Mexico. Fleshy, white pruinose, obovate, thick leaves to about 3 cm long and 2 cm wide, bluntly rounded at the tip, forming small rosettes at intervals along the usually prostrate fleshy branches. Flower reddish.

Pachyphytum viride E. Walth.

A Mexican species with thick erect brownish stem to about 10 cm or more long. Leaves up to 20 at tip of stem, semi-cylindrical, blunt, pale-green to about 12 cm long. Flower reddish-green.

Pachyphytum werdermannii V. Poelln.

A distinctive species from near Jaumave, Tamaulipas, Mexico, having densely arranged leaves along stem up to 25 cm long. Leaves tongue-shaped, thick, somewhat recurved with bluntish tip, pruinose with pinkish shading, not forming a precise rosette. Flowers whitish-red with whitish bracts on long inflorescence.

SEDUM is virtually semi-American, so many species are endemic to North America, the others being generally centred in Europe, Asia and Africa.

Sedum adolphii Hamet

With curved ascending branches with long fleshy thick yellowish-green leaves, tapering bluntly, margins often reddish. Flowers white. Mexico.

Sedum allantoides Rose

Shrub-like to 40 cm high with erect branches and horizontally spreading leaves, about 2 cm long, almost cylindrical with blunt tip, greenish-white. Flowers whitish-green. Oaxaca, Mexico.

Sedum craigii R. T. Clausen

Small bushy plants, prostrate with fleshy stems and leaves. Leaves oblong, somewhat narrow with rounded tip, about 5 cm long, upper side almost flat, rounded on lower side, dark reddish-blue. Flowers white.

Sedum frutescens Rose

A miniature tree-like species with thick succulent stem and branching. Native of southern Mexico on lava flow between Mexico City and Cuernavaca. The stem is covered by thin papery bark which peels readily, with flat linear light green leaves and small white flowers. Two other species have similar habit, *S. tortuosum* Hemsl. and *S. oxypetalum* H. B. et K. but either stem colour is different, or leaves slightly different shape – in the case of the latter, the flowers are red.

Sedum hintonii T. B. Clausen

One of the most beautiful of Sedums from Michoacan, Mexico. Leaves almost forming a rosette, ovate and rounded about 15 mm long, light green and densely covered with fine minute white hairs and white flowers. This plant is rare in cultivation.

Sedum morganianum E. Walth.

A well-known species from Vera Cruz, Mexico, commonly termed the 'Burro Tail'. A pendent plant with long hanging stems covered with spindle-shaped silvery-blue leaves, thick and fleshy about 20 mm long. Flowers at terminal ends in clusters, pinkish-purple.

The genus *Sedum* is represented by about 100 different species in this hemisphere, and those mentioned are reasonably representative.

THOMPSONELLA are peculiar plants closely akin to Echeveria; the flower scape is lateral from the axils of older leaves, has many minute bracts, and flowers are in a loose single spike.

Thompsonella platyphylla Br. & R.

From Guerrero, Mexico. A stemless rosette about 12 cm long, flattish and about 4 cm broad, leaves greyish with red margins. Flowers pinkish-red on panicle. *T. minutiflora* Br. & R. Oaxaca and Puebla is smaller in every respect with rather lax spike and reddish flowers.

Cucurbitaceae

Generally caudiciform plants, represented by three genera.

Cucurbita foetidissima H.B. & K.

Has perennial caudex or tap-root with very elongated trailing stems bearing strong smelling triangular leaves. Flowers are large, yellow like those of marrow. Yellowish fruits about 30 cm diameter. Known as the 'wild pumpkin' in southern States of U.S.A. where it is native.

Ibervillea sonorae (S. Wats.) Greene

Very swollen caudex, either globose or flattened producing a very rampant vine growth. Fairly widely distributed in Mexico, particularly Sonora where it is found at the base of thickets. Leaves small and insignificant, flowers small, yellowish.

Tumamoca macdougallii Rose

A scrambling plant from Arizona with thick, partly subterranean caudex very similar to Ibervillea. Annual branches with thin 3-partite leaves. Has male and female flowers, male 3–6 together, female solitary, pale yellow. Yellowish-red berry-like fruits about 10 mm diameter.

Dioscoreaceae

Are caudiciform plants with only few species in North America.

Dioscorea macrostachya Benth

Member of the Yam family from the forests of Fortin de las Flores, Vera Cruz, Mexico. A roundish, somewhat flattened caudex with long vine-like growth with panicles of yellowish-white flowers. *D. mexicana* reputed to be native of more northerly areas of Mexico is very similar, but with much stouter stem growths, shining and only very few leaves.

Euphorbiaceae

The Spurges have comparatively few representatives in N. America, seeing this is one of the largest of plant families. Includes three genera.

Euphorbia cerifera Alc.

A tall cylindrical stemmed species from Sonora, Mexico, becoming shrubby with many erect waxy greyish branches and small reddish leaves soon deciduous. Flowers several together yellowish-white.

Euphorbia cotinifolia

A West Indian tree-like species with long succulent stem to 6 m high having soft flexible branches and broad ovate, coppery-brown thin fleshy leaves. Not often encountered in cultivation.

Euphorbia pteroneura Bgr.

A Mexican species with pencil like stems, usually 5 or 6-angled, consisting of jointed sections between the leaf-bases. Leaves ovate-lanceolate, deciduous.

Other species of Euphorbia include *E. misera*, a miniature tree-like plant from Baja California with small heart-shaped leaves which are deciduous.

JATROPHA – not all species are succulent, but a few distinctive plants certainly come within that category, some in fact being extreme succulents.

Jatropha multifida, a widely distributed species with narrowly segmented, pinnately lobed leaves and scarlet flowers, is but one of a number found native in the West Indies; others include *J. hastata* and *J. pandurifolia*. *J. berlandieri* Torrey is a native of Texas and has a round caudex-like base and

annual growth from the apex with a charming red inflorescence.

Jatropha podagrica W. J. Hook.

Native of Central America and West Indies having short thickened trunk to about 75 cm high, greyish-green with shedding skin. Leaves from knobbly branches, peltate, 3 to 5 lobed, dark green and leathery about 18 cm long. Inflorescence much branched with many scarlet flowers.

PEDILANTHUS are very similar to Euphorbia, usually with deciduous leaves and 'bird' shaped red flowers.

Pedilanthus carinatus Spr.

Widespread in many of the West Indian Islands, a shrubby plant often to 1 m high, cylindrical stems, erect, green with obovate leaves, fleshy about 12 cm long and red bird-shaped cyathia.

Pedilanthus macrocarpus Benth.

From the Sonora Desert and Baja California, with erect thick succulent stems to about 1 m high, tiny deciduous leaves. Bright red cyathia at terminal ends of stems.

Fouquieraceae

Are stem succulents with often almost bottle-shaped bases, and many branches, usually with spines. Includes two genera.

Fouquieria splendens Engelm.

Widely distributed throughout southern California and in many parts of north Mexico. Spiny tree-like succulent with branches. Leaves small, oval and numerous bright red flowers at ends of stems. The Ocottilla shrub which is so popular in North America as a hedging plant. Other species include *F. diguetii* (v. Tieghem) J. M. Johnst. from Baja California; *F. fasciculata* H. B. et K., the type species of the genus, from north of San Cristobal, Hidalgo, Mexico, with almost bottle-shaped base, a rarity and ideal as a natural bonsai; *F. purpusii*, native of Oaxaca, resembles a small form of Idria.

Idria columnaris Kellog.

The spectacular 'Boogum Tree' which is encountered in 'forests' near Bay of Sebastian Vizcaino in western-central part of Baja California. Huge tree succulent with heavy elongated caudex and

Pedilanthus macrocarpus

numerous branches, greyish leaves and greenish-yellow flowers at apex of plant.

Liliaceae

Includes two genera of plants, both with large-growing species.

Hesperaloe parviflora Coulter

A stemless plant with very long narrow pointed grooved leaves and whitish fibrous hairs along the margins. Flower scape to nearly 2 m long with bell-shaped pinkish-red flowers about 30 mm long. *H. funifera* Trel. very similar but with longer scape and greenish-reddish flowers.

YUCCA are very much the giant 'lilies' of North America. There are many species, mostly tree-like, having thickened stems and rosettes of stiff leaves and generally huge inflorescences. They make spectacular specimens. Some are semi-hardy.

Yucca rigida (Eng.) Trel. from Mapimi, Mexico, bluish leaves, up to 3 m high. *Y. baileyi* a smaller species from Arizona and New Mexico; *Y. neomexicana* Woot. & Standl. another smaller growing species from Des Moines, M. Mexico; *Y. schottii* one of the most showy plants with spectacular fruits from Animas Mountains, Mexico. *Y. whipplei* a native of S. California, flowers only once and dies. *Y. gilbertiana* (Trel.) Rybd. comes from Central Nevada. *Y. filamentosa* is one of the most distinctive having sword-shaped leaves edged with curly white hairs and creamy-white flowers on a 3 m high stem. *Y. aloifolia*, its varieties 'Marginata' and 'Tricolor' are also among the most attractive of this extraordinary family. One species above all others, *Y. brevifolia*, the 'Joshua tree', is widely

Yucca brevifolia

distributed in southern U.S.A. and many parts of northern Mexico.

Yucca faxoniana

(syn. *Samuela faxoniana* Trel.) Tree-like species with long stems up to 4m high, thick and only rarely branching. Leaves at apex, about 1m long, strap-like, with white threads on margins, somewhat grooved with short tapering end. Inflorescence forming pyramid shape with both large bracts and white flowers. This species and others are found in northern Mexico and Texas, U.S.A.

Moraceae

Has only one representative species of consequence.
Ficus palmeri S. Wats.
A species from Baja California, possibly synonymous with *F. brandegeei* Standl. With swollen whitish caudex-like base and multiple stem growths having ovate leaves, somewhat pubescent. Flowers insignificant, but with interesting globose fruits.

Portulacaceae

Includes a number of genera, some of which are low-growing, mat-forming plants while others are more shrubby species.
Lewisia brachycalyx Engelm.
ex Gray and *L. rediviva* Pursh
Are typical of a number of North American species of this genus, with rosette forming growth and attractive flowers, on usually short scaps, white, pink or red.
Talinum guadalupense Dudley
One of the rarest of succulents from Gaudalupe Island off Baja California. A compact very fleshy plant having thick globose mis-shapen caudex with greyish skin, which readily peels. Branches irregular bearing ovate spatulate leaves about 5 cm long, fleshy, bluish-green, edged red. Inflorescence with oval bracts and pinkish flowers.

Talinum includes many other species of extreme succulence, many of which are North American.
Talinum parvulum Rose et Standl., *T. paniculatum* (Jacq.) Gaertn. are perhaps among the better known and of easy culture.

Vitaceae

Provides only one genus of succulent plants.
Cissus tuberosa Moc. & Sesse ex D.C.
Native of Puebla, Mexico, where it is found at an altitude of about 1,500m. A peculiar species with round, succulent caudex and vine-like growth of fleshy greyish-green joints producing aerial roots which seem to encourage swelling of the stem joints. Leaves somewhat fern-like in shape, flowers insignificant.

4 The Succulents of South America

During the last two decades there has been a tremendous upsurge of interest in the plant-life of South America, and this has resulted in the introduction of some exciting new succulents. To a great extent the emphasis has been centred in Peru, Brazil and Bolivia, and from these countries alone many extraordinary new species of cacti have been introduced.

The length and breadth of South America varies enormously both in climate and terrain. This fact undoubtedly contributes to the diverse peculiarities apparent in the species of the Cactaceae, changing continually from those endemic to the northerly countries of Venezuela, Colombia and Surinam to those of Brazil, Uruguay and Argentina in the south. To try to 'zone' South America into climatic groups would prove an impossible task – the 'campos' of Brazil, the 'thorn-savannah' of Argentina, the Andean slopes and valleys of Chile and Peru with their dry winters and humid summers – such variations as these could of themselves account for the countless strange characteristics exhibited by cacti. In addition, the endless coastal regions so widely changeable from north to south in terrestrial, temperature and weather conditions provide further possible causes for the wide range of variation within the cactus world of South America, differences which are even more apparent and more diversified than those of the North American cacti.

All three tribes of the Cactaceae are represented in South America, but with few exceptions species are included within generic titles differing from those of North America. It is interesting to note that no genera of the succulent *Liliaceae* are totally indigenous to the south and likewise no record

of succulents of *Cucurbitaceae* or *Dioscoreaceae*. *Crassulaceae* include only species of Kalanchoë. Sedum, Echeveria and Villadia and *Euphorbiaceae* have sparse representation. On the other hand, some plant families are featured by genera with succulent plants not found elsewhere in the world.

It would seem that our knowledge of the 'other succulents' of South America is extremely limited – so few species have been recorded with so few plant families being represented. Perhaps in the explorative field, the pursuit for new species of cacti has over-shadowed the search for other forms of succulent plant-life? It is conceivable that a vast sphere of opportunity still awaits the imaginative field collector in the realm of the 'other succulents'.

Only sixteen families are involved in this record – some of these are not entirely succulents – for instance, *Bromeliacae*; the terrestrial species detailed are more xerophytic than succulent.

Agavaceae

Agave couci Trel.

A large plant not unlike *A. americana*, having greyish-green leaves armed with reddish-brown marginal spines and terminal spine. Marginal spines rather triangular, those towards the top of the leaf are curved forward, the lower ones recurved. Long branched inflorescence with long yellow flowers. Endemic to Venezuela.

Agave cundinamarcensis Lem.

From the area of Cundinamarca, Colombia. A stemless rosette plant with very thick leaves, first spreading horizontally, then curved towards the centre and finally recurving abruptly. Leaves greyish-yellow with blunted marginal spines and very short terminal spine. Tall inflorescence, pyramid-like with creamy-yellow flowers.

Apocynaceae
Plumiera rubra L.
Similar in many respects to other species of Plumiera native to West Indies. A tree-like succulent with fleshy branches and large elongated leaves having panicles of deep red flowers with yellow throat from the terminal end of the branches. Native of Venezuela and possibly through to Peru.

Basellaceae
Ullucas tuberosus Caldas
An interesting species having large tuberous root and succulent vine-like stems. Leaves generally heart-shaped, sometimes roundish, thick and fleshy. Small whitish flowers in loose racemes. The red tubers are said to be edible. Chile and Peru.

Begoniaceae
Begonia venosa Skan.
A large shrub-like plant from Brazil, often to 60 cm high or more. Stems and leaves covered with a white scurf. Leaves succulent, kidney shape. Flowers white.

Other species are recorded which merit acceptance as succulent plants. *B. epipsila*, a Brazilian plant with succulent stems and roundish, fleshy bright green leaves, under-surface reddish and covered with whitish felt. Flowers white. *B. subvillosa* a beautiful species from Brazil having soft hairy succulent stems, velvety; ovate leaves, very pale green with toothed margins and large white flowers. *B. vellozoana* has very succulent leaves in varying colours from green to bronze and vivid whitish veins. Pinkish-white flowers.

Bombacaceae
Cavanillesia arborea Sch.
A large tree with very succulent barrel-shaped trunk, widening from the base, and then tapering towards the terminal end. Originates from dry forest areas of eastern Brazil, deciduous; its flowers are produced before the leaves. A rare and interesting plant not often seen in cultivation.
Chorisia speciosa A. Saint Hil.
A tree-like species, its succulent trunk studded with stout sharp thorns. Leaves on long stalk, digitately compound toothed leaves. Flowers from the leaf axils, pink 5-petalled flowers about 10 cm diameter with long hairs on the under-side of the petals. Fruits are pear-shaped with silky-floss around the seeds. Known as the floss-silk tree. Native of Brazil. *C. ventricosa* N.M. a very large tree with bottle-shaped trunk with top branches, all of which are spiny. Called the 'Samuru-tree' in Argentina from where it originates, growing in dry forest areas. Flowers, pinkish or yellowish, the outside of the petals woolly.

Bromeliaceae
Abromeitiella brevifolia (Griseb.) Castell
A well-known species endemic to many parts of Bolivia and Argentina. Small compact rosette of elongated triangular leaves about 3 cm long, thick and fleshy with spineless margins. Clusters freely forming mats. Flowers, 'cannon-shaped' bright green. *A. chlorantha* (Haum.) Mez. from Argentina in the region of Tucuman having very small rosettes of elongated triangular leaves about 20 mm long, pale green, clusters freely forming mounds. Leaves very stiff with a small terminal spine and minutely toothed margins. Flowers greenish.
Dyckia sulphurea C. Koch
A spreading rosette about 30 cm diameter, leaves about 20 cm long, dark-green with silvery lines on the under-surface. Flower on long scape, sulphur-yellow, endemic to Brazil. *D. brevifolia* Bak. with rosette very similar to *D. sulphurea*, under-surface of leaves with whitish scales. Flowers yellow, somewhat tubular in shape and borne on long scape with recurved bracts. Also from Brazil. *D. altissima* Ldl. from northern Argentina and south Brazil has rosette of pale green leaves about 25 cm long with margins armed with prominent brown spines. Inflorescence rather horny, branched with bright yellow flowers. Many other species have similar characteristics, some are especially outstanding

such as *D. fosteriana* L. B. Smith, native of Brazil, an ornamental plant, small silvery-purple rosette with silvery marginal spines, bearing bright orange flowers. *D. chloristaminea* Mez. is unique inasmuch as it branches freely with very slender rosettes, almost grass-like leaves, rosettes stemless, offsetting from a common base. Endemic to Brazil. *D. remotiflora* Otto et Dietr.–*D. rariflora* sensu Graham and sensu Lindl. A well-distributed species in Uruguay, S. Brazil and Argentina, rosette with leaves about 20 cm long, strongly recurved, margins with 3 cm long sharp spines. Inflorescence very tall, mealy-white with deep orange-yellow flowers. *D. rariflora* Schult. a Brazilian plant, not to be confused with *D. remotiflora*, is a rather small rosette with hard recurved leaves, green covered with greyish scales, margins with soft blackish spines. Tall inflorescence with only few orange flowers. Many other plants are recognized including some newer discoveries, *D. hebdingii* L. B. Smith from Rio Grande do Sul, Brazil, with yellow flowers and *D. marnieri-lapostollei* Mez. a Brazilian species of particular charm.

Puya alpestris Gay.
Native of Chile. Large rosette over 1 m diameter with long slender leaves about 2 cm wide, having whitish scales on the lower surface and very sharp, hard spiny margins. Long inflorescence with many upward pointing branches, serrated bracts and large greyish-blue flowers. *P. chilensis* Mol. is also from Chile, develops a woody stem with age, often 1 m or more tall from which the rosette growths develop. Leaves 80–100 cm long and 5 cm wide, margins with hard recurved spines. Tall inflorescence covered with brownish hairs and yellowish flowers. Other species include *P. raimondii* Harms., one of the largest species of the genus from altitudes of about 4,000 m in central and south Peru, almost hardy in some protected areas of Britain. *P. laxa* L. B. Smith native of Argentina has loose rosette of long narrow greyish velvety leaves developing on a much branching plant. There are smaller growing species such as *P. nana* Wittm. from Bolivia and *P. medica* L. B. Smith which is endemic to Peru with bluish flowers. These are particularly useful for normal cultivation under glass.

Puya alpestris

Cactaceae

TRIBE I. CEREOIDEAE
In the Britton and Rose classification this tribe was divided into sub-tribes which were ideally suited to plants endemic to North America. The same classification, of course, also applies to South America genera, but due to the tremendous upsurge of interest which has occurred in more recent years, to no small degree owing to the very extensive explorative work undertaken in regions hitherto unknown botanically, additional sub-tribes are likely to emerge. Rather than confuse the issue, the genera of this tribe will be detailed alphabetically without taking into account the possible recognized sub-

97

tribes to which they are presently attached. Not all genera are noted; some are very obscure and might properly be merged with other better-known and understood genera. This does suggest that such nomenclature has no validity. *Cipocereus* Ritt. is allied to *Pilocereus* Lem. non Sch. and concerns species from Minas Gerais, Brazil, namely *C. minensis* (Werd.) Ritt. *Gymnanthocereus* Back. (or *Gymnocereus* Backeb.) relates to *G. chlorocarpa* (H.B.K.) Backeb. from north Peru. *Neobinghamia* Backeb. refers in particular to a Peruvian species, *N. climaxanthus* (Werd.) Backeb. a plant where new growth develops through the previous year's cephalium (as also in *Neodawsonia*). *Ceocardenasia* Backeb. is a monotypic genus created for *N. herzogiana* Backeb., a huge tree-like cactus from Pilquina to Saipina, Santa Cruz, Bolivia, and possibly closely allied to *Neoraimondia* Br. & R. *Praecereus* Buxb. is allied to *Monvillea* Br. & R. and is represented by *P. campinensis* (Backeb. & Voll.) Buxb. a Brazilian species. *Pseudopilocereus* Buxb. are non-cephalium-bearing columnar cacti; a recently described species is *P. magnificus* Buin. & Bred. from Minais Gerais, Brazil and is undoubtedly one of the most remarkable blue stemmed plants yet seen in cultivation. *Pygmaeocereus* Johns. & Backeb. erected this genus for certain Peruvian plants, small and with tuberous roots. Only few species are included such as *P. bylesiana* Andr. & Backeb. with white scented nocturnal flowers. *Raugocereus* Backeb. is considered to have certain characteristics similar to other genera, especially *Browningia*, *Castellanosia*, *Azureocereus* etc. This genus concerns species from Peru such as *R. riosaniensis* Backeb. The genus *Reicheocactus* Backeb. is very much linked to *Neoporteria* and *Neochilenia*. Individual genera have been created for many cerei; some have been isolated for only trivial differences and to refer to each would seem unnecessary.

ACANTHOCALYCIUM Backeb. are globular plants usually with very many acute ribs, long spines and colourful flowers.
Acanthocalycium spiniflora (Sch.) Backeb.
(syn. *Echinocactus spiniflorus* Sch.) Type species from Argentina. Globular to cylindric with about

20 ribs, large white areoles with up to 20 spreading spines, reddish-yellow. Flowers about 4 cm long and broad, rose red. *A. violaceum* (Werd.) Backeb. also from Argentina with dark green body and about 20 ribs, areoles with up to 15 yellowish-brown spines and lilac-purple flowers.
Acanthocalycium aurantiacum Rausch, native of Catamarca, Argentina at 3,000 m altitude, has about 10–16 ribs, pronounced areoles with only few spreading spines and yellowish-orange flowers.
ACANTHOCEREUS (Bgr.) Br. & R. includes species with varying habits, some erect, other clambering and having very prominent spines.
Acanthocereus colombianus Br. & R.
A semi-erect plant, later clambering, native of Colombia. Branches consist of 3-angled joints about 8 cm wide with large areoles having about 8 short radial spines and 2 thick central spines. Very large flower about 25 cm long, white.
AKERSIA Buin. is closely allied to certain other genera particularly Borzicactus, Hildewintera and Bolivicereus.
Akersia roseiflora Buin.
An interesting columnar species from Peru. Erect with many ribs and yellowish-brown spines. Flowers somewhat tubular-campanulate, bright rose-pink. The only representative of this genus.
ARMATOCEREUS Backeb. includes a number of tree-like cerei, closely linked to Lemaireocereus. The flower tube, ovary and fruit are spiny.
Armatocereus humilis (Br. & R.) Backeb.
A low growing trailing plant from Dagua Valley, Colombia, having elongated stems, 4–5 ribs, spreading with rooting branches. Areoles bear white felt, spines about 15. Nocturnal white flowers.
Armatocereus laetus (H.B.K.) Br. & R.
(syn. *Cactus laetus* H.B.K.) Type species. At one time included within the genus *Lemaireocereus*. An erect plant to 6 m high, tree-like with many branches, bluish-green. Ribs about 8 somewhat prominent, areoles with brownish-grey spines about 3 cm long. Flowers nocturnal, white to 8 cm long. Indigenous to southern Ecuador and Peru.

ARROJADOA Br. & R. non Mattf. Cylindrical stems, generally slender with low ribs and many small spines. An apical pseudocephalium develops from which the flowers arise. An interesting genus consisting of only few known species, all from Brazil.

Arrojadoa canudosensis Buin. & Bred.

A tall erect species from Canudos, Bahia, Brazil, to over 1 m high, branching from the base with cephalium of brown bristles and white hairs in which the flowers are produced. Stems continue to grow through the cephalium with the existing cephalium persisting, thus forming bristly rings around the stem. About 14 ribs, areoles close set with white felt and to 15 brown radial spines and 8 usually upward-pointing central spines. Flower tubular, pinkish-green.

Arrojadoa penicillata (Gurke) Br. & R.

A slender erect plant from Bahia, Brazil, about 2 m high with many branches often becoming bushy. About 10 low ribs with closely set areoles bearing short spreading spines. Brownish bristles develop at terminal ends of joints forming a thick ring around the stem. Flowers rose-pink.

Arrojadoa rhodantha (Gurke) Br. & R.

(syn. *Cereus rhodanthus* Gurke) Type species from Piauhy, Brazil, where it is found in very arid areas. Semi-erect, then clambering, cylindrical stems in joints with about 12 ribs, dark green; small areoles having brown slender spines. Flowers from terminal ends, pink about 3 cm long surrounded by brownish bristles which persist and form a ring around each joint.

ARTHROCEREUS Bgr. are generally small-growing species with very spiny stems. Flowers develop from near the top of the stems, nocturnal. This is possibly very closely related to *Setiechinopsis*.

Arthrocereus microsphaerica (Sch.) Bgr.

A small species from near Rio de Janeiro, Brazil, with slender somewhat prostrate stems jointed with many low ribs and spiny. Small whitish nocturnal flowers usually at terminals of joints.

Arthrocereus rondonianus Backeb. & Voll.

A rare species from Diamantian, Brazil, small creeping plant with cylindrical stems to 70 cm long, areoles with numerous bright yellowish spines. Flowers purplish-pink.

ACANTHOLOBIVIA Backeb. consists of globular or oval shaped plants. Very closely allied to

Lobivia, only the flower tends not to open widely, and is borne on the sides of the plant. Very colourful.

Acantholobivia incuiensis Rauh & Backeb.

A globular or caespitose plant with 16–20 ribs somewhat undulated with very pronounced areoles having many spines, the centrals being much longer than the radials. Flowers carmine-red. Native of southern Peru between Chala and Coracora at 3,600 m altitude. The type species is *A. tegeleriana* Backeb. from central Peru.

AREQUIPA Br. & R. concerns principally plants rather globular in shape, from a somewhat confined area around Arequipa, the Peruvian Department which gave the genus its name, and to part of northern Chile. Certain characteristics link this genus with Matucana.

Arequipa leucotricha (Phil.) Br. & R.

(syn. *Echinocactus leucotrichus* Phil.) The type species. A globose sometimes semi-elongated plant having from 10 to 20 ribs, close set areoles with many spines, up to 20, the centrals being about 3 cm long. Flowers on long slender tube, red. Other species are described which appear almost identical, if not synonymous to the species and include *A. rettigii* (Quehl) Br. & R., *A. erectocylindrica* Rauh & Backeb.

AUSTROCACTUS Br. & R. includes only a few species which are sometimes likened to the North American Echinocerei. Low-growing plants, somewhat cylindric with hooked central spines and colourful flowers. Patagonia, south Argentina.

Austrocactus bertinii (Cels.) Br. & R.

(syn. *Cereus bertini* Cels.) Type species of this interesting and rare genus, body olive-green to about 30 cm or more high, 10–12 prominent ribs, felted areoles bearing up to 15 slender spreading radial spines and 4–5 slender, very hooked, blackish central spines up to 3 cm long. Large flower to 10 cm diameter, pinkish-yellow with red stigma lobes. *A. dusenii* (Web.) Br. & R. is very similar, branching from near the base, rose-pink flowers.

AUSTROCEPHALOCEREUS (Backeb.) Backeb. Tall growing cerei with superficial pseudocephalium, which develops on one side of the stem.

Austrocephalocereus dybowskii (Goss.) Backeb.

An attractive much-branched plant from Bahia, Brazil. Tall cylindrical stems nearly 4m high, branching freely from the base, forming clusters. Branches with over 20 ribs with closely set areoles bearing long white hairs and few yellowish radial and central spines, the centrals protruding horizontally, about 3cm long. Nocturnal white flowers about 4cm long, arising from within the white pseudocephalium.

Austrocephalocereus purpureus (Gurke) Backeb.

(syn. *Cereus purpureus* Gurke) Type species. An erect columnar plant, unbranched, to over 3m high

A spectacular clump of *Austrocephalocereus purpureus*.

with broad low ribs 12–16 with depressions above each areole, elongated areoles with white wool and many spines, radials about 18, acicular, short; centrals about 10, 5cm long, brown. Pseudocephalium on one side of the stem, nocturnal white flowers.

AZUREOCEREUS Akers & Johns. includes columnar species with bluish stems, dense woolly areoles and long deflexed spines. Flowers from near the apex on short thick cylindrical tube.

Azureocereus nobilis Akers & Johns.

Type species. A very imposing species from Peru, erect, columnar with few branches, bluish-green, many low but prominent ribs having woolly areoles and long deflexed spines. Flowers nocturnal from upper areoles, white. Another species has been transferred to this genus, *A. hertlingianus* (Backeb.) Backeb. with bright bluish stems and long yellow spines; they might be synonymous. There is considerable doubt as to whether this genus, as such, can be justified – the main factor is undoubtedly the bluish character of the stems which makes these two species among the most attractive of columnar cacti.

BLOSSFELDIA Werd. include some of the more miniature species of the Cactaceae, mostly multiheaded with whitish scattered areoles and no perceptible spines.

Blossfeldia liliputana Werd.

The type species from north Argentina. Small flattish-circular plants, greyish-green with minute greyish-woolly areoles and totally unarmed. Flower whitish-pink produced near to the crown, diurnal. *B. minima* Ritt. is very similar and is likely to prove synonymous.

BOLIVICEREUS Card. includes columnar species from Bolivia – after which the genus was named. Possibly closely related to Cleistocactus.

Bolivicereus samaipatanus Card.

Type species. A most imposing plant from Bolivia, branching freely from the base, very erect. Branches with up to 16 low, transverse ribs with prominent brown woolly areoles and numerous golden yellow radial acicular spines. Flowers are deep red, diurnal.

BORZICACTUS Ricco. This genus along with many others (Matucana, Submatucana, Oroya, Arequipa, Akersia, Hildewintera, Denmoza, Cleistocactus etc.) has been the subject of much research by botanists on both sides of the Atlantic and to date no all-embracing formula has yet been produced which is generally acceptable to all. Many of the original generic names will 'die hard', and while there is no intention to ignore the work of very eminent scientists, for the purpose of this record the better-known generic title is being used.

Borzicactus acanthurus (Vaup.) Br. & R.

Low spreading procumbent plant from Matucana, Peru, with long branches up to 30 cm long and about 4 cm diameter. Stems with about 18 low rounded ribs, small woolly areoles and numerous yellow short bristly spines, with few somewhat longer centrals. Flowers red. At one time included within the genus *Loxanthocereus*. Also seemingly legitimately placed is *B. roezlii* (Haage Jr.) Backeb. with pronounced rounded ribs, up to 20 radial spines and one central protruding horizontally. Flowers, reddish, towards the terminal of stem.

BRACHYCEREUS Br. & R. Short-stemmed plants from Galapagos Islands, with close set areoles and many acicular spines.

Brachycereus thouarsii (Web.) Br. & R.

(syn. *Cereus thouarsii* Web.) Type species. One of the few endemic species of the Galapagos Islands where it is fairly widely distributed. A rare plant in cultivation. Stems to about 1 m high and branching from base. Ribs about 20, with closely set areoles bearing numerous bristly spines about 3 cm long which completely cover the branches, so dense is the formation. Flower nocturnal, whitish.

BRASILICEREUS Backeb. Allied to Cephalocereus. Tree-like plants, all from Brazil.

Brasilicereus phaeacanthus (Gurke) Backeb.

(syn. *Cereus phaeacanthus* Gurke) Type species. An erect slender plant, branching freely from the base, endemic to Bahia, Brazil. Branches have about 12 ribs, low and narrow, closely set white woolly areoles with numerous brownish spines to 1·5 cm long. The flowers are white, funnel-shaped and nocturnal.

BROWNINGIA Br. & R. Attractive erect plants, sometimes branching at the top. Stems with numerous ribs and very spiny.

Browningia candelaris (Meyen) Br. & R.

(syn. *Cereus candelaris* Meyen.) Type species. Erect tall tree-like, from high altitudes in northern Chile and southern Peru. Stems to over 4 m high forming a stout trunk and branching at the top. Many rounded ribs with pronounced areoles bearing numerous brownish-black spines. Flowers pinkish-white, nocturnal. Other species include *B. altissima* (Ritt.) Buxb. with erect, almost spineless, prominently ribbed stems and nocturnal whitish flowers, earlier known as *Gymnanthocereus altissimus* Ritt. and originates from Cajamarca, Peru. *B. pilleiffera* (Ritt.) Hutchis. and hitherto known as *Gymnanthocereus pilleiffera* Ritt. from Balsas, Peru, with small greenish-white flowers at terminals of branches.

BUININGIA Buxb. Species of particular interest and attraction, segregated from Coleocephalocereus as its flowers and seeds are more similar to Melocactus. Plants with pseudocephalium.

Buiningia brevicylindrica (Buin.) Buxb.

(syn. *Coleocephalocereus brevicylindrica* Buin.) Type species. A fascinating plant, short cylindrical stem with about 17 broad acute ribs, having pronounced areoles bearing approximately 10 spreading radial spines and 3 or 4 centrals, yellowish but becoming greyish. Cephalium develops firstly across 3 or 4 ribs eventually spreading and covering half the stem with yellowish bristles set in thickish yellowish-white wool which becomes blackish with age. Flowers small, yellowish-green. *B. aurea* (Ritt.) Buxb. is very similar in many respects, offsets freely from the base with heavily spined plantlets. Both species are from southern Brazil. Closely allied to Coleocephalocereus.

CALYMMANTHIUM Ritt. includes only two species from Peru. Tall erect plant, the unique characteristic among cacti is undoubtedly the flowers with a 'double Perianth'—one within the other.

Calymmanthium substerile Ritt.

Type species. A rare plant from Peru and Bolivia,

erect, branching from the base 4–5 angled, fresh green with large areoles and spines of unequal length. Also recognised is *C. fertile* Ritt. with 3–4-angled branches.

CASTELLANOSIA Card. was erected for one species with upper areoles having brownish-grey bristles and the lower areoles with awl-shaped spines.
Castellanosia caineana Card.
Type species. A tall growing species to about 5 m or more. Stems cylindrical with 9 rounded ribs. Pseudocephalium develops towards top of branches. Flowers deep red, diurnal somewhat funnel-shaped. A species from Bolivia which has close association with *Browningia*.

CEREUS Mill. Tall, stately plants, generally much branched. All with nocturnal flowers and generally red fruits.
Cereus jamacura De Cand.
One of several of this large genus which are very well-known in cultivation. Tall growing to 10 m high, branching freely, bluish-green erect branches with up to 6 ribs having large areoles and many spines–on mature plants these become very long. Flowers on long tube, white, nocturnal to about 25 cm long. Widely distributed in Bahia, Brazil. This is often confused with *C. peruvianus* (L.) Mill., a plant to be seen in many parts of south-east South America, and not necessarily native to Peru which its name would suggest. Stems are dark green, usually 4 to 9 ribs, dark brownish-black spines. Flowers also white, large, nocturnal. The type species of the genus is *C. hexagonus* (L.) Mill. from more northerly regions of South America which has generally 6-angled stems, thin, ribs, small felted areoles and short spines. Flowers very large, nocturnal, white.

CEPHALOCLEISTOCACTUS Ritt. Plants producing slender branches, low ribs, densely set areoles and very spiny. Develops a cephalium with age which can grow to more than 1 m long.
Cephalocleistocactus chrysocephalus Ritt.
Type species. A tall growing plant with many cylindrical branches, characterised by 11–14 low ribs and areoles bearing about 15 radial spines and

6 centrals. Branches develop very long cephaliums, consisting of yellowish-brown bristly spines. Flowers reddish about 5 cm long. Endemic to Bolivia and for which this generic title was created.

CHAMAECEREUS Br. & R. are small caespitose plants with cylindrical joints with numerous flowers.
Chamaecereus silvestrii (Speg.) Br. & R.
One of the most popular and well-known cacti from mountainous regions of Tucuman, Argentina. Plant consists of small joints forming prostrate clusters. Joints with 6 to 9 ribs and soft white spines. Flowers, large for the plant, to about 7 cm long, orange-red. Easy in cultivation and readily propagated by rooting the small joints. A number of interesting cultivars have been introduced through cross-pollinating Chamaecereus with Lobivia species resulting in diminutive plants similar to Chamaecereus, but with even larger and differing colours of flowers.

CLEISTOCACTUS Lem. Slender plants of erect or clambering habit. The flower is the main characteristic, the perianth tube being almost closed and only the stamens and style protrude.
Cleistocactus baumannii (Lem.) Br. & R.
(syn. *Cereus baumannii* Lem.) Type soecies. Plants having erect stems with many ribs and closely set areoles bearing numerous very short brownish spines, from yellowish areoles with orange-red diurnal flowers, endemic to Argentina. *C. strausii* (Heese) Backeb. is possibly the best known of the genus, having greyish areoles and white spines. Flowers reddish, diurnal, from mountainous areas of Bolivia. *C. wendlandiorum* Backeb. from west Argentina is one of the finest of the genus, with very short golden-yellow spines and deep orange flowers, the bright green stigma just protruding. A very rewarding group which are easy in cultivation and begin to produce flowers when about 75 cm long.

CLISTANTHOCEREUS Backeb. Large growing plants, branches with few ribs and notches between the areoles. Day flowering, from the apex of the plant.

A well-grown group of Cleistocactus species.

Cleistocactus strausii

Clistanthocereus fieldianus (Br. & R.) Backeb.
(syn. *Borziactus fieldianus* Br. & R.) Type species
for a genus which has become re-united with
Borzicactus but is still recognized by the Backeberg
title. A tall growing plant, forming thickets to 5 or
6 m high, many elongated branches which often
tend to become pendent and almost prostrate.
Ribs 6–7, broad and stout, pronounced, large
circular areoles with about 8 whitish spines of unequal length, some to over 5 cm long. Flowers
from terminal ends of branches, reddish. *C. hertlingianus* Backeb. is now known as *Azureocereus
hertlingianus* (Backeb.) Backeb.

COLEOCEPHALOCEREUS Backeb. were separated
from Cephalocereus on account of the naked
funnel-shaped flowers emanating from the bristly
woolly pseudocephalium borne in a groove.

Coleocephalocereus fluminensis (Miqu.) Backeb.
(syn. *Cereus fluminensis* Miqu.) Type species.
Found on rocky cliff faces near the coastline, Rio de
Janeiro, Brazil, tall, erect or clambering, densely
branched. Stems have about 12–17 ribs, acute, with
closely set areoles and short acicular yellow spines.
Pseudocephalium on only one side of the terminal
ends consisting of dense white wool and yellowish
bristles. Flowers nocturnal, pinkish-white. *C.
goebelianus* (Vaup.) Backeb. endemic to the states
of Bahia and Minas Gerais, Brazil, is possibly the
largest of this genus, often to 6 m high. Stems with
up to 25 ribs, closely set areoles with about 16 radial
spines and about 6–8 stiff straight centrals. Cephalium covers half the stem consisting of whitish wool
and dark brown sometimes black-bristles. Flowers
pinkish-white. Other more recent introductions
include *C. decumbens* Ritt. from Minas Gerais,

A collection of very fine Copiapoa species and forms.

Brazil, a smaller-growing species somewhat decumbent in habit. *C. paulensis* Ritt. is another densely branching and clambering plant from the island of Ilhabela near Sao Paulo, Brazil.

COPIAPOA Br. & R. contains many of the most spectacular globular cacti all originating from Chile. The title is derived from the provincial name, Copiapo. It includes many species, some of which might possibly be considered synonymous with others, or alternatively be reduced to varietal status.

Copiapoa marginata (S.-D.) Br. & R.
(syn. *Echinocactus marginatus* S.-D.) The type species from the coastal hills of Antofagasta, Chile, is a clustering plant, sub-cylindrical, about 12 low ribs and very closely set areoles from which emanate up to 10 spines of unequal length, one usually much longer. Flowers yellow, from the crown of the plant which becomes closely set with many brownish hairs. *C. cinerea* (Phil.) Br. & R. from near Taltal, western Chile, is one of the most distinctive species, somewhat cylindric whitish-grey stem, dense white wool in the apex, about 18 broad ribs with closely set areoles and black spines. Flowers yellow. Three distinct varieties of *C. cinerea* are recognized, *C. cinerea* v. *dealbata*, usually with long spines, singly from the areoles; *C. cinerea* v. *columna-alba* has generally shorter spines than the species, taller and whiter. *C. longistaminea* Ritt. is yet another outstanding plant, with greyish-green body, somewhat flattened with white wool at the apex, round areoles with brownish felt and 3–6 brownish spines, generally spreading. *C. krainziana* Ritt. is exceptional on account of its covering of fine, white, hair-like bristles and golden spines.

CORRYOCACTUS Br. & R. Short erect plants with prominent ribs and large diurnal flowers, very symmetrical, borne from the upper areoles.

Corryocactus brevistylus (Sch.) Br. & R.
(syn. *Cereus brevistylus* Sch.) Type species. A tall growing plant to about 3 m high and branching

freely from the base forming thickets. Slender branches with about 6 pronounced ribs, large, roundish, areoles about 3 cm apart with dense wool and about 15 brownish spines of unequal length. Flowers large, about 10 cm diameter, yellowish. Indigenous to the mountainous areas of south Peru at altitude of nearly 3,000 m. A Bolivian species, *C. melanotrichus* (Sch.) Br. & R. is a smaller growing plant from barren hills around La Paz at over 3,000 m, with yellow spines and large yellow flower.

DENMOZA Br. & R.–an anagram of Mendoza, Argentina, signifying its habitat. Somewhat cylindrical plants with very straight parallel ribs and clusters of uneven reddish-brown curved spines.
Denmoza rhodacantha (S.-D.) Br. & R.
(syn. *Echinocactus rhodacanthus* S.-D.) Globular-cylindric, becoming more elongated with age. With straight ribs somewhat undulated, grey felted areoles about 2 cm apart each bearing about 10–11 curving red spines. Flowers red with style protruding beyond the petals and stamens. Endemic to the western mountainous areas of Argentina. *D. erythrocephala* (K. Sch.) Berg. is very similar but with more slender spines and bristly hairs at areoles, also from Argentina.

DISCOCACTUS. Pfeiff. is a genus of consequence due in no small degree to the many expeditions which have resulted in the discovery of a number of new species during the last two decades. The names of Buining and Horst are particularly associated with such expeditions and they, probably more than any others, have been instrumental in introducing new species of Discocactus, Melocactus, and other of the more rare, little-understood Brazilian plants. The genus is characterized by the body of the plant, being globose and somewhat flattened; the cephalium which is more apparent with some species than with others; the large nocturnal white fragrant flowers, and the naked fruits.
Discocactus placentiformis (Lehm.) Sch.
(syn. *Cactus placentiformis* Lehm.) The type species. Low, globular, bluish-green plant, with woolly cephalium. Has about 10–14 broad, low ribs, and 6–8 areoles on each rib bearing usually 6, some-

times 7 stout recurved dark brownish spines and rarely 1 solitary central spine. Large white flower, fragrant. Endemic to Brazil. *D. heptacanthus* (Rodr.) Br. & R. from Mato-Grosso, Brazil, is about 12 cm diameter with up to 12 rather tuberculate ribs and areoles bearing usually 7 stout recurved radial spines. Cephalium bristly, and flower white, large, scented. *D. alteolens* Lem. from Brazil, a very flattish plant with few ribs and few spines. A very rare species with the typical large white scented flower. One of the most fascinating plants to be discovered in recent years is *D. horstii*, a small Brazilian species with up to 20 acute ribs having closely set areoles and minute 'comb-like' spines. The plant body measures about 2–3 cm diameter, reddish-greyish-green with pronounced woolly cephalium from which large white nocturnal flowers emerge.

ECHINOPSIS Zucc. comprises species, many of which are well-known in cultivation. Some species have been used for cross-pollination with plants of other genera, notably Lobivia, resulting in some remarkably attractive cultivars in a great many different coloured flowers.
Echinopsis eyriesii (Turp.) Zucc.
(syn. *Echinocactus eyriesii* Turp.) The type species. A popular species originating from south Brazil, Uruguay and Argentina. Generally of clustering habit, short globular plants with many pronounced acute ribs, areoles bearing whitish wool and to 18 very short spines. Flowers from side of plant to 25 cm long, pure white, scented, lasting only one day. *E. multiplex* (Pfeiff.) Zucc. with which *E. eyriesii* is often confused, is endemic to southern Brazil. It differs in respect to the spine formation, viz. up to 15 ascending radial spines about 1–2 cm long and 4 or 5 even longer central spines. Flower lilac-pink. *E. leucantha* (Gill.) Walp. is an oblong plant to 30 cm high, having about 12–15 ribs, close set areoles with 8 somewhat curved brown radial spines and 1 elongated curved central to 10 cm long. Large flower about 16 cm long, white.

ERDISIA Br. & R. are slender-stemmed plants, branching from the base with few ribs, and spiny areoles, flowers colourful but smallish. Easy.

Erdisia squarrosa (Vaup.) Br. & R.
(syn. *Cereus squarrosa* Vaup.) The type species from over 2,000 m altitude in the highlands of Peru. Long slender stems to 2 m having about 8 ribs with fairly closely set areoles from which emanate about 15 yellowish spines of unequal length, longest to about 4 cm. Flowers at terminal ends of stems, yellowish-red. Other species include *E. tenuicula* Backeb. with orange-red flowers.

ERIOCAREUS (Bgr.) Ricco. have their counterpart in the genus *Harrisia* which includes a number of West Indian species, all with yellowish fruits. Eriocereus have red fruits, and originate generally from S. America.
Eriocereus martinii (Lab.) Ricco.
A well-known species from Argentina, much branched, clambering to 2 m or more. Branches with about 4–5 angled, areoles with a row of short radial spines and 1 long stout central. Flower very large to 20 cm, nocturnal, white. *E. tortuosa* (Forb.) Ricco., also from Argentina around Buernos Aires, has about 7 low rounded ribs, areoles with up to 10 awl-shaped spines spread radially and 1 much longer central. Flowers whitish-pink. *E. bonplandii* (Parm.) Ricco., with 4-angled stems, areoles about 2 cm apart with 6–8 acicular spines to 4 cm long, reddish-grey. Flowers nocturnal, white.

ERIOSYCE Phil. is a small genus of large globular to semi-columnar plants with many ribs and spines, and very woolly at the apex.
Eriosyce ceratites (Otto) Br. & R.
A large growing plant to 1 m high, native of Chile with 25 or more ribs and up to 20 long, thick, blackish spines, mostly straight but some curved. The apex of the plant becomes very woolly with age. Flowers from the top of the plant, about 3–4 cm long, yellowish-red.

ESPOSTOA Br. & R. includes many columnar species with pseudocephalium. Areoles with longish spines and white hairs and usually small nocturnal flowers, with short style and stamens.
Espostoa lanata (H.B.K.) Br. & R.
(syn. *Cactus lanatus* H.B.K.) The type species from hills of Ecuador and Peru at an altitude

of over 2,000 m. A white-haired columnar plant to over 4 m high, often branching freely in habitat. Over 20 ribs, rounded with large areoles bearing numerous brownish needle-like spines intermingled with long white hairs. Pseudocephalium develops at tops of branches through which the reddish flowers emerge. *E. melanostele* (Vaup.) Berg. from Peru is a more robust plant producing a brownish cephalium through which the pinkish-white flowers appear.

EULYCHNIA Phil. includes a few interesting and attractive species, erect, branching, sometimes procumbent with many ribs, spines and very small flowers.
Eulychnia acida Phil.
A tall-growing, tree-like plant, to over 3 m high, sometimes with different habit, with shorter branches, becoming procumbent. Stems have about 12–13 low but broad ribs, areoles with many spines of unequal length protruding almost horizontally some very long to almost 16 cm. Flowers rather top-shaped, about 5 cm long, pinkish-white.

FACHEIROA Br. & R. is a somewhat obscure genus originally created for one species. It has been proposed that the genus should be merged with Thrixanthocereus, but the title still persists and newer discoveries may support its retention.
Facheiroa pubiflora Br. & R.
The type species which has its origin on the Serra de Cannabrava, Bahia, Brazil. An erect, tall, much-branched plant, lightish to greyish-green. Ribs about 15, the brown-felted areoles bearing up to 12 brown radial acicular spines and usually 4 centrals somewhat longer than the radials. Branches with long brownish pseudocephalium consisting of masses of brownish-red hairy bristles extending from the top downwards, flowers small, whitish, nocturnal. *F. ulei* (Gurke) Werd. is another rare member of this genus, from Serra do Ignacio, Brazil, its pseudocephalium reputedly brown and very soft.

FRAILEA Br. & R. consists of a great number of relatively small-growing species, globular, sometimes becoming elongated and branching. Many tuberculate ribs and small spines. Flowers small from apex of plant. Flowers can be pollinated without opening.

Frailea cataphracta (Dams.) Br. & R.

(syn. *Echinocactus cataphractus* Dams.) The type species which is native of Paraguay. Small globose to about 2 cm diameter, dull velvety purplish-green with about 10–15 low ribs with flattened tubercles and under each a crescent shaped band, maroon coloured. Spines very small and adpressed. Flowers, pale yellow, open in full midday sunshine. *F. asterioides* Werd. is synonymous with *F. castanea* Backeb. – very similar to *F. cataphracta* but with even smaller spines on a reddish-brown body. *F. pumila* (Lem.) Br. & R. is caespitose, deep green, with up to 15 ribs and areoles with yellowish-brown spines, radials about 14, centrals only 1 or 2, flowers yellow. *F. gracillima* (Lem.) Br. & R. has greyish-green stems covered with minute bristly

spines, flower yellow – a species from Paraguay. *F. matoana* Buin. & Bred. from the southern part of Mato Grosso in Brazil is one of the more recent discoveries, being globose with depressed crown to only 25 mm diameter, reddish to dark brown with 15 ribs divided by transverse minute furrows into small globular tubercles. Areoles with small spines to 4 mm long, brown and flower yellow.

GYMNOCALYCIUM Pfeiff. a popular genus of mainly globular plants, often solitary but sometimes caespitose, ribs either rounded or acute which are divided into tubercles. Flowers usually bell-shaped, sometimes more funnel-shaped, flower tube with broad scales having naked axils. Includes many species.

Gymnocalycium denudatum (Link & Otto) Pfeiff. The type species of this important genus. Native of southern Brazil. Plant body is glossy dark green, somewhat depressed, about 15 cm diameter with

Gymnocalycium denudatum

5–8 broad, low ribs, tubercles hardly discernible, and to about 8 slender, rather curved adpressed radial spines. Flowers from apex of plant, white. *G. westii* Hutchis. from Bolivia, has about 14 somewhat spiralled ribs, areoles yellowish felted having about 11 radial spines, white, erect or slightly curved and 4 centrals, all tipped brown. Flowers bright golden yellow. *G. horstii* Buin. a Brazilian species having many similar characteristics to *G. denudatum*. Plant dark glossy green with about 6 broad well-defined ribs, felted areoles having spreading radials and often 1 long central. Flowers peach-pink, lasting for several days. A varietal form, *G. horstii v. buenekeri* Buin. found about 200 km north of the species has much darker rose flowers. *G. chuquisacanum* Card. from Chuquisaca, Bolivia, is greyish-green with 13 ribs consisting of very pronounced tubercles, grey felted areoles with about 7 spreading curved radial spines and 1 central to nearly 3 cm long curved upwards, all greyish with brown tips. Flowers pinkish. *G. platense* (Speg.) Br. & R. from near Cordoba, Buenos Aires, Argentina, about 10 cm diameter, bluish-green, with about 10–14 ribs divided by transverse furrows forming tubercles, the areoles with usually 7 radial adpressed spines. Flower whitish. *G. mihanovitchii* (Fric & Gurke) Br. & R. is of considerable interest. Native of Paraguay. Body reddish-greyish-green with 8 sharp ribs divided by transverse furrows above and below the areoles which have small radial spines. Flowers yellowish-green. The variety *G. mihanovitchii v. friedrichiae* has rose-pink flowers. Interest has also centred around the 'freak' forms of the species where the plant body is either red, orange, yellow or white, generally referred to as *G. mihanovitchii* '*Hibotan*' – these colorations are due to chlorophyll deficiency and the plant can only exist when grafted. Many species really deserve mention if space permitted. *G. saglione* (Cels.) Br. & R. is important from Catamarca, north Argentina, globular often to 30 cm diameter, up to 32 ribs, low and broad, divided into large round tubercles, large areoles with about 10 outward curved spines and usually 1 central. Flowers pinkish-white. A variety *G. saglione v. tilcarense* Backeb. was segregated and placed into a new genus *Brachycalycium* it has now been re-united with Gymnocalycium.

HAAGEOCEREUS Backeb. includes a large number of species varying considerably in many respects one from the other. Generally they are associated with yellowish-golden spines and undoubtedly many attractive plants are involved, but it would nevertheless seem to be of doubtful origin.
Haageocereus decumbens (Vaup.) Backeb.
A clambering sprawling plant from south-west Peru and north-west Chile where it is found on rocky hillsides. Slender branches with about 20 low ribs almost hidden by numerous golden-yellow spines, about 30 radials and 5 centrals. Flowers whitish. *H. setosus* (Akers) Backeb. is a beautiful species with yellow spines and the stem with many white hairs and reddish flowers. *H. acranthus* (Vaup.) Backeb. represents a number of species with coarser spines, stems densely covered with yellowish woolly areoles and numerous yellowish radial spines. Flowers whitish. Endemic to Peru.

HELIANTHOCEREUS Backeb. is closely related to Trichocereus and Lobivia. Small day flowering plants.
Helianthocereus huasha (Web.) Backeb.
A clump forming species with many semi-erect cylindrical stems, having about 12–18 low rounded ribs. Areoles closely set with numerous acicular yellowish-brown spines. Flowers variable in colour, yellow or red. Native of Catamarca, Argentina. *H. grandiflorus* (Br. & R.) Backeb. is also from Argentina, small clustering plant, stems with about 14 ribs and about 15 yellowish radial spines. Flowers pink.

HILDEWINTERA Ritt. A genus erected for the following species.
Hildewintera auriespina (Ritt.) Ritt.
A beautiful plant within a very doubtful genus. The generic names of *Winteria* Ritt. and *Winterocereus* Backeb. have also been used in connection with this species, but it would now appear the correct classification is in the genus *Borzicactus*. A cylindrical stem, of pendent habit, branching freely from the base, slender with many ribs and a profusion of golden-yellow spines completely covering the body of the plant. Flowers orange-reddish, with protruding yellow stigma, diurnal.

Hildewintera auriespina

A very fine cristate form of *Hildewintera auriespina*.

ISLAYA Backeb. consists of only a few species, all of which are from Peru. Globose or semi-cylindrical, generally heavily spined with yellowish flowers and large red fruits.
Islaya paucispinosa Rauh. & Backeb.
Globular plants from Chala, Arequipa, Chile. Stem reddish-grey about 8 cm diameter with about 12–16 ribs, pronounced areoles with stiff spreading greyish-brown spines. Flowers from apex of plant, golden yellow. Other species include *I. grandis* Rauh & Backeb., *I. bicolor* and several others which have many characteristics in common and the more they are grown together in cultivation the more similar they appear to be.

JASMINOCEREUS Br. & R. includes only species from the Galapagos Islands – named such because of the perfumed jasmine-like flowers.
Jasminocereus galapagensis (Web.) Br. & R.

(syn. *Cereus galapagensis* Web.) The type species is a tree-like plant with many branches composed of short joints. Ribs about 15 with closely set brown-felted areoles bearing many slender, sometimes bristle-like brown spines varying in length. Flowers on slender tube, funnel-shaped, brown with yellowish stripes. Other species have been recorded. *J. sclerocarpus* Sch. is undoubtedly synonymous with the type. There is also mentioned *J. howellii* and its variety *delicatus*, which may be distinctive, but little is known of it.

LEOCEREUS Br. & R. contains a few species of slender growth, clambering, almost vine-like, cylindrical stems with very indistinct ribs, small flowers on scaly tube, the scales having hair-like bristles in the axils.
Leocereus bahiensis Br. & R.
The type species is native of Joazeiro, Brazil. Long slender and trailing with about 12 low ribs, closely set areoles and numerous radial, few central yellowish spines, all spreading. Flowers about 4 cm long, white. *L. glaziovii* (Sch.) Br. & R. from Minas Gerais, Brazil, with about 12 ribs, small elongated white felted areoles and numerous brownish spines; flower about 6 cm long, white. *L. melanurus* (Sch.) Br. & R. is also endemic to the same region; there seems little to distinguish this from *L. glaziovii*, and it is possibly synonymous.

LEUCOSTELE Backeb. includes only the species for which this genus was erected.
Leucostele rivierei Backeb.
A tall columnar plant, rarely branching, up to 2 m high. Branches with many distinct ribs, areoles woolly with long white spines densely arranged. Flowers from near terminal ends, diurnal, said to be reddish.

LOBIVIA Br. & R. is composed of many species, globular or somewhat cylindric, usually clustering freely. It is sometimes difficult to associate one species with another, the more so as some would seem on the one hand more similar to Echinopsis, and on the other hand to Rebutia. It would certainly appear a difficult genus and further research might well produce a new classification. All species have colourful flowers. The generic title is an anagram of Bolivia, the country where many of the species originate, but more recent exploration has located closely allied plants in Peru.
Lobivia pentlandii (Hook.) Br. & R.
(syn. *Echinocactus pentlandii* Hook.) The type species which is of Bolivian origin. Stems simple or caespitose, greyish-green with about 12 ribs deeply crenate, forming tubercles. Areoles with about 5 to 8 radial spines, brownish and curving backwards. Funnel-shaped flowers about 4 cm long, reddish-orange. *L. cinnabarina* (Hook.) Br. & R. from the Bolivian Andes has about 20 irregular ribs with 8–10 backward curved radial spines and 2 or 3 centrals, grey, slender. Flowers to 4 cm diameter, bright scarlet. *L. ferox* Br. & R. from Oruro, Bolivia, is a large species, solitary to about 30 cm diameter or more with many very long upcurved spines, the centrals being to 15 cm long. Flowers reddish. *L. aureolilacina* Card. from Chuquisaca, Bolivia, very spiny, the radials somewhat pectinate, the centrals subulate, strong, whitish-grey and slightly hooked at tip. Flowers very beautiful, lilac and yellow. *L. larae* Card. from Cochabamba, Bolivia, is about 12 cm diameter with spreading incurved spines, flower funnel-shaped lilac and magenta, a rare species. *L. cariquinensis* Card. from Cariquina, Bolivia, at about 3,900 m altitude, a clustering plant with golden-yellow spines and orange-yellow flowers, and which might well be a variety of *L. pentlandii*. *L. zudanensis* Card., greyish-green stem to about 15 cm diameter, heavily spined from grey-felted areoles with centrals being up to 8 cm long. Flowers deep blood-red. Native of Zudanez-Tarabuco, Bolivia. *L. intermedia* Rausch., from Challuanca, Peru, with dark green stem, armed with many slender radial and central spines, centrals being much longer and somewhat curved. Flowers bright scarlet. *L. leptacantha* Rausch is also from Peru, at Paucartambo at 3,000 m altitude. Bright green stems with long brownish-yellow spines and large flowers, somewhat variable colourwise, either reddish-orange or yellowish-orange. A group of very easily cultivated plants, decorative with pleasing appearance of stem and flower alike.

LOXANTHOCEREUS Backeb. is a genus much

under discussion and closely allied to Borzicactus with which, according to current research, it could possibly be merged. Slender, short-stemmed plants, somewhat columnar with more or less terminal flowers.

Loxanthocereus gracilis (Akers & Buin.) Backeb.
Originating from Peru at over 3,000 m altitude in the Andes. When first introduced was included in the genus *Maritimocereus* which was erected for this particular plant, but now this has been merged with Loxanthocereus. A low decumbent species, branching quite freely with about 10 or 11 low ribs, tubercled. Areoles bearing 10 small protruding spines, greyish. Flowers zygomorphic, diurnal, orange-red. Other species are still recognized as being included in this genus, *L. splendens* from Peru among them, but in view of the uncertainty surrounding this and other closely related genera, no definite mention is being made.

MALOCOCARPUS S.-D. non Fisch. & Mey. is one of the genera included in the sub-tribe Echinocactanae. This genus now includes species originally known as *Wigginsia*. Malacocarpus have a close kinship with Notocactus. Plants are globose or short cylindrical with straight, but sometimes tuberculate ribs. Crown of plant often densely woolly. Flowers from the centre, small with ovary densely scaly and axils with numerous bristly hairs.

Malacocarpus sellowii Sch.
A globular species from Brazil, Uruguay and Argentina, about 15 cm diameter with woolly apex. Ribs about 20, acute and slightly undulate on margins, pale green. Areoles well apart bearing about 6 straight spines to 2 cm long. Flowers from the top, yellow. *M. erinaceus* (Haw.) Lem. ex Först. with strongly undulate ribs, areoles with about 8 yellowish radial spines to 2 cm long and 1 central. Flowers large to about 6 cm diameter – this is possibly synonymous with *M. corynodes* S.-D. which it certainly resembles in many characteristics, both being from Brazil, Uruguay and Argentina. *M. langsdorfii* (Lehm.) Br. & R. from central and southern Brazil is more oblong in shape, developing a very woolly crown, ribs about 17 with slender spreading spines, the 1 central being over 2 cm long. Flowers yellow.

MATUCANA Br. & R. includes several species or varieties originating from Peru. Current opinion suggests that these should be merged into the genus *Borzicactus* due basically to flower characteristics. The plants here are generally globular, but some becoming short-cylindrical with age. Numerous broad and low tuberculate ribs, usually with many spines and slender tubular flowers.

Matucana haynei (Otto) Br. & R.
(syn. *Echinocactus haynei* Otto) The type species which is native of Matucana in central Peru. Mostly globular plants to about 10 cm diameter with dense spine formation, white with brownish tips, to over 3 cm long. Flowers orange-red or even deeper red on a long slender tube. Many new discoveries have been made during the last few years due to the extensive efforts of Rauh, Ritter, Lau and others – varying characteristics have been noted with many of the newer plants, but it may well be determined that some are varietal forms of *M. haynei*. However, newer species include *M. blancii* Backeb. from Rio Parron, Cordillera Blanca, Peru, a very densely spined stem covered with numerous whitish spines, flowers reddish. *M. herzogiana* Backeb. from Cordillera Negra, Peru, with yellowish-white somewhat curved and spreading bristle-like spines and scarlet flowers. *M. variabilis* Rauh & Backeb. from Churin, Oyan, Peru; *M. crinifera* Ritt. from Machua Huari, Peru; *M. yanganucensis* Rauh & Backeb. from Casma Pass, all have very similar characteristics as far as spination is concerned. *M. winterae* Ritt. from Santiago de Chuco, while similar in spination generally, has a distinctly different-coloured flower, lilac-red.

MEDIOLOBIVIA Backeb. was originally intended for species intermediate between Rebutia and Lobivia. These are currently considered nearer to Rebutia and have been merged with that genus. They consisted of colourful flowering plants, mainly from Argentina and Bolivia.

Mediolobivia aureiflora (Backeb.) Backeb.
(syn. *Rebutia aureiflora* Backeb.) The type species from Salta, Argentina, at over 2,000 m altitude. Stems dark greenish-red usually clustering freely. Ribs not too distinct, tubercles irregularly disposed. Areoles have about 20 whitish-brown bristly spines.

Large flowers bright orange with whitish throat. *M. aureiflora* v. *rubriflora* (Backeb.) Backeb. differs from the type in respect to the flower colour which is rosey-red. This species was for a long time known as *M. kesselringiana* Cullm.

MELOCACTUS Link & Otto is the distinctive genus, the species of which are often referred to as the 'Turks cap' Cactus. Several are indigenous to North America and West Indies, but there are many which are native of South America, and some of the more recent discoveries have been in Brazil. All species with cephalium.
Melocactus melocactoides De Cand.
A charming, medium-sized species from coastal areas of Brazil, particularly around the regions of Rio de Janeiro, Bahia and Pernambuco. Sometimes called *M. violaceus* Pfeiff. (the two are synonymous). Fresh green stem with about 10 broad obtuse ribs, areoles about 6 to each rib, bearing about 5–8 radial spines, brownish-grey to about 1 cm long, sometimes a little curved. Cephalium compact with white wool and brownish bristles and deep pink flower. *M. neryi* Sch. from the state of Amazonas, Brazil, is very similar, but with pronounced terete spines all curved and spreading outwards–rose-pink flowers. *M. erythracanthus* Buin. & Bred. from western slopes of Serra do Espinhaco, Bahia, Brazil, a recent discovery with globose body, about 12 sharp pronounced ribs, rounded areoles and 7 yellowish-brown spines, one of which is bent downwards about 13 cm long. Small tubular flower, lilac-red. *M. giganteus* Buin. & Bred. from Serra Santo Inacio, Bahia, Brazil, is another new discovery (1968) which has about 15 ribs, greyish areoles with greyish-brown spines–8 radials about 18 mm long and 1 central about 17 mm long slanting upwards. Flower deep lilac.

One of the most outstanding discoveries has been *M. glaucescens* Buin. & Bred. with greyish-blue body. Native of the western slopes of Serro de Espinhaco, Bahia, Brazil, with about 11 ribs, areoles have 8 greyish spines, radials spreading and one curved downwards, 1 central protruding, somewhat ascending, with slightly hooked tip. Flower red. *M. cremnophilus* Buin. & Bred. from Serra do Espinhaco, Bahia, Brazil, a dark green plant about

14 cm diameter with up to 13 somewhat obtuse ribs, slightly sunken areoles with 8–9 radial spines of varying lengths, one lower one directed downwards to 7 cm long. Central spines 4, the lower one directed downwards to 4 cm long, the other 3 about 3 cm long. Flower carmine-red.

MICRANTHOCEREUS Backeb. includes a few fascinating plants, mainly rare in cultivation with distinctive pseudocephaliums from which many small flowers emerge.
Micranthocereus polyanthus (Werd.) Backeb.
(syn. *Cephalocereus polyanthus* Werd.) The type species from near Caetete, Bahia, Brazil. A low

Micranthocereus polyanthus

Micranthocereus polyanthus in habitat.

slender plant, branching from the base, the stems being almost completely covered with whitish-yellowish spines, and even more so towards the apex where the pseudocephalium develops and many rose-red flowers are borne. *M. violaciflorus* Buin. from Minas Gerais is a recent introduction of considerable merit, slender stems with many ribs and short rather interlaced spines. The pseudo-cephalium extends well down one side of the stem consisting of brownish-red-purplish bristles and white wool with reddish-purplish flowers. *M. auri-azureus* Buin. & Bred. native of Grao Mogol, Minas Gerais, Brazil, at an altitude of about 1,000 m. A tall slender plant to just over 1 m, bluish-grey body with 18 rounded ribs and areoles with yellow wool and many yellowish-brown spines of unequal length. Pseudocephalium develops with thickening whitlsh wool from which the lilac-pinkish flowers emerge.

MILA Br. & R. are Peruvian plants, caespitose with small yellowish flowers. The generic name is an anagram of the capital of Peru – Lima.
Mila caespitosa Br. & R.
The type species from near Santa Clara on the low hills bordering Remac Valley. Small plant to about 15 cm high and clumping freely. About 10 ribs with straight margins, areoles densely brown-felted with 20 radial spines and several longer centrals, all yellowish-brown. Flowers about 1·5 cm long, at apex of stems. *M. densiseta* Rauh & Backeb. also from central Peru is rather longer, up to 25 cm, heavily spined with typical yellow flowers. Other species include *M. kubeana* with whitish spines and *M. nealeana*, a smaller species with soft whitish spines.

MONVILLEA Br. & R. are night-flowering plants with slender, semi-erect stems and flowers on long slender tube. The peculiarity of the flower is centred in the stamens which instead of being in definite rows are scattered over the throat.
Monvillea cavendishii (Monv.) Br. & R.
(syn. *Cereus cavendishii* Monv.) The type species from Brazil, Paraguay and northern Argentina. A tall growing plant, generally branching from the base with about 9 low rounded ribs bearing small

areoles and to 12 brownish spines. Flower whitish, about 12 cm long, nocturnal. *M. spegazzini* (Web.) Br. & R. from the Chaco Territory, Argentina, is a distinctive species, bluish-green stems, marbled white and grey, 3-angled with pronounced tubercles, areoles with black spines, flower whitish-pink. *M. diffusa* Br. & R. native of the hillsides of Catamayo Valley, Ecuador, a tall species having 8 ribs bearing areoles with about 10 radial and 1–3 central black-tipped greyish spines.

MORAWETZIA Backeb., a monotypic genus erected for this one species. A tall-growing plant with pronounced terminal cephalium of brownish bristles and white wool.
Morawetzia doelziana Backeb.
Native of southern and central Peru. An erect slender plant, branching freely from the base, and forming groups. Ribs about 10, low, bearing prominent woolly areoles having about 20 yellowish-brown erect spines. Flowers from the cephalium at apex, zygomorphic, carmine-red.

NEOCHILENIA Backeb. has become a very popular genus. This is one of a group of genera which has received considerable attention at the hands of botanists and laymen alike, and it is reasonable to expect that in the foreseeable future a new classification will be approved. The names of *Nichelia* Bull. and *Chilenia* Backeb. have also been used for this genus.
Neochilenia jussieui (Monv.) Backeb.
(syn. *Echinocactus jussieui* Monv.) The type species native of Chile, globular plant, blackish-greenish-red, slightly woolly at top with no spines, about 14 acute ribs divided into pronounced tubercles, yellowish felted areoles armed with 7 or more dark brown spreading radial spines and 1 central to 2·5 cm long. Flowers from near the apex, pale pink with darker midrib. *N. fusca* (Mühlpf.) Backeb. from the Chilean Andes, dark green with 12 ribs, somewhat tubercled, areoles with brownish spines, about 7 radials and 4 centrals, flowers yellow. *N. esmeraldana* (Ritt.) Backeb. from Esmeraldas, north Chile, purplish-reddish stem and numerous tubercles; areoles woolly with up to 12 brownish radial spines, with or without centrals. Flower

yellowish. *N. residua* (Ritt.) Backeb. from near Antofagasta, north Chile, about 8 cm diameter with about 12 ribs, blunted tubercles, areoles having many brownish spines, about 12 radials and 5 or more centrals, flower yellowish.

NEOPORTERIA Br. & R., very closely allied to Neochilenia, and possibly well-nigh inseparable; the plants usually associated with this genus and with those of *Pyrrhocactus, Horridocactus* and *Neochilenia* undoubtedly call for a complete review and an acceptable classification.
Neoporteria subgibbosa (Haw.) Br. & R.
(syn. *Echinocactus subgibbosus* Haw.) The type species for which this genus was created. A somewhat cylindrical-shaped plant to 30 cm high with about 20 ribs, close set areoles and numerous brown acicular spines, mostly straight. Flowers at apex, pinkish-red. Native of Valparaiso, Chile.

NEORAIMONDIA Br. & R. constitutes a monotypic genus. The distinctive characteristic is the areoles. These are considerably enlarged, being brown felted, thick and often becoming elongated and branching, producing a bristly cephalium effect.
Neoraimondia macrostibas (Sch.) Br. & R.
A tall species branching from the base, very spiny, 12 or more to each areole, some elongated to 24 cm long. Flowering areoles become very enlarged. Flowers about 4 cm long, white. Endemic to desert area of western Peru. This is a very rare species, of which little is known in cultivation.

NEOWERDERMANNIA Fric. includes a few species, from widely varying localities, which are specifically recognized, but in fact appear very similar.
Neowerdermannia vorwerkii (Fricc.) Backeb.
The type species originating from around Lake Titicaca in Bolivia and Jujuy in Argentina. A globular plant with about 16 ribs divided into low tubercles; the areoles centred in the depressions between the tubercles bear about 10 spreading somewhat curved spines, one upper spine being much longer and hooked. Flowers pinkish-white. *N. chilensis* Backeb. from Chile is very similar, and reputedly flowers of varying colours occur.

NOTOCACTUS (K. Sch.) Bgr. Constitutes one of the most popular genera of the Cactaceae. It has been subject to careful study and research, and has been sub-divided into other genera, viz. *Brasilicactus, Eriocactus*, but now the trend is to re-unite these, together with *Malacocarpus* (*Wigginsia*) into a single genus, *Notocactus*. Generally globular plants, sometimes semi-cylindric or short-columnar, all free-flowering; some bloom as very young plants. Mentioned here are only those which have been included in Brasilicactus, Eriocactus or Notocactus.
Notocactus ottonis (Lehm.) Bgr.
(syn. *Cactus ottonis* Lehm.) The type species from Brazil. Usually clustering, with bright green bodies having about 10–15 ribs; areoles with yellowish radials and brownish centrals about 1 cm long. Flowers golden yellow with reddish stigma and lobes, the tube covered with brown hairs. Widely distributed throughout Brazil, Uruguay, Paraguay and Argentina. There are a number of varieties of the type. *N. rutilans* Dan. & Krainz. from Uruguay, has elongated bluish-green body, tubercled, areoles with brownish-red tipped spines; flowers pale purplish with yellowish throat. *N. scopa* (Spreng.) Bgr. endemic to Brazil and Uruguay, is one of the most attractive of the genus, whitish slender spines from white woolly areoles. Flower from the centre, bright yellow with red stigma. *N. mammulosus* (Lem.) Bgr. from Brazil, Uruguay and Argentina. A globular species with up to 25 ribs, strongly tuberculate and covered by numerous almost interlocking spines. Flowers golden-yellow with reddish-brown stigma. *N. leninghausii* (Haag. Jr.) Bgr. with pale green body and up to 40 low ribs, closely set areoles and numerous golden spines, large golden yellow flowers. A S. Brazilian plant included in *Eriocactus*. *N. uebelmannianus* Buin. from the Rio Grande do Sul, Brazil. Body globose, somewhat depressed, dark green, with about 16 ribs having chin-like tubercles; areoles bear about 6 adpressed whitish spines, the lowest being the longest. Flower reddish-purple about 5 cm diameter. *N. uebelmannianus* v. *flaviflorus* Buin. is similar in all respects except the flower is golden-yellow. *N. magnificus* (Ritt.) Krainz is another outstanding species from Serra Geral, Rio Grande do

Sul, Brazil, with greyish-green body, pronounced ribs with closely set areoles and hairy spines, flowers clustering at the apex, yellow. *N. herteri* Werd., another distinctive plant, native of Uruguay, having many ribs, tubercled, slender spines and reddish-purple flowers. *N. buiningii* Buxb. has peculiar differences with bluish-green body, wavy undulating ribs, stiffish radiating spines and yellow flowers. Native of Uruguay on the borders with Brazil, south-west of Livramento–Riviera. *N. graessneri*

Notocactus graessneri v. *albisetus*

(K. Sch.) Bgr., also from Rio Grande do Sul, at one time included in the genus *Brasilicactus*, densely spined, with masses of long yellowish hairy spines adpressed against the body of the plant and with almost greenish flowers. *N. minimus* Fric. & Krzgr. is one of the more recent discoveries with smallish semi-cylindric body, grouping freely with large yellow flowers.

OREOCEREUS (Bgr.) Ricco. includes several cereoid plants with large areoles usually developing long hair. This genus has a close relationship with *Borzicactus* and a new classification might well bring about a merger of the two genera.
Oreocereus celsianus (Lem.) Ricco.
(syn. *Pilocereus celsianus* Lem.) The type species from the Andes, Bolivia, Peru and Chile. Sturdy stems, branching freely from the base, sometimes semi-prostrate. Branches with 10 obtuse ribs, divided into tubercles, areoles with long hairs and

several straight rigid yellow spines protruding horizontally. Flowers from the top of the branches, red, diurnal. Other species include *O. hendriksenianus* Backeb. from Peru and Chile with much wool and golden spines, orange-red flowers. *O. trollii* (Kupp.) Backeb. is another beautiful plant almost entirely covered with whitish hair and wool and yellow spines, having carmine-red flowers.

OROYA Br. & R. are all Peruvian species, named after the type locality – Oroya – includes a number of semi-globose plants with elongated areoles and widely spreading spines. Flowers from the crown, short, funnel-shaped. This is another genus with a close affinity with Borzicactus.
Oroya peruviana (Sch.) Br. & R.
(syn. *Echinocactus peruvianus* Sch.) The type species for which the genus was erected. A globose depressed plant, deep green with broad ribs having humped tubercles and long narrow areoles, small somewhat pectinate radial spines, few centrals stronger than the radials. Flowers from near top, yellowish, with very short tube. From south of La Oroya, Peru. *O. neoperuvianus* Backeb. from north-east of La Oroya, a larger plant with more ribs and less pronounced tubercles, flowers yellowish. *O. borchersii* (Boed.) Backeb. from Cordillera Negra at 4,000 m altitude. Stem short-cylindrical or somewhat globular and depressed, light green, with rather broader areoles having deep yellow to brownish-red spines evenly distributed. Flowers greenish yellow. Other recognized species include *O. laxiareolata* Rauh & Backeb. from Mantero Valley, south of La Oroya and *O. subocculta* Rauh & Backeb., also from Mantero Valley. There is a great similarity of characteristics and it is feasible that some will be reduced to synonymity or varietal status.

PARODIA Speg. comprises many species of globular plants with distinct ribs, woolly areoles and highly coloured spines. Most species of easy culture, producing flowers as quite young plants.
Parodia microsperma (Web.) Speg.
(syn. *Echinocactus microspermus* Web.) The type species, the specific name suggests small seeds, and

this feature is general of all *Parodia* species. It was earlier known as *Nickenia microsperma* Web. Stem globose or short cylindrical to about 10 cm diameter. Ribs are divided into low tubercles, spirally arranged, areoles with about 10–25 white acicular spreading radial spines and 3 or 4 reddish-brown centrals, the lower one being hooked at the tip. Flowers from the crown, golden yellow. A most attractive species from Tucuman, Argentina. *P. microthele* Backeb. has light green stem, pronounced areoles, whitish spines and beautiful orange-red flowers. *P. sanguiniflora* Fric ex Backeb. endemic to Cochabamba, Bolivia, at an altitude of over 2,000 m has thick white radial spines and brown centrals which are hooked at the tip. Flowers large, blood-red. *P. nivosa* Fric ex Backeb. a very beautiful 'white' species, densely covered with whitish spines and having deep reddish flowers at the crown. *P. chrysacanthion* (Sch.) Backeb. has numerous golden-yellow spines, glistening and shining, densely set. Flowers golden-yellow. There are over 40 recognized species, native of Bolivia, Argentina, Brazil and Paraguay, and without exception rewarding plants for the layman.

PHILIPPICEREUS Backeb., a monotypic genus created for one species segregate from the genus *Eulychnia*.
Philippicereus castanea (Sch.) Backeb.
(syn. *Cereus castaneus* Sch.) Type species for this species from Aconcagua, Chile. Shrubby plant, spreading from the base with long cereoid stems having low rounded ribs, yellow-greyish spines, flower pinkish-white on very hairy tube.

PILOCEREUS Lem. non Sch. *Pilosocereus* Byl. & Rowl. includes many columnar plants, some from North America and West Indies, others from South America. Mostly erect, tall, developing pseudo-cephaliums.
Pilocereus glaucescens Lab.
An erect, branching plant with dark-bluish rounded ribs, somewhat inflated, close-set areoles with numerous whitish bristles and hairs. Spines of varying length, 12 or more radials and about 6 more centrally disposed, yellowish-brown. Whitish woolly pseudocephalium develops on one side of the

branches from which the flowers emanate. This species is of Brazilian origin and has also been referred to as *Pseudopilocereus glaucescens* (Lab.) Buxb.

PSEUDOLOBIVIA (Backeb.) Backeb. includes a number of attractive globular plants with colourful flowers, many of which were originally included either in *Echinopsis* or *Lobivia*. This genus constitutes intermediate status.
Pseudolobivia kermesina Krainz.
Very similar in appearance to *Echinopsis* as far as the body is concerned. Plant about 12 cm diameter, glossy green having about 20 ribs, areoles furnished with yellowish wool, about 15 radial spines with brownish tips and 4–6 reflexed centrals to 2 cm long. Flowers from crown of plant, deep carmine-red. Native of Argentina. *P. aurea* (Br. & R.) Backeb. a compact species from Cordoba, Argentina, having about 14 ribs, areoles with short brownish wool and 10 radial spines to 1 cm long, centrals about 4 and longer than radials. Flowers lemon-yellow. *P. ancistrophora* (Speg.) Backeb. from Salta and Tucuman, Argentina, have rather flattened plant body, about 18 ribs with somewhat sunken areoles bearing 7 radial spines and 1 hooked central. Flowers white.
   In 1974 this genus was merged into Echinopsis.

REBUTIA Sch. comprises a great number of small, globular plants, mostly caespitose with flowers of varying colours. All are very easy in cultivation, rewarding inasmuch as they produce flowers within a year or two of germination. Some species have been included in the genus *Aylostera* which is currently united with Rebutia.
Rebutia minuscula Sch.
The type species from Tucuman, N. Argentina. A very popular and well-known plant, clustering, bright green bodies about 5–6 cm diameter, low ribs consisting of rounded tubercles, areoles with numerous very small whitish spines. Flowers red. *R. krainziana* Kesselr. which is native of Bolivia, has distinctive white woolly areoles with minute white spines and large red flowers. *R. senilis* Backeb. from Salta, Argentina, is typified by the dense covering of whitish bristle-like spines, flowers

carmine-red. A variety, *R. senilis* v. *kesselringiana*, is similar but with yellow flowers. Another yellow-flowering species is *R. marsoneri* Werd. from the Jujuy province of north Argentina, the body being dark green with brownish-yellow spines. *R. fiebrigii* (Gurke) Br. & R. – *Aylostera fiebrigii*, a Bolivian species to about 7 cm tall, dark glossy green, 15–18 spirally arranged ribs divided into tubercles with numerous bristly-white spines from the areoles, flowers orange-red. *R. calliantha* Bew., a globular species with whitish areoles and whitish spines has lilac-pink flowers and comes from Argentina. In recent years a number of new species have been discovered, considerably extending the scope for research and study and in this respect the names of Donald and Buining are most prominent. Newer species include *R. kariusiana* Wess. – *R. calliantha* v. *kariusiana* Buin. & Don. with deep pink flowers. *R. albiflora* Ritt. & Buin. having white flowers.

ROSEOCEREUS Backeb. are closely related to Trichocereus. Tall bushy plants with large white nocturnal flowers.
Roseocereus tephracanthus (Lab.) Backeb.
(syn. *Cereus tetracanthus* (Lab.) The type species endemic to Bolivia. An erect plant with many low ribs having somewhat sunken woolly areoles and several brownish-tipped spines. Flowers funnel-shaped, white, on long tube with swollen reddish scales and white hairs in the axils. The flowers are very beautiful and large, sometimes to over 15 cm long.

SETICEREUS Backeb. is allied to the genus *Haageocereus* to which genus many species have been transferred. Plants with beautiful golden spines and colourful flowers.
Seticereus icosagonus (H.B.K.) Backeb.
(syn. *Cactus icosagonus* H.B.K.) The type species which originates from northern Peru and Ecuador. A grouping species, somewhat erect stems with about 20 ribs, transversely furrowed. Close set areoles with numerous needle-like spines and long red-orange flowers.

SOEHRENSIA Backeb. are closely allied to Lobivia and Echinopsis. Large globular somewhat de-pressed plants having short funnel-shaped small flowers on short tube, pilose and without bristles. Includes only few species.
Soehrensia bruchii (Br. & R.) Backeb.
(syn. *Lobivia bruchii* Br. & R.) The type species which originates from Tucuman, Argentina. Large greyish-green plant with about 50 ribs or more, tuberculate, areoles with whitish wool and spreading, sometimes protruding spines. Flowers deep red, from near the crown of the plant. Other species include *S. grandis* (Br. & R.) Backeb., *S. formosa* (Pfeiff.) Backeb., a very beautiful species with whitish wool and spines from Quebrada de Toro at 2,800 m in Argentina. *S. korethroides* which is sometimes considered an Echinopsis, from Salta at 4,000 m in Argentina, has beautiful red flowers.

SETIECHINOPSIS (Backeb.) de Haas includes a very popular and well-known species for long associated with the genus *Echinopsis* to which it certainly does not belong. Slender, plants with very long flower tube having bristle-like elongated scales.
Setiechinopsis mirabilis (Speg.) de Haas
(syn. *Echinopsis mirabilis* Speg.) The type species from the Province of Santiago del Estero, Argentina. An erect cylindrical plant to about 15 cm tall, dull greyish-yellowish-green with 11 ribs, slightly undulated having up to 14 slender radial spines and 1 erect central. Flowers from near the apex, white.

STEPHANOCEREUS Bgr. at one time included with Cephalocereus. Has the peculiarity of developing an apical cephalium consisting of masses of wool and bristles, forming a ring around the stem, through which the stem continues its growth after flowering.
Stephanocereus leucostele (Gurke) Bgr.
(syn. *Cereus leucostele* Gurke) The type species originating from the deserts of southern Bahia, Brazil. An erect plant with about 13–15 low ribs, numerous whitish spines, the radials spreading, centrals longer. Flowers at the top of the plant in the woolly bristly cephalium, nocturnal, white with yellow stamens and stigma lobes. A plant which closely resembles species of Arrojadoa.

STETSONIA Br. & R. is a unique genus containing only one species. An erect plant with pronounced ribs and stiffish spines, endemic to north-west Argentina.

Stetsonia coryne (S.-D.) Br. & R.

Stems columnar, tree-like, in habitat up to several metres high. Stems pale green having 7–9 obtuse ribs, areoles with wool and up to 10 stout greyish-black spines of unequal length. Flowers white on longish tube, slightly scaly, nocturnal.

SUBMATUCANA Backeb. is related to Borzicactus, Matucana, Oroya and certain other genera for which a new classification is under consideration. A number of species were included in this genus, many being of more recent discovery.

Submatucana aurantiaca (Vaup.) Backeb.

A beautiful species from Catamarca, Peru, having about 16 ribs, areoles somewhat elliptical and 15 or more reddish brown spreading spines, some to 1 cm long and one even longer. Flowers from the crown of the plant, tubular, scarlet. *S. madisoniorum* Hutch. very much resembles a Lophophora, greyish-green body with few areoles, sometimes with very long spines. Flowers reddish. *S. madisoniorum v. pujupattii* Lau & Don. from Puente de 24 Julio, on the River Maranon, Peru, is similar in many aspects, but the stem has a beautiful bluish-white bloom, flowers red.

SULCOREBUTIA Backeb. constitutes a genus of plants mainly from Bolivia. At first many of the species were considered Rebutia, and named such. It would now seem there is a greater affinity to *Weingartia*. Plants are caespitose, small and somewhat tuberculate, usually with pronounced areoles and spines, flowers very colourful.

Sulcorebutia steinbachii (Werd.) Backeb.

The type species from Colomi, Bolivia. A small globular plant, usually caespitose with darkish green body, tuberculate ribs having groove on upper surface of tubercle, long narrow areoles with small spreading brownish spines. Flower deep red. *S. arenacea* (Card.) Ritt. has dark brownish-green body, areoles with whitish spines, tipped brownish and golden-yellow flowers. Native of Ayopana, Bolivia. *S. rauschii* Frank, one of the

newest discoveries from near Zudanez, Chuquisaca, Bolivia, having a blackish-green-grey body, ribs divided into round flattened tubercles, small elongated areoles set with black appressed spines. Flowers magenta-rose with white throat. *S. tiraquensis* (Card.) Ritt. from Tiraque to Monte Puncu at over 3,000 m, densely covered with bristle-like spines to over 1 cm long, yellowish-red and flowers reddish. This species can be variable particularly in respect to spine colours. *S. totorensis* (Card.) Ritt. native of the region around Totora, has long dark red spines and deep red flowers. *S. glomeriseta* (Card.) Ritt. is a yellow flowering species from Rio Cotacajes, Ayopana, Bolivia, densely covered with numerous whitish bristle-like spines. *S. candiae* (Card.) Buin & Don. has dark green body with yellowish pectinate spines from pronounced areole and yellowish flowers. From Tiquirpaya, Ayopana, Bolivia. Another very similar plant, *S. menesesii* (Card.) Buin. & Don. found at 1,600 m near Naranjito, Ayopana, Bolivia with pinkish-white pectinate spines, somewhat bristle-like, flowers yellow. Other popular and well-known species include *S. kruegerii* (Card.) Ritt. with yellow flowers and likewise the same colour of flower from *S. caineana* (Card.) Don.

THRIXANTHOCEREUS Backeb. include species of erect habit, often with long bristle-like hairs at the base of the plant, particularly when young. Forms pseudocephalium on one side at top of branches with nocturnal flowers from older part of pseudocephalium.

Thrixanthocereus blossfeldiorum (Werd.) Backeb.

(syn. *Cephalocereus blossfeldiorum* Werd.) The type species from Peru. A tall species, sometimes branching from the base, straight 20 ribs with woolly areoles set with whitish-brownish bristly spines. The pseudocephalium develops at the terminal ends of mature stems and extends downwards with masses of brownish-whitish bristles and whitish wool. Flowers nocturnal, somewhat funnel-shaped. Other species include *Thrixanthocereus senilis* Ritt. from Ancash, Peru, a distinctive plant covered with white silvery bristly spines and hairs, older growth tends to develop long yellowish spines also, these often with reddish-brown tips. Flowers emanating from the pseudocephalium, purplish-red, nocturnal.

TRICHOCEREUS (Bgr.) Ricco. is one of the best-known of columnar cerei. Plants of easy culture, erect, often branching from base with large nocturnal flowers. Young plants of some species are to be recommended for grafting purposes.

Trichocereus macrogonus (S.-D.) Ricco.
(syn. *Cereus macrogonus* S.-D.) Type species. An erect plant, somewhat bluish-green having 7 low rounded ribs with large areoles about 2 cm apart, radial spines short, acicular, brown and 1 longer central about 2 cm long. Flowers nocturnal, whitish. *T. pachanoi* Br. & R. native of Ecuador, has about 6 ribs, dark green; above each areole a deep horizontal depression, only very few spines, usually small, occasionally to 2 cm long. Flowers near to terminal, white, nocturnal. *T. pasacana* (Web.) Br. & R. endemic to Argentina and Bolivia – a well-known species with about 25 or more pronounced ribs, areoles with long yellowish stiff spines. Flowers whitish.

The genus *Trichocereus* has now been largely absorbed into *Echinopsis* (1975). The wisdom of this is in doubt and there may well be further reclassifications.

UEBELMANNIA Buin. includes some of the newest discoveries of recent years and whose introduction caused great interest. Most species are still rare in cultivation. All known species are of Brazilian origin.

Uebelmannia pectinifera Buin.
An extraordinary plant with a globose or cylindrical body to about 15 cm diameter. Dark reddish-brown in actual colour, but with a white scaly covering giving the effect of a greyish-bluey-white body. Ribs 14–18 areoles very closely set with pectinate blackish perpendicularly arranged spines, almost comb-like. Areoles in crown of plant somewhat felted and with greyish-white wool from which the small yellow flowers are borne. From an altitude of 1,000 m is Minas Gerais, Brazil. *U. pectinifera* v. *pseudopectinifera* Buin. is similar to the species but with non-pectinate greyish-black spines, untidily spreading, flowers yellow. From the vicinity of

Trichocereus huasha—one of the Trichocereus species now absorbed into Echinopsis.

Uebelmannia gummifera in habitat.

Diamantina, Minas Gerais, Brazil. *U. gummifera* (Backeb. & Voll.) Buin.–*Parodia gummifera* Backeb. & Voll. is an interesting plant, thought to be identical to *Echinocactus centeterius* Pfeiff. and from the same habitat, Minas Gerais, Brazil. Dull greenish body with many ribs, tubercled, areoles with about 7 spines, the 2 centrals one points upwards, the other down. Crown of plant woolly, flowers small, yellow. *U. buiningii* has a reddish body with ribs strongly tubercled, few whitish spines and yellowish flowers. *U. meninensis* Buin, is almost completely covered with pronounced tubercles and 2 stiff spines from each areole.

VATRICANIA Backeb. includes only one species from Rio Grande Valley, Bolivia at an altitude of 1,000 m or more. Similar to Cephalocereus and Espostoa.
Vatricania guentheri (Kupp.) Backeb.
(syn. *Cephalocereus guentheri* Kupp.) The type species. An erect columnar plant branching from the base. Branches with about 27 somewhat tubercled ribs; areoles have yellowish wool and about 15 bristly yellowish-brown spines and 1 central. Flowers nocturnal, about 7 cm long, whitish-pink arising from the pseudocephalium which develops on one side of the branch.

WEBERBAUREOCEREUS Backeb. are distinctive plants, originally included with Trichocereus. Branches very spiny. Flowers somewhat curved at base and tube very scaly.
Weberbaureocereus fascicularis (Meyen) Backeb.
(syn. *Cereus fascicularis* Meyen) The type species from high altitudes in southern Peru and Chile. Erect slender plant with about 16 low ribs; areoles with brownish felt and numerous brownish-yellow spines, the centrals being stouter and longer than the radials. Flowers about 10 cm long, pinkish-white from near the ends of the branches. Other species are *W. rauhii* Backeb. a very lovely plant with creamy-yellow flowers at the branch tips. *W. seyboldianus* Rauh & Backeb. a Peruvian species with deep red flowers.

WEINGARTIA Werd. globular plants with turnip-like roots, but having a small 'neck' between the body of the plant and the root. Very tubercled with numerous spines. Possibly related to Sylcorebutia.
Weingartia fidaiana (Backeb.) Backeb.
(syn. *Echinocactus fidaiana* Backeb.) The type species from Bolivia. Globular or somewhat oval olive-green body with flattened tubercles and pronounced woolly areoles bearing about 6–8 brownish-yellow spines. A dwarf growing variety with orange-yellow flowers. *W. westii* (Hutch.) Don. from south of Potosi in Bolivia at 3,500 m altitude. Somewhat elongated and offsetting freely from near the base; strongly tubercled with about 14 brownish spines of unequal length. Flowers golden-yellow. *W. torotorensis* Card. native of Mina Asientos, Bolivia is heavily tubercled with numerous yellowish spines and rose-pink flowers. *W. neocummingii* Backeb., also known as *W. cummingii* from Peru and Bolivia has very pronounced tubercles and orange-yellow flowers.

ZEHNTNERELLA Br. & R.–a genus of Brazilian plants, tall and erect with very spiny ribs with small nocturnal flowers scattered along the upper ends of the branches.
Zehntnerella squamulosa Br. & R.
The type species from east of Joazeiro, Bahia, Brazil. Stems long and slender branching from the base. Branches have about 18–20 low ribs, set closely together with small areoles and 15 or more brownish acicular spines, some to 2–3 cm long. Flowers nocturnal, small, white.

TRIBE 2. OPUNTIOIDEAE
Includes many well-known species, sometimes associated with Austrocylindropuntia, Brasilopuntia or Tephrocactus which are now united with Opuntia. Other genera within the tribe include many rare and desirable species.
Opuntia brasiliensis (Willd.) Haw. (Brasilopuntia)
A well-known species widely distributed in Brazil, Argentina, Peru and other South American countries. Tall erect plant to 4 m high with cylindrical main stem, flattened branches and many bright green flat, thin terminal joints with few spines. Flowers yellow from terminal joints, fruit yellow. This species is very similar to *O. argentina* Gris. which has geenish-yellow flowers and red fruits.

Pseudolobivia aurea

Chamaecereus silvestrii

South America

ABOVE *Portulaca grandiflora*

ABOVE *Fascicularia bicolor*

BELOW *Opuntia erectoclada*

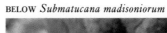

BELOW *Submatucana madisoniorum*

Opuntia tunicata (centre)—a very dwarf, fiercely spiny species.

An Opuntia of the Tephrocactus group.

Opuntia floccosa S.-D. (Tephrocactus)
One of the very attractive species from Peru. Plant consists of oblong joints with long white hairs from the areoles almost hiding the joints entirely. Flower yellow. *O. lagopus* (K. Sch.) and other similar species are possibly synonyms, the main difference seeming to be in the colour of the hairs!

Opuntia galapageia Hens. (Platyopuntia)
A very rare and beautiful species from the Galapagos Islands which in habitat grows into a large compact bush-like plant. Joints oblong-elongated, dark green with pronounced felted areoles and numerous long golden-yellow-brownish spines. **Flowers yellow. This is a spectacular cactus.**

Opuntia ignescens Vaup. (Tephrocactus)
An interesting species from Peru with bluish-green erect or spreading joints, forming clusters. Joints somewhat pointed, few areoles covered with felt and numerous glochids with up to 15 erect, acicular yellow spines. Flowers scarlet from near the top of the joints.

Opuntia miquelii Monv. (Austrocylindropuntia)
An uncommon species from Chile with cylindrical bluish-green stems to about 1 m high with many branches. New growth is bright green, turning bluish with age, having flattened tubercles, areoles rounded and pronounced with many glochids and up to 12 spines in clusters. Flower pale or rose-pink about 5 cm diameter.

Opuntia pachypus Schumm. (Austrocylindropuntia)
A rare species from Peru and possibly Ecuador, in habitat a tall much-branching plant over 3 m high, cylindrical, dark green, tubercles slightly elevated with numerous short yellowish-white spines from depressed woolly areoles. Flowers rather small, red, to about 2 cm diameter developing near the tips of the plant. Not often seen in cultivation.

Opuntia quimilo Sch. (Platyopuntia)
A large branching species from northern Argentina with obovate joints, large and thick, dark greyish-green, only few areoles and usually a solitary spine from each areole about 14 cm long. Large flowers to about 7 cm diameter, bright red. This can grow to large dimensions in cultivation and it is reputed that in habitat it can reach to 4 m high and cover many square meters.

Opuntia salmiana Parm. (Austrocylindropuntia)
A very slender erect bushy plant from Brazil, Argentina and Paraguay. Elongated cylindrical terete stems, greenish-purple having small woolly areoles, yellowish glochids and few spines. Flowers yellowish-white with red fruits. *O. spegazzinii* Web. is possibly only a variety, having pure white

flowers, as also is *O. ipatiana* with lilac-pink flowers. *O. colubrina* is very similar, but inclined to be far more bush-like in habit and with larger bright yellow flowers.

Opuntia subterranea R. E. Fries (Tephrocactus)
A very rare and unusual species from northern Argentina and Bolivia. Very thick tuberous root, stem usually solitary, occasionally branching, cylindrical to only 4 or 5 cm long with many low dark green tubercles, very small areoles with few short whitish spines, adpressed. Flowers whitish-brown.

Opuntia subulata (Muehl.) Engelm.
(Austrocylindropuntia)
A popular well-known species originating from Chile and Argentina, it has been widely naturalized in parts of southern Europe. Large plant to 4 m high, bright green, cylindrical, developing many long pointed cylindrical leaves near the apex of branches. Has yellow flowers near terminal ends. *O. exaltata* Berg. which is distributed widely in Peru, Chile, Bolivia and Ecuador, is also very similar, but with very tuberculate dark green stems and reddish flowers.

Opuntia vestita S.-D. (Austrocylindropuntia)
A very popular plant which originates from Bolivia. Somewhat erect stems with many branches forming clusters. Joints are cylindrical, rather slender, with rounded areoles having short wool, few spines and long white hairs, also quickly deciduous minute leaves. Flowers red from near the terminal ends of the joints.

Pterocactus kuntzei Sch.
An unusual species on account of its very large tuberous root, forming almost a caudex. Has erect slender stems, sometimes quite elongated, soft, greyish-purple and only about 1 cm in diameter. Areoles with numerous minute white adpressed spines. Flowers yellow. *P. tuberosus* (Pfeiff.) Br. & R. is very similar in most respects and is possibly synonymous.

Maihuenia poeppigii (Otto) Web.
One of the outstanding miniature species of the Opuntieae indigenous to the high mountains of Chile. A shrubby prostrate plant forming masses with cylindrical joints to about 6 cm long, slender with small cylindric leaves and 3 spines to each

areole. Flowers yellow at terminal ends. Other species include *M. valentinii* Speg. from Chubut, southern Argentina, with whitish or creamy-yellow flowers and *M. patagonica* (Phil.) Br. & R. with white flowers. All are of similar appearance and habit and exceedingly rare in cultivation.

Maihueniopsis molfinoi Speg.
An uncommon species endemic to Argentina from high altitudes of over 3,000 m. Prostrate, densely branched with many small oval joints, small areoles bearing glochids and few minute spines, often absent. Flowers at terminal ends, pinkish.

Quiabentia zehntneri Br. & R.
A species of Brazilian origin. A very shubby plant, cylindrical stem and horizontal branches usually in whorls. Leaves fleshy. Large felted areoles with numerous acicular whitish spines, glochids on upper part of areole. Flowers large, red, at terminal ends of branches. Rare in cultivation, closely resembling Pereskiopsis but with even more succulent stems and branches. Other species are recognized: *Q. chacoensis* is also native of Brazil; *Q. pereziensis* Backeb., a tree-like species from Perez, Bolivia at 1,600 m.

Tacinga funalis Br. & R.
An erect cylindrical branched species from Bahia, Brazil. Tall growing plant with greyish-blue stems and branches and scarcely discernible ribs. Areoles have short glochids, deciduous and sometimes soft brownish spines. Flowers usually at terminal of branches, reputedly nocturnal, green or greenish-white. This is still a rare species not too frequently seen in cultivation. Considered to be an intermediate between Opuntia and Nopalea–the monotypic genus was erected for this one species.

TRIBE 3. PERESKIOIDEAE
Pereskia humboldtii Br. & R.
A slender erect species from southern Peru, with rounded stem and thin branches with generally few spines. Leaves oblong, rather elongated about 4 cm long, solitary and arranged alternate. Flowers in clusters at terminal end of branches, reddish.

Pereskia sacharosa Gris.
A tree-like plant to over 6 m high with succulent stems and branches, heavily spined. Leaves about 10 cm long and very pointed. Flowers in clusters,

usually pink with hard large fruit about 4 cm diameter. This is native of Argentina and Paraguay, and while similar to *P. aculeata* (Plum.) Mill. in many respects, has different flower colour.

Rhodocactus moorei (Br. & R.) Knuth

A stout-stemmed bushy plant indigenous to Brazil to about 1 m high, freely branching with up to 4 long spines of unequal length to 7 cm long, somewhat black or yellow tipped black. Leaves almost round and tapering at tip. Flowers in clusters at apex, large to nearly 5 cm diameter, rich purplered or magenta. Fruits green with 1 to 3 seeds. One of the most spectacular of this tribe; young, short cuttings root very quickly and flower easily and profusely.

Commelinaceae

Would appear to have more succulent species within the family than are at present recognized. If the definition of a succulent concerns the stem and leaves, then several of the genus *Commelina* could be included, particularly some of those endemic to America.

Tradescantia navicularis Ortg.

Half-creeping succulent species with short segmented stems. Leaves boat-shaped, grey-green set in 2-ranks, often purplish on the underside. Flowers purplish-pink. From Peru.

Compositae

Espeletia grandiflora Humb. et Bonpl.

A short tree-like succulent to about 1 m tall with short stem covered by old dried leaves and surmounted by a tuft of long leaves covered with numerous whitish hairs. An unusual plant rarely cultivated having insignificant flowers. Native of Colombia to Venezuela. Other species include *E. killipii* Cutar, also from Venezuela, which is very similar but having a very erect rosette of leaves above the dried leaves.

Crassulaceae

Echeveria columbiana v. Poelln.

From an altitude of over 3,000 m near Vetas,

Colombia. Branching with fleshy stems, rosettes at terminals, somewhat dense, wedge-shaped leaves with blunt tips, tapering, about 3 cm long. Long flower scape with yellow flowers. *E. ballsii* E. Walth. with short stems and thick, oblong-obovate leaves, bright green, tall inflorescence, often two to each rosette, yellow flowers, endemic to Colombia. *E. bracteolata* Lk., Klotzsch et Otto. from Venezuela. A plant very similar to *E. gibbiflora* D.C. but having leaves alternate and horizontally spreading rather than rosulate. Very fleshy leaves, keeled on underside, pruinose. Flowers yellowish-red. Other South American species include *E. quitensis* (H.B.K.) Lindl. from Ecuador, Colombia and Bolivia; *E. eurychlamys* (Diels.) Bgr. and *E. excelsa* (Diels.) Bgr. both native of Peru.

Kalanchoë brasiliensis St. Hil.

Of shrubby habit having stems covered with short hairs. Leaves ovate lanceolate, tapering with serrated edges, upper leaves smaller with smooth edges. Terminal flowers in clusters, pink, the stalks being covered with dense hairs. Brazil. *K. pinnata* (Lam.) Persoon is widely distributed in many parts of South America as well as West Indies and most other tropical and sub-tropical parts of the world. An erect plant, very succulent to 1 m high. Leaves at first simple, then pinnate with leaflets 3–5 together, oblong and rather bluntly tapering with crenate margins, flowers bell-shaped, hanging pendent on slender branching inflorescence, greenish on the outside becoming reddish towards the stalk and whitish tips to petals.

Sedum backebergii v. Poelln.

An erect shrubby plant from central and south Peru about 7 cm high with woody stems and many branches. Leaves bluish-green, alternate, oblong and rounded both sides with keel on lower surface, upper surface papillose. Flowers yellow.

Villadia andina (Ball.) Baehni et MacBr.

A low, small clustering species native of Peru. Leaves semi-globose and very small. Flowers with short stalks, blackish-red. *V. berillonana* (Hamet) Baehni et MacBr. from an altitude of 3,000 m at Ayacucho, Peru, has short stems with greyish-green fleshy leaves, almost round. Flowering stems longer, very succulent with yellow flowers. *V. grandyi* (Hamet) Baehni et MacBr. from Chacha-

poyas, Peru, an erect little plant with stems to
3–4 cm long with roundish leaves, more long than
wide with blunt tip. A rather long flowering stem
with leaf-like bracts and few yellowish flowers.

Euphorbiaceae
Euphorbia phosphorea Mart.
Erect, somewhat stick-like with angled stems,
jointed with very small terminal leaves. A species
from Bahia, Brazil, which is said to shed phos-
phorescent light due to a bacteria which is associated
with this plant. *E. caracasana sanguinea* a bush-like
plant native to Venezuela through to Peru having
succulent stems with reddish branches and fleshy
deep red oval leaves, becoming bluish-green in
maturity with red veins and midrib. *E. sipolisii* N. E.
Br., somewhat similar to the *E. phosphorea*. From
the Minas Gerais, Brazil, an erect pencil-shaped
stemmed plant, 4-angled, jointed with small, soon
deciduous leaves. Stems are dull green, the angles
give the effect of blunted 'ribs'. Flowers red-
maroon. *E. weberbauri* Mansf. native of Cajamarca,
Peru, is also of similar character to *E. sipolisii* and
E. phosphorea. *E. neutra* is a very large species
endemic to Brazil. A succulent columnar plant, 5–6
angled, and constricted into longish joints set with
pairs of short stout horny spines.
Jatropha macrantha Müll. Arg.
Endemic to central Peru at an altitude of over
2,000 m. A beautiful flowering species to 1 m high
with glossy pinnate leaves usually from near
terminal ends of stems with pinkish-red flowers in
clusters on short succulent stalk. *J. curcas* is a tall
plant, indigenous to several parts of tropical
America and West Indies, tree-like to sometimes
5 m high having a thick 'ivy-shaped' leaf, flowers
yellowish-green. The seeds are used for their oil. *J.
peltata* H.B.K. from Amazonas, Brazil through to
Peru, a species to about 1 m high with very succulent
fleshy stem, leaves five-lobed. Flowers deep red.

Gesneriaceae
A family of exotic plants, mostly non-succulent
but all bearing attractive foliage and generally
exquisite flowers.

Rechsteineria leucotricha Hoehne
With a thick rounded tuberous root often to 30 cm
diameter which is mostly exposed. Stems densely
covered with silvery hairs as are the broad obovate
leaves set in the form of a whorl. The pinkish-
orange flowers are terminal in centre of whorl.
Native of Brazil.

Melastomataceae
Mostly tropical shrubs or trees, generally exotic
with pronounced veined leaves and attractive
flowers. Only one genus is known to include
succulent species.
Monolena primuliflora Hook. f.
An interesting caudiciform, leaf scars persisting
giving a tubercled effect. Leaves learge, smooth,
dentate, red on underside and red veins. Pinkish
flowers with white centre, usually three together.
Colombia.

Oxalidaceae
Species of this family are found in many parts of
the world. The majority tend to be somewhat
succulent, others develop from a bulbous base.
While species of the 'wood-sorrels' are to be found
in Europe and Africa, the most interesting succulent
plants are endemic to South American countries.
Oxalis carnosa Mol.
Small shrubby plant with tuberous roots and thick
fleshy stem with few branches. 'Clover-like' leaves
from the terminal ends in clusters on longish stalks,
bright green and fleshy. Flower stems from between
the leaves, 4 or 5 in a cluster flower yellow.
Native to coastal areas of Peru, Chile and Bolivia.
O. peduncularis from Equador with fleshy petioles
in rosettes at branch terminals and fleshy leaves.
Flowers on long stem, deep yellowish-orange. *O.
herrerae* is a smaller edition of *O. peduncularis*,
short stem with very thick fleshy leaf stalks and
bright green leaves. Flowers rather smaller, yellow.
O. sepalosa Diels. from Peru and Bolivia, stems to
about 40 cm high and very much swollen at the
base. Leaves densely arranged at the top with yellow
flowers. *O. ortgiesii*, from the Peruvian Andes, a
succulent tree-like plant to about 50 cm tall with

reddish-green leaves, maroon on the under-side. Flowers yellow. *O. succulenta* Barn. An attractive small species with many branches and numerous small glaucous leaves having minute hairs on the under-surface. Native of Chile and Peru.

These plants are not difficult in cultivation – in fact if due attention is not given they can spread out of all proportions! They mainly require to be grown 'hard' – too much moisture encourages rampant growth and they quickly lose their attraction.

Phytolaccaceae
A rather mixed group of plants, some tree-like or shrubby while others are just herbaceous plants; the roots of some of the latter are poisonous.
Phytolacca dioica L.
Fairly well distributed throughout much of South America. A tall succulent tree with thick fleshy roots and equally fleshy trunk and branches. Leaves at terminals of branches, somewhat spirally arranged, oval to elongated, tapering sharply at the tip about 25 cm long and about 15 cm wide, bright green with reddish veins. Flowers pendent on long stalks, whitish and inconspicuous.

Piperaceae
Peperomia dolabriformis Kunth.
Species from Peru. Shrubby habit to about 10 cm tall, fleshy spatulate leaves folded together so that only the under-side of the leaf is visible, the edges having a translucent appearance, creating a 'window' which allows light to penetrate. Flowers are inconspicuous, erect, 'catkin-like'. *P. nivalis*, a Peruvian species, with numerous leaves, keel-shaped, almost folded, forming rosettes. Leaves are scented like aniseed. *P. incana* native of Restinga in Brazil, with fleshy stiff heart-shaped leaves, greyish and completely covered with whitish felt. A very succulent species. *P. ornata* has short succulent stem with clusters of elliptical leaves on red stalks, and beautifully veined. Endemic to south Venezuela. *P. perskiaefolia* from north Brazil and Venezuela with habit much resembling Pereskia. Succulent plant with obovate waxy leaves from reddish stems. *P. polybotrya* originates from Colombia, erect succulent stem, vivid green leaves, purple edged, thick, shield-shaped, inflorescence branched with multiple 'catkins'.

Portulacaceae
Calandrinia spectabilis Otto et Dietr.
Native of Chile. A somewhat shrubby plant with elongated compressed leaves to 4 cm long, pruinose. Flowers very beautiful, about 5 cm diameter, rich purple. Several other South American species are recorded with similar habit and flower colour including *C. discolor* Schrad. (Chile); *C. ciliata* D.C. (Equador) and *C. umbellata* D.C. (Peru).
Portulaca werdermannii v. Poelln.
A prostrate species from Bahia, Brazil, with oblong cylindrical leaves, set alternate, having many hairs in the leaf axils. Terminal flowers, purplish-red. *P. pilosa* L. distributed throughout much of tropical America, a beautiful prostrate plant with dense white hairs and small fleshy leaves. Flower reddish-yellow. *P. poellnitziana* Werd. from near Rio de Janeiro, Brazil, is very similar to *P. pilosa* but with more erect stems having whitish hairs, and bright yellow flowers. *P. grandiflora* Hook, a low, spreading plant with cylindrical leaves, fleshy and hairy. Flowers of various colours, yellow, red, purple etc. often used as a decorative bedding plant for a sunny position and treated as an annual. Native of Brazil.

Urticaceae
Includes many xerophytic plants, generally shade-loving, but not epiphytic. Several have succulent growth and are well-known as houseplants.
Pilea globosa Wedd.
Endemic to Peru and to other Andean regions. Has small sub-globose leaves crowded towards the tips of the stems, only 3 mm long and broad. Upper surface hemispherical, somewhat flattened on lower surface. Flowers small, purple.

5 Succulents of the Old World

It would be an almost impossible task adequately to provide a comprehensive review of the hosts of succulent plants to be found throughout so much of the world outside the Americas in a book of this size. To consider only those from the African mainland would be a stupendous undertaking, and when those from various parts of Asia and Australia need to be included as well the task is far beyond the scope of this chapter.

Many important works have been published on specific families and genera, e.g. Mesembryanthemaceae, Euphorbiaceae, Stapeliaceae, the Aloes etc. and indeed on succulent plants as a whole. All that can be compassed within this chapter is a cross-section of some of the many intriguing succulents especially those which have been recognized and enjoyed for very many years, and others of more recent discovery which, because of this, may have a special appeal to many amateur growers.

The continent of Africa is the homeland of scores of succulents, and while they can to a degree be compressed into a comparatively few genera, the species involved are multitudinous. Five major families dominate the flora of Africa – Stapeliaceae, Liliaceae, Crassulaceae, Mesembryanthemaceae and Euphorbiaceae – and it would be exceedingly difficult to locate an area, excluding the extreme desert-lands, where species could not be found. Other families of no less significance and importance are more restricted in distribution due to their particular environmental requirements. To those of Africa must be added the succulents of Asia and Australia, together with the many islands in close association with the continents – and these islands often produce the plants of greatest interest and charm.

The 'other' succulents have and are increasingly becoming of more and more significance. The African Succulent Plant Society in Britain was formed for the sole purpose of meeting this challenge, and, coupled with the work of the prominent Aloe Society in South Africa, is contributing much-needed information.

The 'common' plant is not necessarily 'usual' or beyond consideration. This selection will contain many such species – with lesser-known plants in an attempt to provide a guide-line to the better comprehension of succulents generally.

Agavaceae

Are represented by one genus only outside the New World. *Sansevieria* are a widely distributed group embracing very many species, many of which are true succulents; indeed, some are epiphytic and have been referred to elsewhere. We have authentic knowledge of only few – new species are being discovered and remain, so far, undescribed. Some species have made ideal houseplants.

Sansevieria canaliculata Carr.
A very slow-growing species, producing only 2 or 3 new leaves annually. These are medium green, slightly curved and flexible with regular grooves longitudinally arranged. Flower whitish. Tropical Africa.

Sansevieria cylindrica Bojer
A most distinct species having sharp elongated cylindrical leaves, often with furrows, dull dark green. Flower stem short with very white flowers. Southern tropical Africa, Natal.

There are also varietal forms of this species, differing in the thickness of leaf, flower colour.

A fine collection of Aloes—the showiest of the succulent Liliaceae.

Sansevieria hahnii HORT.
An interesting 'sport' of *S. trifasciata* v. *laurentii* found in New Orleans in 1939 with the habit of a low vase-like rosette, clustering freely from the base. Leaves dark green with pale green cross-bands. Flower whitish.

Sansevieria stuckyi Godefr. Leb.
With creeping rhizomes forming colonies. Leaves cylindrical to about 1 m long with light green cross-bands and mottling. Flower whitish. From the region of the Victoria Falls in Rhodesia.

Sansevieria thyrsiflora Thbg.
Has thick, creeping rhizome sending up numerous rosettes of erect, flat smooth leaves, tapering at the apex, upper surface slightly channelled, lower surface with slight keel. Flowers greenish-white, and sweetly scented. South-east Africa.

Sansevieria trifasciata v. *laurentii* (Willdem.) N. E. Br.
A most attractive species, making an ideal house-plant – commonly known as 'mother-in-law's tongue'. Leaves sword-like, very erect with marginal yellow stripes and whitish crossbands. Flowers whitish. From the Congo, tropical Africa.

There are several other species worthy of note: *S. guineensis* from Nigeria, *S. pearsonii* from Angola and the more miniature *S. parva* from East Africa are of particular interest and merit, but there are many others also.

Amaryllidaceae

Consists of many bulbous species, most of which are not generally considered succulents. Two genera are included in this record, both of real botanic interest.

Ammocharis coranica (Ker-Gawl.) Herb.
Large bulbous species with strap-like leaves, green and spreading. Inflorescence on long flattish stem with umbels of rose-pink flowers. Leaves deci-

duous. In common with some other bulbous species, the flower precedes the leaves. From many areas of South and South West Africa.

Haemanthus albiflos Jacq.

A popular species with flowers like a shaving brush – white with golden anthers. Quickly grouping with evergreen leaves having ciliate margins. South Africa.

Haemanthus coccineus L.

Species having a flattish bulb, producing deep red flowers with orange anthers before leafing. Usually has only two wide lingulate leaves annually which are deciduous. Fruit in the form of purple berries. South Africa.

Apocynaceae

Is of especial interest to connoisseurs of unusual succulents. Some are from the New World and are mentioned elsewhere.

Adenium obesum

Adenium multiflorum Kl.

An attractive succulent shrub with thick swollen trunk to 3m high. Many branches, leaves at terminal ends, spirally arranged, simple, ovate-lanceolate, smooth, dark green, deciduous. Flower funnel-shaped, white with crimson edges. The milky sap is poisonous. Transvaal, Southern Rhodesia. Known as the 'Impala lily'.

Adenium obesum Balf.

Has thick, succulent caudex with many short fleshy branches to 2m high. The swollen roots often protrude above ground. Leaves spirally arranged at branch terminals, glossy dark green, fleshy, obovate with pinkish midrib. When young, leaves often have minute hairs. Flowers numerous, showy with spreading petals, carmine-red. Sometimes called 'desert rose'. Kenya, Tanzania, Mozambique and other areas of East Africa.

Adenium oleifolium Stapf.

A rare species with elongated tuberous caudex, pale brown skin. Branches develop from the upper portion, erect, fleshy. Leaves at end of branches in clusters, linear and narrowing into the stalk, glossy grey-green. Flowers pinkish-red with deeper red markings. A poisonous plant from Great Namaland.

Other species of Adenium are recorded, mostly having the same characteristics with slight differences in leaf shape or flower colour.

PACHYPODIUMS have created considerable interest since their introduction into cultivation. These succulent shrubby plants, all with fleshy trunks or caudices are still considered rarities although two species are now being grown in Europe as useful houseplants.

Pachypodium baronii v. windsori (H. Poiss.) Pichon

An unusual species with almost globose caudex to about 80 mm diameter. Few branches, round with many spines and rough skin. Leaves at terminal ends, short stalk, thick, ovate and usually two together, opposite, margins crenate, about 5 cm long. Inflorescence between the leaves with red flowers. S. Madagascar.

Pachypodium brevicaule Bak.

With stone-like fleshy swollen caudex often to 65 cm diameter. Leaves sessile, elliptical on short eleva-

Pachypodium lamerei

tions 3 cm long, having few spines between leaves. Flower yellow. Madagascar.

Pachypodium densiflorum Bak.

A multiheaded small caudiciform species, having many rounded branches covered closely with subulate spines. Leaves green with whitish felt on under surface. Flowers very decorative, orange. Madagascar.

Pachypodium geayi Const. et Bois.

Tree-like species, long slender stem to 10 m high, fleshy with many spines, very dark or brownish-green. Leaves at apex, linear-lanceolate. Flowers white. From the dry western coastal areas of Madagascar at low altitudes.

Pachypodium giganteum Engl.

Tall succulent tree-like plant to 6 m high. Stem bottle-shaped, branching at apex, all furnished with many hard spines. Leaves sessile, ovate-elongate coming to a point, margins ciliate. Flower white, scented. Gt. Namaland.

Pachypodium horomboense H. Poiss.

Low-growing species with caudex and many thick fleshy branches all with spines. Leaves oval to about 6 cm long. Flower bright yellow, cup-shaped on long stem. Madagascar where it grows on granite rocks.

Pachypodium lamerei Drake

An erect, sometimes much-branched species with conical fleshy trunk to 2 m high. Leaves 25 cm long and 3 cm wide. Flower white. From dry forest areas of Madagascar.

Pachypodium lealii Welw.

Arborescent species, clavate, narrowing at the apex with numerous erect branches. Leaves small and narrow, set between stout spines, also from shorter stems having somewhat larger leaf and less-stout spines. Flower white at ends of branches. South Africa, Cape Province around Namaqualand.

Pachypodium namaquanum Welw.

Tree-like succulent to nearly 2 m high. Stems fleshy

Pachypodium namaquanum

Pachypodium namaquanum in cultivation.

and furnished with many spines, only very rarely branched. Leaves develop in tufts at apex, smallish and undulated, deciduous in dry season. Flowers from leaf axils, numerous, velvety reddish-brown, striped yellow inside. Known as the 'Ghost-men' by native population. Namaqualand, Cape Province.

Pachypodium rosulatum Bak.
Low and thick caudex, fleshy, branching with cylindrical and densely spined branches. Leaves at terminal ends, in form of rosette, narrow, oblanceolate. Flowers on long stalks, sulphur-yellow. Madagascar.

Pachypodium saundersii N. E. Br.
Very succulent species with caudex sometimes rounded, otherwise elongated to over 1 m high. Leaves oblanceolate, dark green, somewhat undulate, from numerous twisted branches. Flower white with reddish stripes. Zululand.

Pachypodium succulentum D.C.
Caudex short and thick with long tapering tuberous root, very succulent. Branches erect from the upper portion of the caudex. Leaves lanceolate, set at the base with 2 spines. Flower pale pink. L. Namaqualand, Cape Province.

Araliaceae
A family of plants most of which have glossy leaves, palmately divided or lobed – some are vines, such as the *Hedera* species, others are shrubs or trees, often with aromatic foliage. Very few can be considered succulent, the best representation is found in the genus *Cussonia* which are evergreen shrubby trees with caudex-like trunks which store moisture. Branches are woody, flowers terminal.

Cussonia spicata Thunbg.
Very swollen caudex, developing into a sizeable tree. Leaves soft green, digitately lobed, flowers in dense clusters and erect, elongated fruits. Distribution from South Africa to Tanzania.

Other species include *C. thyrsiflora* and *C. holstii*, both African species and *C. myriacantha*, native of Madagascar.

Asclepiadaceae
Provides one of the most extraordinary and fascinating families – very widely distributed throughout the Old World and containing genera with extremely varying characteristics but also distinctive features which are readily appreciated as per-

taining to a particular genus. Only a very limited cross-section is mentioned and these are representative of hundreds of species mostly with unusual and colourful flowers.

BRACHYSTELMA includes many small growing species with very tuberous roots resembling a caudex. Stems and leaves are deciduous in resting season and plants should then be kept completely dry.

Brachystelma grossarti Dtr.
Round tuber and branching to 20 cm long, erect. Leaves elliptical to 33 mm long. Flowers in umbels with longish stalks, and 5 recurved triangular lobes, yellow or greenish-yellow. South West Africa.

Several other species are now in cultivation and although of recent introduction have become much sought after. *B. foetidum* Schltr., *B. barberiae* Harv. ex Hook. and the even more miniature species, *B. pygmaea* N. E. Br. are of considerable interest.

Brachystelma modestum R. A. Dyer
Forming round tuber, generally subterranean and thin branches. Leaves small, oval-elliptical with minute hairs on upper surface. Flower simple or usually in pairs, spreading with 5 triangular recurved lobes, very dark red. Natal.

Brachystelma stellatum Bruce et Dyer
Globular tuber, branching from the terminal, short and semi-erect. Leaves rounded about 1 cm long, minutely hairy, margins ciliate. Flowers from leaf axils, on short stalks, – inside creamy-white and purple markings, 5 spreading lobes, yellowish with white hairs, oval triangular. Transvaal.

CARALLUMA includes very many species, usually creeping plants, sometimes subterranean 'stolon'-like growths which spread and then appear above ground with erect stems. Very similar to Stapelia.

Caralluma aperta (Mass.) N. E. Br.
Stems to 7 cm high, often erect, sometimes pros-

Brachystelma foetidum

trate, 4-angled, bluntly dentate, greyish-green. Flowers on stalks at base of stems, oblong lobes, somewhat blunted, margins with fine papillae and darkish brown at bottom, yellowish and brownish furrows and many dots above. L. Namaqualand, Cape Province.

Caralluma baldratii White et Sloane
Stems simple or branching often from subterranean growths, 4-angled, rather deeply furrowed, greenish-white and many reddish spots, margins toothed. Flowers pale maroon with pinkish-reddish spots and minute hairs, short pronounced lobes lanceolate. Ethiopia to Kenya.

Caralluma burchardii N. E. Br.
Stems erect with many branches forming cushions, stems to 20 cm high, 4-angled, edges, pronounced teeth, greyish to bluish-green. Flowers small in clusters, corolla glabrous, dark olive-green covered with whitish hairs, giving almost the effect of a greyish-blue flower. Canary Islands.

Caralluma dummeri (N. E. Br.) White et Sloane
Stems somewhat 4-angled but rounded with marginal teeth, pale greyish-green and red markings. Flowers several together on stalks about 15 mm long, cup-shaped, lobes spreading and tapering sharply, inside surface with hairs, outside rather smooth, darkish brownish-green. Tanzania and Kenya.

Caralluma europaea (Guss.) N. E. Br.
Erect stems and branches, 4-angled with blunt edges slightly dentate, grey-green and many reddish spots. Flowers small in umbels, 5 ovate lobes, margins minutely ciliate, greenish-yellow, corona dark brown. From Mediterranean countries and southern Spain. A well-known species with many varietal forms.

Caralluma frerei (Dalz.) Rowl.
Long known as *Frerea indica* until transferred to Caralluma. One of the few species with leaves. Stems somewhat rounded, spreading, rarely branched, olive-green, sometimes becoming pale-green. Flowers at ends and along the branches, solitary with short stalk, petals broadly triangular with fine hairs, maroon to brownish. India.

Caralluma lutea N. E. Br.
Stems branching from the base forming clusters to 10 cm high. Stems 4-angled, glabrous, sharply

toothed, grey mottled purple. Star-like yellow flowers with red cilia at edges. Transvaal, Cape Province and other parts of South Africa and possibly East Africa.

Caralluma mammillaris (L.) N. E. Br.
Branching from the base forming clusters. Stems stout to 14 cm high, fresh green or brownish-green, 5 or 6-angled with spreading teeth. Flowers in clusters near apex of branches, corolla deeply 5-clefted, lobes lanceolate and very narrow, margins recurved. Inside surface deep purple, outer surface whitish and many spots. From many areas of Cape Province.

Caralluma retrospiciens (Ehrenbg.) N. E. Br.
One of the tallest species of the genus. Stems erect, smooth, 4-angled almost horny edges, dentate, irregularly branched, pale greyish or olive-green. Flowers freely from tips of branches in umbels, lobes triangular-ovate, dark brown and very dark red cilia. Ethiopia and certain Red Sea islands.

Many other species could be described; all have great eye appeal, and generally speaking are the most easily cultivated of the Stapeliaceae.

CEROPEGIA species are extremely varied in flower character, resembling lanterns or parachutes. The majority are climbing or pendent plants, few are shrubby. Many have a very tuberous, caudex-like root system.

Ceropegia ampliata E. Mey.
Thin-branched species, climbing. Leaves very small, soon falling. Flower very large to 6 cm long with a swollen, balloon-like base becoming tubular and purple petals united at the tips, inside of tube almost white with greenish nerves. Mozambique, Natal and South West Africa.

Ceropegia dichotoma Haw.
An erect cylindrical stemmed species to 1 m high, greyish-green, divided into joint-like sections, and from the nodes developing greyish-green leaves during growing season. Flower towards terminal ends of branches, yellow with lobes remaining attached. Canary Islands.

Ceropegia elegans Wall.
A trailing species with elongate or oval leaves minutely ciliate, not fleshy. Flowers usually 2 to-

gether cylindrical expanding funnel-like, white and purple blotches, lobes remain united in the centre and are edged with dark hairs. India and Ceylon.

Ceropegia fusca C. Bolle.

A very distinctive species somewhat resembling *C. dichotoma* in habit. Stems erect and then spreading to 40 cm high. Branches cylindrical constricting at joints, greyish or purplish. Leaves small, flowers brown and yellow. Canary Islands.

Ceropegia haygarthii N. E. Br.

A climbing, trailing species with strong stem, very succulent. Leaves on stalks, long-cordate. Flowers most attractive about 4 cm long, tube curved at base and expanding funnel-like towards the tip, pale pink and purplish spots, the 5 lobes almost touch in the centre, then unite into a pistil-like stalk topped by red knob with whitish hairs. Endemic to Natal.

Ceropegia nilotica Kotschy

Species with tuberous roots, climbing and twining branches, 4-angled. Leaves ovate, gradually tapering on short stalk, fleshy. Flowers with corolla to 3 cm long, clavate, dark brown – usually 2-flowered. Lobes triangular, united at the tips, and brown hairs inside and yellow spots at the base. Ethiopia through to Uganda.

Ceropegia radicans Schlecht.

Succulent climbing species with long stems. Leaves about 40 mm long, ovate, dark green. Flowers solitary from leaf axils, in form tubular, widening towards the tip, where the erect lobes are united at the tips, purple, green and white. Cape Province.

Ceropegia robynsiana Werderm.

Climbing species, robust, fleshy with many nodes along the stems. Glabrous leaves, ovoid becoming pointed at tips. Flower, inflated balloon-like at base, above strongly constricted and expanding to whitish-green funnel with brownish spots and the long lobes, pointed, beak-like. West Africa.

Ceropegia sandersonii Decne

One of the most outstanding of the genus. Climbing succulent species having small ovate fresh green leaves. Flowers on short stalks – like a parachute, green and mottled darker green – corolla to 7 cm long, expanding broadly funnel-like. Lobes at first narrow, then much widened and uniting at the sides, margins upturned with whitish hairs. Natal.

Ceropegia sandersonii

Ceropegia stapeliaeformis

Ceropegia stapeliaeformis Haw.

Trailing species having thick stem, somewhat rounded and shortly jointed and many knots, greyish-green with purple mottlings and whitish spots. Flowers upturned and tube becoming funnel-like, widening broadly, lobes spreading, outer surface brownish with whitish spots, inner surface hairy, white. Cape Province.

Ceropegia woodii Schlecht.
Creeping with slender threadline branches, forming tubers at nodes. Leaves heart-shaped, bluish-green, white marbled, 2-together. Flowers about 2cm long, slightly curved, inflated at base, expanded above, lobes united at tip, purple. Natal.

CYNANCHUM is a more obscure member of this family, usually of climbing habit, having many thick branches and small flowers.

Cynanchum marnierianum Rauh
Low bushy species with many branches, dark green, covered by irregular tubercles and minute hairs.

Cynanchum marnierianum

Leaves at internodes, deciduous. Flowers lantern-like, being five petals uniting at the tips, greenish-brown. Madagascar.

Cynanchum messeri (Buch.) Junelle et Perr.
Climbing species, somewhat branched, woody, cylindrical, with roughened skin, reddish and waxy. Flowers small on short stalk, petals tapering, yellowish with short hairs on upper surface. Madagascar.

Cynanchum perrieri Choux.
Four-angled branches, erect and leafless. Branches consist of swollen internodes, flowers small, pale greenish-white. Madagascar.

Cynanchum rossii Rauh
Four-angled or rounded stems, creeping growth forming dense clumps, dark green and a complete coating of curly hairs. Flowers solitary, having hairy peduncle, petals olive-green with white edges on the upper surface, yellowish-green on the lower, corona papillose, olive-green. Madagascar.

TAVARESIA was for many years known as *Decabelone* and includes few species of distinctive characteristics making them easily distinguishable from others of the Stapeliaceae.

Tavaresia angolensis Welw.
(syn. *Decabelone elegans* Decne.) Stems 6 or 8-angled, spreading teeth each with 3 whitish spines. Flowers several together from the base of the dark greenish stems, corolla tube curved 8cm long, lobes triangular, recurved and tapering to short point. Outside yellowish and many brownish spots, inner with numerous papillae within the tube and minute hairs. Angola.

Tavaresia grandiflora (K. Sch.) Berg.
(syn. *Decabelone grandiflora* K. Schum.) Stems 10 to 14-angled, tubercled with white bristle-like spines at tips of tubercles. Flowers from base of the greyish stems, corolla curved to 12cm long, lobes spreading, broadly triangular and tapering to point. Outside surface has minute papillae, somewhat rough, yellowish and brownish spots and furrows, inner surface with many papillae. South West Africa.

DIPLOCYATHA is closely related to the genus *Huernia*, but differs in respect to the campanulate tube of the flower from which another tube develops with a thickened margin.

Diplocyatha ciliata (Thunbg.) N. E. Br.
Stems 5cm long branching from the base forming clumps. Branches 4-angled, with acute teeth, greyish-green and reddish markings. Flower about 8cm from stalk, short campanulate funnelled tube with acute lobes, ovate, spreading, whitish, papillosem edges and long white hairs, also in the centre of the tube, cup-shaped papillose annulus with thickish margins. From many areas of Cape Province.

DUVALIA includes a number of species closely allied to Stapelia. Usually with prostrate stems, short and often thick or rounded, and frequently very pronounced corolla and annulus, with long flower stems.

Duvalia caespitosa (Mass.) Haw.

Branching from the base. Stems to 4 cm long somewhat rounded, 4-angled. Flower from the middle or base of young growth, corolla greenish and brown, glossy, fleshy raised annulus, with minute hairs. Lobes spreading horizontally, edges folded back, ciliate towards the middle. Karroo, Cape Province.

Duvalia maculata N. E. Br.

Stems prostrate, forming clumps, angled with blunt edges and long teeth, darkish green. Flower from centre of new growth, corolla and lobes brownish-red, corolla 20 mm, lobes 7 mm and folded right back, fleshy, and minute hairs. Annulus 7 mm, white with red spots. South and South West Africa.

Duvalia polita N. E. Br.

An attractive plant with prostrate stems, darkish-green, 6-angled, rather rounded, teeth having inclined tips and grooves over the teeth. Flowers from centre of growths, corolla with pale hairy ring in the middle, lobes broadly triangular, brownish-red, smooth. S.W. Africa.

ECHIDNOPSIS – a group of rambling and mis-shapen plants, very irregular in their method of growth. Stems usually elongated with shorter branches, many angled and tubercled. Flowers very small.

Echidnopsis cereiformis Hock. f.

Stem usually erect, rarely prostrate, spreading and forming large clusters. Branches and stems having many ribs with blunt, tubercled angles, darkish-green or brownish-green, tuberculate. Flowers very small, usually 3 or 4 together, brown. Tropical Africa.

Echidnopsis framesii (Pill.) White et Sloane

Stems prostrate becoming erect with few branches from base, 6-angled, somewhat rounded and edges divided into angular tubercles. Stems purplish or ashy-grey. Flowers in small clusters, purple.

EDITHCOLEA – closely allied to Caralluma but with particularly large flowers. A rare species in cultivation which seems to have difficulty to survive in most European climates.

Edithcolea grandis N. E. Br.

Bushy plant up to 30 cm high. Stems somewhat erect, 5-angled with many hard thorn-like teeth, greyish-green. Branches irregular, leafless. Flowers especially showy, solitary at branch tips on short stalk, circular in the centre with 5 triangular-ovate lobes 5 cm long joined together half-way to centre, yellow and numerous red or brown spots. Throat tuberculate round the deep tube with purple hairs. Kenya, Ethiopia.

Another species is recorded from Socotra, *E. sordida* N. E. Br. which has similar characteristics excepting the flower colour which is deep purple.

FOCKEA includes a number of caudiciform species having large tuberous roots and many long thin clambering branches. Rare in cultivation.

Fockea crispa (Jacq.) K. Sch.

Probably the best-known of the genus having round, turnip-shaped caudex, very warty and roughened up to 3 m diameter – much of which is buried underground. Leaves opposite, oval-acute, 2 cm long, dark green, very wavy edges. Flowers 4 or 5 together, greenish with small brown spots. Karroo, Cape Province. This species lives to a great age; several such examples are to be found in botanic gardens throughout the world. Smaller plants are available for pot culture, and the great essential is a totally dry resting season.

Fockea edulis (Thbg.) K. Sch.

Large somewhat rounded caudex, covered with brownish skin. Branching freely from apex with glossy smooth leaves, dark green. Flowers yellowish-green. South and South West Africa. The tubers are said to be edible.

Other species are recorded, but have many similarities to those mentioned. *F. natalensis* is very similar to *F. edulis*. *F. multiflora* K. Sch. grows to great heights with thick succulent caudex, stems and branches. The sap is used for making rubber.

Folotsia aculeatum (B. Desc.) B. Desc.

A slender trailing species, branching from the base, stems being segmented and covered with silvery-white powder. Inflorescence consists of several white terminal flowers. Native of Madagascar.

Folotsia floribundum B. Desc.

A shrubby plant with numerous segmented branches, inter-tangling and forming masses.

Inflorescence with terminal flowers, white and scented. Endemic to Madagascar.

HOODIA are related to Stapelias. Not considered an easy plant in cultivation, requires good sunlight and airy conditions. Plants of distinction with most unusual flowers.

Hoodia bainii Dyer

Stems erect with compressed tubercles, spirally arranged, rarely branching, greyish-green. Flowers at terminal ends, subcircular, the tips of lobes being slightly raised, dull brownish-yellow. Cape Province.

Hoodia gordonii (Mass.) Sweet

Species having many stems from central growing point, erect and firm, rarely branching. Has 12 to 14 ribs, irregularly longitudinal furnished with tessellate tubercles and hard spines, greyish-green. Flowers usually at terminal end, subcircular with lobes hardly apparent, margins outcurved, brownish-pink with obscure furrows and rough. L. Namaqualand, Cape Province.

Hoodia macrantha Dtr.

Stems erect forming clusters from central growing point to 80 cm high. Many ribs, sharply tuberculate. Flowers at terminal ends, subcircular, forming shallow bell-shape with tips of lobes somewhat recurved, purplish-yellow, the largest flowers of this genus being up to 20 cm across. South West Africa. Very rare in cultivation.

HUERNIA includes a great many species of the Stapeliaceae, having short stems and forming thickish clusters with many varied, colourful and unusual flowers. Only a few are mentioned here.

Huernia confusa Phill.

Erect 5-angled stems, dull green, angles furnished with short triangular teeth spreading acutely. Clusters freely. Flower on short stalk from near base of growths, corolla circular 3 cm, shallow tube, glabrous, pinkish with thick annulus, yellowish-green and spotted. Lobes triangular, short-tapering, pale green and reddish markings, slightly papillose. Transvaal.

Huernia pillansii N. E. Br.

Stems forming clusters to 4 cm high with spirally arranged ribs and soft maroon spines. Flowers

from young stems on short stalk having 5 pronounced lobes, triangular and tapering, each to 12 mm long. Outer surface yellow with reddish spots. Cape Province.

Huernia primulina N. E. Br.

An interesting species with short erect stems to 8 cm high, 4 or 5-angled, somewhat dentate and teeth which rapidly become blunted, pale greenish or greyish-green, with reddish spots. Flowers in clusters on short stalks, corolla has pale purplish tube and fleshy triangular lobes, broadly tapering, slightly recurved, inside yellow-white with few blackish spots around throat. South Africa.

Huernia schneideriana Bgr.

Stems to 18 cm long, 5 to 7-angled, sparsely toothed, clustering, light green. Flower bell-shaped, outside surface brown, inside velvety-black with paler papillose margins and edges, lobes recurved. A popular species. Mozambique and Malawi.

Huernia zebrina N. E. Br.

Thick clustering species, stems to 8 cm high, tapering towards the apex, green and flecked red, angled with reddish teeth. Flower on short stalks, broadly bell-shaped, narrowing around the mouth of the tube and a broad ring around the mouth. Lobes triangular, very acute. Rather small flowers, yellow with transverse purple bands. Zululand, Transvaal, South West Africa.

HOYA are mainly climbing plants, only few are shrubby while others are epiphytic. Most species are succulent; there are exceptions, but even some of these have a tendency to succulence, either in the stem or leaves. Known as the 'Wax-flower', some species have become popular as houseplants. This genus includes more species than is generally recognized; many are of easy culture. All species are fragrant.

Hoya australis R. Br.

A robust climber with broad oval pointed leaves, thick, fleshy, green and several whitish spots. Flowers in umbels, whitish-pink with red centre. Australia.

Hoya bandaensis

A rampant climber with very long stems and large oval pointed fleshy dark green leaves, glossy.

Buiningia aureum

Nococactus scopa v. *candicans*

Flowers in umbels on long stalks, white with reddish centre. Malaysia.

Hoya bella Hook.
A well-known shrubby species, fairly straight stems and short branches, but sometimes dropping at the ends. Leaves small, thick, ovate lanceolate, deep green. Flowers in umbels, white with purple centre. India and Malaysia.

H. sikkimensis and *H. parasitica* are also dwarf-growing species similar to *H. bella*, and might possibly be synonymous or a variety of this species.

Hoya carnosa (L.) R. Br.
Trailing fleshy palnt with elongated stems and branches. Leaves ovate-elongate and shortly tapering, dark green, fleshy and waxy. Flowers in pendent umbels, pink with reddish spots in centre. China and Australia. The species usually considered the 'Wax-flower'.

H. carnosa v. *marmorata* (syn. var. exotica) Hort. is in all parts the same as the species, but with yellow mottled or striped leaves. *H. carnosa* v. *variegata* de Vries. is also similar, but the leaves are white variegated. The flower in both instances is identical.

Hoya imperialis Lindl.
A trailing species with stems, leaf ribs and stalks covered with felt. Leaves very tough, elliptic, somewhat downy. Flowers very beautiful on pendent umbels, darkish purple with a greenish centre.

Hoya longifolia Wall.
A smaller-growing species with slender stems and long linear leaves channelled above and roundish under. Flowers in umbels, delicate waxy-white and a rich carmine centre. A very distinctive species from the tropical Himalayas.

Hoya macrophylla Bl.
Slow-growing species with twining habit. Leaves large, fleshy, ovate, light or coppery-green, tapering towards the tip, having prominent pale veins and a quilted surface. Flowers in umbels, white and papillate hairy. Java.

Hoya imperialis

Hoya moteskei
Rampant climber with broad elliptic waxy leaves, somewhat leathery with irregular whitish spots and markings. Flowers in umbels, pinkish-white with maroon centre. Indonesia.

Hoya multiflora (Decne.) Bl.
A trailing plant, but more shrubby than some other species with large elliptic glossy leaves tapering sharply at both ends. Flower in umbels, straw-yellow with brownish centre. Malacca.

Hoya obovata
(syn. *H. kerrii*) A robust climber with stout stems. Leaves thick, fleshy and very succulent, heart-shaped to 8 cm long, dull green. Flowers in umbels creamy-white with rose-purple centre. Thailand, Java and possibly Fiji.

Hoya pallida Lindl.
Long twining species having elliptic waxy leaves, pale green. Flowers in umbels, pale yellow with reddish centre. An unusual species and rare in cultivation. China.

This comprises one of the most exotic climbing genera of succulents and the flowers can offer endless pleasure.

PECTINARIA related to *Piaranthus* and *Duvalia*. Low-growing species, angled and tuberculate. Flowers with the corolla lobes connate at the apex having narrow openings between.

Pectinaria asperifolia N. E. Br.
Freely clustering with many stems, often erect to 8 cm long, rounded with 6 to 8 ribs consisting of sharp tipped tubercles. Flower drooping, outside surface, purplish-brown, inside white and purple dots. Cape Province.

Pectinaria saxatilis N. E. Br.
Forming clumps with somewhat procumbent stems, acutely 4-angled to 5 cm long, angles compressed and furnished with acute teeth. Flowers in clusters from the younger shoots, ovate, lobes connate at the tips, blackish-purple and hairy. Cape Province.

PIARANTHUS are small-growing species usually with 4-angled stems and blunt edges. Flowers erect on stalks, round corolla with bell-shaped tube, hairy triangular lobes.

Piaranthus foetidus N. E. Br.
Stems subglobose to 4 cm long with 4 and sometimes 5-angled, toothed edges, greyish-green, sometimes reddish. Flowers from near top of stems, outside greenish-red, fleshy and inside yellow with transverse lines and hairs. Cape Province.

Piaranthus globosus White et Sloane
With procumbent stems, oval and obscurely 4-angled with few small teeth along the edges, light green. Flowers have no tube, back surface glabrous, inside pale greenish-yellow with reddish spots, hairy. Cape Province.

Pseudopectinaria malum Lavr.
A relatively new discovery in Somalia. Very fleshy succulent stems, elongated and somewhat bluntly angled. Leaves insignificant and quickly fading. Flower borne on short pedicel, fleshy, circular, corolla purplish inside and papillose outside, incurved triangular lobes and yellow outer corona.

Piaranthus pillansii N. E. Br.
Procumbent stems to 4 cm long, club-shaped with 4-angles rather obtuse. Light pinkish-green. Flowers in pairs, outside glabrous, inside yellowish-green, hairy. Cape Province.

RAPHIONACME contains species which are either tuberous-rooted or with caudex. These are a recent introduction into cultivation and only few of the nearly 30 species have yet been seen.

Raphionacme galpinii Schltr.
Caudex to about 14 cm diameter. Short annual stems to about 7 cm long with elongated, pilose leaves about 3 cm long. Flower smallish, greenish-yellow. Transvaal.

Other species are widely distributed throughout East, West, South and South West Africa – many are little known, but obviously are of considerable interest. *R. procumbens* from South West Africa has an exceptionally large tuber. *R. daronii* from Ghana has almost a horizontally flattened caudex. *R. vignei* also from Ghana with an almost vertical caudex, very elongated and with greenish flowers.

Raphionacme hirsuta (E. Mey.) Dyer
Large caudex to 20 cm diameter. Annual shoots appear from the apex producing small lanceolate leaves. Small flowers, purple. East Cape Province, Natal, Orange Free State and Transvaal.

SARCOSTEMMA includes about 14 species, mainly with thin, somewhat elongated stems, often segmented, invariably leafless and with small flowers in umbels.

Sarcostemma brunoniana Wight et Arn.

Having fairly strong twining stems, often prostrate, jointed with segments about 5 cm long, cylindrical, bright green. Flowers in umbels, white. India.

Descriptions of other species differ very little from those mentioned; the main distinction with some are the varying flower colours and size of flower. The distribution is most extensive—Asia, Africa and Australia, also in South America where perhaps the larger-flowering species are found.

Sarcostemma viminale R. Br.

Erect cylindrical branches, becoming rather pendent, jointed with triangular leaf scales, greyish-green. Flowers white in umbels. From tropical and sub-tropical Africa. The best known of the genus.

STAPELIA is undoubtedly one of the best known genera of succulent plants—all fleshy stemmed with angular branches, usually 4-angled, forming clumps and having remarkably attractive flowers. For classification purposes the genus has been divided into sections, taking into account the peculiarities of the flower structure. Only selected species will be noted without reference to the section to which they belong.

Stapelia asterias Mass.

With light green, soft downy, 4-angled stems to 15 cm high, forming clusters. Flowers star-like, long dark brown lobes with transverse lines and reddish cilia. Karroo, Cape Province.

Stapelia clavicorona Verd.

Stems to 30 cm long with compressed angles armed with teeth and sides deeply furrowed. Star-shaped flower, light yellow with purplish-brown transverse lines, margins partly ciliate. Transvaal.

Stapelia comparabilis White et Sloane

Very succulent stems to 15 cm long, sometimes to nearly 2 cm thick, 4-angled, toothed. Flowers nearly 10 cm diameter—star-like hairy flowers, brownish-purple with yellowish transverse lines. Cape Province.

Stapelia erectiflora N. E. Br.

Slender 4-angled stems, erect to about 14 cm high, angles with small distant teeth, pale green. Flower

Sarcostemma viminale

A newly introduced and so far unidentified species of Stapelia.

Stapelia erectiflora

on long stalk, small about 14mm purplish, and densely covered with white hairs. Cape Province.

Stapelia gigantea N. E. Br.

Stems angled, ascending, thick and fleshy to 20 cm high, small teeth on angles, dull green, velvety. Flower very large to 35 cm diameter, pale yellow with many undulate, crimson transverse lines. Natal, Transvaal and Zululand.

Stapelia grandiflora Mass.

Has clavate stems, angled with teeth, very erect to 30 cm high, dark green and densely soft-hairy. Flowers large to 16 cm across, flat, deeply lobed, purple-brown and purplish and whitish hairs on margins of lobes. Cape Province.

Stapelia hirsuta L.

With erect stems, clustering to 20 cm long, 4-angled and minute teeth, dark greyish-green, soft-hairy. Flowers rather large to 12 cm, star-like, yellowish-red with many purplish hairs on margins and lobes having transverse lines of purplish-red.

Cape Province. This species has many varietal forms.

Stapelia kwebensis N. E. Br.

Fleshy erect stems, branching freely from the base to 14 cm high, 4-angled, pronounced dentate with small 'leaves', fresh-green. Flowers from near the base, smallish, starlike, on stalks, chocolate-reddish, fleshy with many wrinkles and transverse lines. Transvaal.

Stapelia leendertziae N. E. Br.

Slender and erect stems, loosely clustering, slightly angled with small fleshy teeth and minutely papillose. Flowers have bell-shaped tube about 6 cm long and pointed recurved lobes, dark purple, covered with dark purple hairs. Transvaal.

Stapelia mutabilis Jacq.

Stems to 14 cm high, clustering, thick with pronounced teeth, greyish-green. Flowers roundish with recurved lobes, yellowish and purplish transverse lines and margins ciliate. South Africa.

Stapelia nobilis N. E. Br.

A much-branched species with stems to 14 cm long, pale green, angles have minute teeth and slightly hairy. Flowers star-shaped with bell-shaped tube, yellow, reddish transverse lines, back surface purple. From Transvaal.

Stapelia pillansii N. E. Br.

Branching freely into clusters, stems 12 cm long, bluntly angled with few teeth. Flowers star-shaped and having slender lobes, purplish-brown, fleshy, smooth. Back surface covered with soft hair and purplish hairs or margins. Cape Province.

Stapelia variegata L.

The best known of the genus, often called the 'Star-flower'. Many branches in clusters and stems to 10 cm long, angled, spreading teeth, dark green. Flowers very showy, greenish-yellow with purplish-brown spots, lobes wrinkled having many transverse lines. Cape Province. There are several varieties of the species.

Stapelia virescens N. E. Br.

With erect, greenish-grey stems, brownish mottled, bluntly angled and small teeth. Flowers like starfish, flat, lobes spreading and margins recurved, yellowish-green with covering of small pointed papillae, outside whitish tinged purple. Cape Province.

This comprises one of the most colourful groups of succulents and those recorded are typical of the exotic nature of the flowers—others of the genus are no less fascinating. The great disadvantage associated with these plants is the evil smell of the flowers, resulting in their being referred to as 'carrion plants'.

STAPELIANTHUS includes only few species with distinctive stem shapes, many angled and smallish flowers. Closely related to the genus *Huernia*. All known species are endemic to Madagascar.

Stapelianthus madagascarensis (Choux.) Choux.

Stems greyish-green, somewhat erect to 10 cm long, 6 to 8-angled, dentate with pronounced teeth and spiny tip. Small flower, bell-shaped, reddish, spotted purplish, with papillae, tube narrow, lobes tapering.

Stapelianthus pilosus (Choux) Lavr. et Hardhy (syn. *Trichocaulon decaryi* (Choux.) An attractive and unusual species covered with numerous hairy-like conical tubercles, stems erect or prostrate to 18 cm long. Flower from base of stems on stalk, broadly bell-shaped, reddish, with minute hairs, lobes tapering, triangular.

STULTITIA—related to Stapelia—separated on account of the flower characteristic—Stultitia have flowers which show a distinct ring around the mouth of the tube. Includes only few species.

Stultitia araysiana Lavr. & A.S. Bilaidi

Stems to 8 cm long, spreading and forming clusters, 4-angled with conical teeth, greyish-green also brown spots. Flowers star-like, with slender lobes, deeply set, margins rounded, inside surface bright red-brown, shiny, tubercles densely arranged with short white bristle, outside surface greyish-green, tuberculed. South Yemen.

Stultitia conjuncta White et Sloane

Procumbent with many creeping branches to 15 cm long, 4-angled, greyish-green, mottled deeper green and brown, angles with teeth. Flower bell-shaped, short lobes, smooth, pale purplish-brown and creamy-white. Transvaal.

Stultitia cooperi (N. E. Br.) Phillips

Stems erect to 3 to 4 cm long, 4-angled and pronounced teeth, greyish-green, mottled red and dark green. Flowers star-like, outside surface green and purplish stripes, smooth: inside surface wrinkled, yellow with purple lines, and small hairs on recurved margins. Cape Province.

Stultitia hardyi Dyer

Species with subterranean growths, somewhat prostrate stems, 4-angled and pronounced teeth, pale green with brownish or darker green mottled. Flower campanulate having spreading recurved lobes, brownish-red, and yellowish-white spots; under surface yellowish. Transvaal.

TRICHOCAULON have thick fleshy often globose or cylindrical stems with densely arranged tubercles. Flowers rather small, from between the tubercles. Most species are still rare in cultivation.

Trichocaulon cactiforme N. E. Br.

Stems cylindrical or oval-cylindrical, densely tuberculate, greyish-green. Flower at apex, pale yellow, spotted red, short lobes spreading.

Trichocaulon keetmanshoopense Dint.

Stems globose about 15 cm long, greyish-brown or purplish-brown, and covered with rounded tubercles. Flowers small, yellowish with brownish spots, lobes broadly ovate, tapering abruptly. From Keetmanshoop, South West Africa.

Trichocaulon melforme Marl.

Stem almost round or oval, greyish-green with blunt obtuse tubercles. Flower near apex, somewhat campanulate, inner surface yellow spotted purplish, lobes broad, oval and tapering abruptly, under surface dark reddish. Gr. Namaland.

Trichocaulon pedicillatum Schinz

Thick cylindrical stems completely tuberculed with minute bristle. Greyish-green. Flowers from near apex, small, dark brown and reddish, spreading lobes and inner surface with minute papillae. Namib Desert.

Trichocaulon pillansii N. E. Br.

Stems branch freely, many angled but generally cylindrical, grey-green, covered with tubercles and bristle at tip. Flowers several together, yellowish, campanulate with lobes spreading. Cape Province.

Several other genera are included in this family, often with only small representation, and individual species have been selected for particular mention.

Decanema bojeriana Decne

An erect-stemmed species very similar to Sarcostemma. Branches cylindrical, leafless with many joints. Flower at apex, cup shaped, greenish. Madagascar.

Hoodiopsis triebneri Luckh.

An elegant species, erect stems branching from the base, 8 or 9-angled, very pronounced, with marginal teeth, light green and purplish lines. Flower solitary, bluntly star-shaped to about 10–11 cm diameter, lobes flat spreading, margins recurved, outside surface greenish-pink, inside surface deep brownish-red, longitudinal grooves, all covered with papillae. Gr. Namaland.

Huerniopsis decipiens N. E. Br.

Stems semi-prostrate to 7 cm long, 4 or 5-angled, rounded also sharp teeth, grey-green with purplish blotches. Flowers somewhat bell-shaped, triangular lobes and edges so recurved as to appear rounded, spreading. Inside surface purplish with yellowish spots, outside greenish and spotted.

Kinepetalum schultzei Schltr.

Has very tuberous root, almost caudex-like. Many erect stems to 1 m high, cylindrical, and minute hairs. Leaves long and narrow, somewhat grooved, tapering, green, covered with small hairs. Flowers have bell-shaped tube, with very thin, thread-like lobes about 3 cm long, white spotted, green, with many purplish hairs. Gr. Namaland.

Closely related to Ceropegia.

Luckhoffia beukmanii (Luckh.) White et Sloane

A rare member of the Stapeliaceae, erect stems branching from the base, tall, usually 8-angles with many blunted tubercles, greyish-green. Flowers at apex of branches, somewhat rounded and flat, greenish-pink on outside and inside papillate with black hairs, lobes brown and yellow spotted with longtitudinal ribs, margins recurved, minutely ciliated. From Cape Province.

Pseudolithos migiurtinorum (Chiov.) Bally

(syn. *Lithocaulon sphaericum* Bally.) With almost completely round or oblong stems, and totally

Pseudolithos migiurtinorum

covered with irregular tessellations, dull whitish-green when young, greyish-green on older plants. Flowers small in clusters, brownish-green. From Flowers small in clusters, brownish-green. Somalia.

Rhytidocaulon piliferum Lavr.

Erect stems and branches, 4 to 6-angled, bluntly tessellated, rough and covered with waxy papillae densely arranged, grey or brown. Leaves small, deciduous. Flowers fleshy, small, somewhat tubular with very narrow spreading lobes, whitish below, dark purple above. Somali Republic.

Siphonostelma stenophyllum Schltr.

Species with flattened caudex, few short stems from apex, somewhat jointed and minute hairs. Leaves narrow and elongated, dark green. Flowers small, bell-shaped with elongated lobes which unite above, brownish-green and yellow inside. Closely related to Ceropegia. Gr. Namaland.

Balsaminaceae

Are usually considered herbaceous plants, but certain of the genus *Impatiens* can be classified as succulents.

Impatiens mirabilis Hook. f.

With fleshy pale green stems, later turning reddish-brown, very succulent – leaves grouping at the apex, somewhat ciliate and waxy. Flowers golden-yellow, large. Isle of Langkawi, Sumatra.

A number of other species, obviously true succulents, are recorded – but these appear to be rare in cultivation, and very little is known about them. It is generally assumed they constitute 'stem' succulents. *I. balfouri* from West Himalayas with pink flowers and yellow spots. *I. holstii*, from Kenya and Tanzania with purple-scarlet flowers, is closely linked to the typical 'busy Lizzie', one of the most popular of this genus.

Bombacaceae

Includes many tree-like succulents; several are associated with the Americas. One of the most outstanding genera of the family is *Adansonia* – species of which are found in Africa, Madagascar and Australia.

Adansonia digitata L.

A huge tree with trunk up to 18 m high and of considerable girth. The swollen trunk consists of pulpous wood and with no growth rings. Leaves large digitate with leaflets, deciduous. Pendulous flowers, about 10 cm, white with purple stamens and long woody fruits, somewhat hairy about 25 cm long. Leaves and fruit are edible. This features very much in savannah areas in tropical Africa.

Commonly known as the 'baobab tree', 'dead-rat tree' and 'monkey bread tree'.

Other species have mainly the same characteristics, but flower colour varies – yellow, pink and red.

Bombax malabaricum

Has very spiny trunk of similar structure to Adansonia. Large palmate leaves with leaflets and pendulous red flowers in clusters. From many parts of Asia, India and the Far East.

Burseraceae

Has one representative in the Old World – others in the Americas. The genus *Commiphora* includes a few borderline species which may or may not be succulent; one only is a true succulent.

Commiphora dulcis Engl.

A small tree with thick tuberous caudex, sparsely branched, spreading horizontally. Leaves very small, narrow with insignificant flowers. An interesting plant, a natural bonsai – Namib Desert, on quartz rock face.

Campanulaceae

Includes only few succulent species contained within two genera.

Campanula vidalii

A shrubby species to 25 cm high, much branched with succulent spatulate toothed leaves. Flowers in racemes, white with yellowish base, bell-shaped. Endemic to the Azores, Madeira.

Lobelia rhynchopetala (Hochst.) Hemsl.

Caudiciform species having elongated fleshy trunk to about 4 m high. Leaves long and wide developing palm-like fans at the terminal end. Endemic to Ethiopia and Tanzania.

Commelinaceae

Mostly trailing and clustering plants of which Tradeseanlia is possibly better known – invariably all genera have attractive foliage, but insignificant flowers.

Cyanotis lanata Benth.

A densely leafy plant, very succulent and hairy to 7 cm long from fleshy stems covered with wool.

Flowers in clusters, generally purple or pink. Indigenous to many parts of tropical Africa.

Convolvulaceae

Is one of the largest plant families with representation in most parts of the world. Only few genera include succulents, and these generally have caudiciform root systems.

Ipomoea holubii Bak.

With large caudex, (in habitat) usually buried. Grass-like leaves. Flower variable–from deep pink to dark purple. Widely distributed in North Transvaal on grasslands.

Ipomoea inamoena Pilg.

Very large caudex with thick brownish skin. Leaves elongated, ciliate on the margins. Flowers from leaf-axils, lilac to white. Fairly widespread in parts of South West Africa.

Ipomoea batatas

The well known 'sweet potato'–having tuberous roots and succulent stems. Leaves variable, sometimes digitately lobed or ovate. Flowers pinkish-white. Originally from Asia.

The other genera, *Merremia* and *Turbina*, are possibly identical to *Ipomoea*–and seemingly

Turbina holubii

synonymous as far as the succulent species are concerned. *Turbina holubii* is an example–although species so named have rather larger stem and leaf growths with larger, more purple flower.

Compositae

The largest of all plant families, many of the genera contain succulent species, particularly *Senecio* and *Othonna*. In recent years some genera have become merged: *Kleinia* and *Notonia* and certain species of *Cacalia* were united with SENECIO.

Hertia cheirifolia (L.) O. Ktze.

A creeping glabrous grey-green shrub with fleshy purplish-green leaves having distinct veins. Flowers in panicles, yellow. Endemic to Algiers and Tunisia.

Some species of *Gynura* are succulents, also *Pteronia*, which are of little interest and considered difficult in cultivation.

Othonna capensis L. H. Bail.

Creeping or procumbent species with many stems and branches. Leaves almost cylindrical, fleshy, slightly furrowed. Flower at terminal end, yellow. Eastern Cape Province.

Othonna euphorbioides Hutchins.

A dwarf succulent shrub with short stems, sparingly branched, covered with greyish powder. Leaves in tufts at ends of branches, elongate-spatulate–like long spoons, light green, white pruinose and long white spines between the leaves. Deciduous. Flowers yellow on short stalk. South West Africa.

Othonna herrei Pill.

Curious succulent with short thick stems notched by persistent leaf bases. Rarely branching. Leaves irregularly obovate, undulate, fleshy on short stalk, glaucous green, deciduous. Numerous small yellow flowers. Namaqualand, South Africa.

Othonna lepidocaulis Schltr.

A very dwarf species, rarely branched, thick and roughened with persistent leaf bases. Leaves produced at the apex as small rosette, fleshy, linear about 5 cm long. Bright yellow flowers. A rare species from mountainous areas in Namaqualand, Cape Province.

Othonna pygmaea Compt.

Small, almost caudex base with short stem and

Senecio haworthii

branches. Fleshy succulent leaves, spatulate, somewhat obtuse, slightly crenate at the tips, deciduous. Inflorescence from apex of stem with short peduncle bearing yellow flowers. A very interesting miniature from rock faces, Clanwilliam Div. Cape Province.

Senecio chordifolius Hook. f.
A tall shrub with slender, elongated cylindrical leaves, slightly tapering at the apex, fresh green. Long flower scape of pale yellow flowers. Albert Div. Cape Province.

Senecio haworthii (Haw.) Sch. Bip.
Long known as *S. tomentosa*. Stems and branches either erect or semi-erect, covered with soft white wool. Leaves cylindrical and pointed and having white coating. Long flower scape with yellow flowers. Endemic to South Africa.

Senecio stapeliaeformis Phill.
An erect branching angular species, with purplish-brown and grey stems rising from the base – branches invariably underground at first. Angles 5 to 7 toothed with minute leaves which quickly

wither and leave cushions. Flower on long stalk, bright red. Eastern Cape Province.

Senecio macroglossus

A variegated or green wax-vine, branching freely and climbing. Has small ivy-shaped leaves, succulent, variegations green and white or yellowish. Large yellow flowers. Green form endemic to Eastern Cape Province, the variegated form from Kenya.

Crassulaceae

Are widely distributed throughout the Old World and form one of the largest of succulent plant families. Most species are in cultivation, being generally of easy culture, some as hardy plants. Many genera are involved.

ADROMISCHUS has over 50 known species, primarily miniatures with small stems and rather insignificant flowers of white or brownish-red. Propagation easy from leaves or seeds.

Adromischus bolusii (Schoenl.) Bgr.

Has small green spatulate leaves with waxy covering, margins have hard reddish edge. Flower red on unbranched inflorescence. Mosselbay and Riversdale, Cape Province.

Adromischus festivus C. A. Smith

Small branches with grey-green and silver mottled leaves, cylindrical and truncate towards the apex. Graaff Reinet, Cape Province.

Adromischus roaneanus Uitew.

Erect, zig-zag stems, branching freely and becoming procumbent. Leaves round or oblong narrowed into a stalk, apex with a small spine, margins rounded, grey-green, covered by waxy mottlings. Flower whitish or purplish. Little Namaqualand, Cape Province.

Adromischus tricolor Sm.

Short stem with few branches, spindle-shaped leaves with silver and maroon markings. Flower purplish-red. Clanswilliam Div. Cape Province.

Adromischus trigynus (Burch.) v. Poelln.

Short stems, clustering with leaves compressed, elliptical, light green with silver-grey and brownish-red markings. Flower purplish. Transvaal to Orange Free State.

AEONIUM are indigenous to Canary Islands, Madeira, parts of N. Africa and Cape Verde Islands, and some other of the islands in the Mediterranean.

All species have an attractive leaf structure in the form of a rosette. The flowering stem often dies after the seeds are formed.

Aeonium arboreum (L.) Webb et Berth.

A popular species up to 1 m high, erect and topped with rosette of thin leaves, ciliate on margins. Flowers in long racemes, golden-yellow. There are varieties of this species, *A. arboreum* v. *atropurpureum* with dark purple leaves, and variegated forms, v. *albovariegatum* and v. *luteo-variegatum* with white and yellow mottlings respectively.

Aeonium nobile Praeg.

Very large rosette on short stem. Leaves darkish green and sticky. Flowers reddish or coppery colour – a most attractive species.

Aeonium smithii (Sims) Webb et Berth.

A rarity with distinctive characteristics. Usually short stems which become covered with brownish hair when mature. Leaves undulated with many soft hairs, deep green with red stripes on both sides. Flower yellow.

Aeonium simsii (Sweet) Stearn

Short stemmed plant, grouping freely. Broad leafy rosette, grass-green with reddish lines and margins ciliate. Flowers golden-yellow.

Aeonium tabulaeforme (Haw.) Webb et Berth.

Low, almost stemless species with almost flat rosette, growing on rock faces. Leaves narrow and spatulate, margins ciliate, fresh-green. Flower yellow.

AICHRYSON are allied to Aeonium and endemic to the same areas. Annuals and biennials.

Aichryson dichotomum (D.C.) Webb et Berth.

Stems branching in pairs, hairy and succulent. Leaf spoon-shape, bright green, sometimes purplish. Flower pale yellow.

Aichryson villosum (Ait.) Webb et Berth.

Densely branched species, stems having white hairs, sticky. Leaves spatulate covered with long hairs. Flower golden-yellow.

COTYLEDON includes many species, shrubby or

prostrate, usually compact with thick fleshy leaves and terminal inflorescence with pendent flowers.

Cotyledon buchholziana Steph. et Schuldt.

Miniature branching species having cylindrical stems and branches, dark grey-green with brownish-red scale leaves; these soon disappear. Growing points spirally arranged, having small linear leaves. Inflorescence about 15 mm long with pinkish-purple flower. A rare species of considerable charm. Namaqualand, Cape Province.

Cotyledon cacalioides L.f.

A short, thick stemmed, little branching plant. Stems tubercled, somewhat spiral. Leaves cylindrical-acute, greyish-green. Long inflorescence with many yellowish-red flowers. From the Karroo region of Cape Province.

Cotyledon jacobseniana v. Poell.

A pretty semi-procumbent plant, much branched with brownish skin. Leaves small and thick, oblong, narrowing towards base and apex. Flower scape erect, thin with reddish-green blooms. Endemic to Namaqualand, Cape Province.

Cotyledon ladismithiensis v. Poelln.

Dwarf shrubby plant, freely branching. Leaves at terminal ends, very thick and fleshy, pale fresh green, obovate with dentate apex – the surface covered with minute white hairs. Inflorescence hairy with pendent apricot-yellow flowers. South Africa.

Cotyledon orbiculata L.

Large thick stemmed species, usually erect, sometimes procumbent. Leaves obovate covered with a waxy silver-whitish bloom, margins red. Long flower scape with yellowish-red blooms. There are varieties of the species, with leaves or/and flowers differing. Gr. Namaland, South West Africa.

Cotyledon paniculata L.f.

Thick stemmed tree-like species often to 150 cm high. The swollen trunk is covered with thin papery brownish skin. Branches few, fleshy obovate leaves bluntly tapering, pale green with somewhat yellowish margins. Deciduous during resting season. Flowers red with greenish stripes. Karroo region of Cape Province.

Cotyledon papillaris L.f.

Low miniature species, much branched. Leaves only few, somewhat wedge-shaped, or sub-obtuse, dark green. Margins rounded at base and sharp towards apex. Flowers on long scape, reddish-yellow. Other varieties are recorded, *C. papillaris v. glutinosa* (Schoenl.) v. Poelln. where the flowers have sticky hairs, *C. papillaris v. robusta* Schoenl. et Bak. which resembles the species but more robust and *C. papillaris v. subundulata* v. Poelln. with leaves wavy towards the tip and reddish-brown. Karroo regions of Cape Province.

Cotyledon undulata Haw.

One of the most attractive of the genus, shrubby with opposite broad wedge-shaped leaves and distinctive crinkled apex, all stems and leaves covered with silvery-grey pruinose. Flower on long stalk, orange or golden-yellow becoming reddish near the apex. From Cape Province.

CRASSULA include many species of considerable interest and variation, their attractiveness being centred more in their vastly differing foliage forms rather than the flower, although when in full bloom they provide a most beautiful setting. Many Crassula species are non-succulent, others are aquatics, which are omitted here. The genus has been divided and sub-divided for classification purposes and particular references to this classification are not included. Several species of outstanding character are deserving of mention.

Crassula barbata Thbg.

Forming clusters of dense rosettes, usually curved inwards, dark green, margins with many whitish hairs. Leaves almost rounded with fine point at apex. Flowers white, erect. A monocarpic species, old growth dies after flowering, but new growth developing from the base. From dry deserts of S. Africa.

Crassula cephalophora Thunb.

A short branching species forming flattish rosettes, leaves ovate and fleshy, flat upper surface and covered with whitish hairs, margins closely set with white cilia. Flowers yellowish. Well distributed in Cape Province, Orange Free State and Basutoland.

Crassula cornuta Schoenl. et Bak.

Small species with densely leafed stems, fleshy, leaves keel-shaped, silver grey. Short inflorescence with small white flowers. South West Africa and Cape Province.

Crassula falcata Wendl.

An attractive plant with thick, fleshy, somewhat flattened, oblong-falcate leaves, grey-green. Flower on fleshy stalk with many beautifully bright crimson or orange-red blooms. One of the best flowering species of the Crassulas. Cape Province to Natal.

Crassula hemisphaerica Thunb.

Miniature species forming cushions, with round leaves, flat with raised tips, being closely set together and overlapping, giving rosette effect, dark grey-green, and with white ciliate margins. Flower white. South West Africa.

Crassula lycopodioides Lam.

A well-known species of many varietal forms, having thin brittle stems, leafed densely the whole length with pointed triangular scaly leaves, bright green. Flowers very minute, white. The species and varieties all originate from South West Africa.

Crassula pyramidalis Thunb.

An attractive miniature, densely leafed in four rows, leaves being three-cornered, flat, of equal size, close together forming an attractive column. Flowers white, in clusters at apex of column. Namaqualand, Cape Province.

Crassula tecta Thunb.

A small growing species, somewhat branched and closely set, fleshy semi-circular or boat-shaped leaves, dark green and covered with short but thick white hairs. Flowers white. South West Africa and Cape Province.

Crassula tetragona L.

Resembling a miniature pine tree. An erect shrubby plant, with few branches, slender and roundish. Leaves spindle-shaped, set closely together. Flower small and white. Eastern Cape Province.

GREENOVIA is also closely related to Aeonium and endemic to the Canary Islands.

Greenovia aurea (C. Sm.) Webb et Berth.

Forms close clusters with cup-shaped rosettes which tend to close tight during resting season. Leaves thin, spatulate and bluntly rounded at the tips, bluish-green, pruinose. Flower deep yellow.

Greenovia dodrantalis (Willd.) Webb et Berth.

Dainty rosettes forming clusters with numerous spoon-shaped leaves, vivid bluish-green with waxy surface. Flower bright yellow.

KALANCHOË is a genus of tremendous variety. Since *Bryophyllum* and *Kitchingia* have become merged with *Kalanchoë*, classification has divided the genus into three sections, Kitchingia, Bryophyllum and Kalanchoe. Species very widely distributed throughout many parts of the tropical and sub-tropical world – those from the Americas will be considered elsewhere. This genus includes some of the most attractive succulents.

Kalanchoë beharensis Drake del Cast.

Tall slender stem, notched, becoming hard and woody, with brownish hairs. Leaves broadly arrow-shaped, lobed, fleshy, olive-green to dark green, brownish hairs on upper surface, whitish hairs on lower surface. Flowers yellowish-cream with purplish throat. Madagascar.

There are forms and varieties of this species – the forms involve the leaf colorations provided by the hairs. Some remain green or grey on the upper surface. Another varietal form, *K. beharensis* v. *glabra,* has wavy margins to the leaves, glaucous with no hairs, also from Madagascar. (Sect. Kalanchoë)

Kalanchoë beharensis

Kalanchoë beauverdii v. *beauverdii* Hamet

A climbing species with elongated leaves, blunt developing adventitious buds or 'plantlets' at the tip. Inflorescence has many flowers, deep violet or blackish-violet. S. Madagascar.

Other varieties occur of this species, varying on account of flower and fruit. (Sect. Bryophyllum)

Kalanchoë blossfeldiana v. Poelln.

Compact bushy plant, with erect stems and branches. Leaves glossy-green, small obovate, edged red, somewhat crenate towards apex. Flowers in clusters, bright red. Mont Tsaratanana, Madagascar. (Sect. Kalanchoë) This species has been used for hybridizing to produce some most popular houseplants in quite a range of colours.

Kalanchoë gastonis-bonnieri Hamet et Perr.

Large species, fleshy with large lanceolate leaves, margins coarsely crenate, surface whitish pruinose, especially on young growth. Flower pale pink. Endemic to Madagascar and also possibly Kenya. (Sect. Kalanchoë)

Kalanchoë grandiflora Wight et Arn.

Erect species with obovate toothed leaves, covered with bluish waxy coating. Flowers yellow. One of the finest species, somewhat rare. East Africa and Eastern India. (Sect. Kalanchoe)

Kalanchoë longiflora Schltr.

A robust erect species with 4-angled stems. Leaves oval to oblong and pronounced dentate in the upper part, very fleshy, pale grey-green or copper coloured. Flowers pale orange with slight fragrance. Natal. (Sect. Kalanchoë)

Kalanchoë mangani Hamet et Perr.

Numerous woody stems and branches forming a thick somewhat prostrate or pendent shrub. Small leaves, fleshy, obovate, dark green loosely arranged. Urn-shaped flowers brick red. Massiv of Andringitra, Madagascar. (Sect. Bryophyllum)

Kalanchoë marmorata Bak.

Stout fleshy stem, erect, branching usually from the base. Leaves obovate with scalloped margins, pinkish or bluish-green, grey pruinose and many brownish mottlings. Flowers elongated, white. Ethiopia. (Sect. Kalanchoë)

Kalanchoë pumila Bak.

Bushy plant with erect becoming prostrate growth. Has closely set obovate leaves crenate in the upper

Kalanchoë rhombopilosa

part, purplish-grey with covering of white bloom. Flowers at terminal end, pitcher shaped, reddish-violet or lilac. Popular species making excellent houseplant from central Madagascar. (Sect. Kalanchoë)

Kalanchoë rhombopilosa Mann. et Boit.

A small distinctive species, mostly erect and little branched. Small leaves somewhat triangular, rounded above, apex indented and sinuate, grey-green with silver and red markings. Flowers small, yellowish. There are other varieties of this species, *K. rhombopilosa* v. *alba* with wholly white leaves, and *K. rhombopilosa* v. *viridis* which has very thick, wider deep or fresh green leaves. Madagascar. (Sect. Kalanchoë)

Kalanchoë scapigera Welw.

An interesting and uncommon glabrous plant having thick stems and branches, with fleshy obovate leaves, margins entire, dark green or greyish-green. Leaves at apex of stems. Large red or orange-red flowers makes this one of the most beautiful of the genus. Socotra and parts of East Africa.

Kalanchoë thyrsiflora Harv.

Tall growing plant, up to 60 cm, with almost oval leaves densely arranged diagonally, light green, margins red. Stems and leaves are densely white pruinose. Flower urn-shaped, yellow. A very beautiful and desirable species from Transvaal, Cape Province. (Sect. Kalanchoë)

Kalanchoë tomentosa Bak.

Sometimes called the 'panda plant'. Has erect branching stems, densely leafy forming a compact shrub. Leaves spoon-shaped, entirely covered with white felt and the tips deep brown and dentate. There are a number of forms, some with small leaves, others having rather larger leaves than the species. Madagascar. (Sect. Kalanchoë)

Kalanchoë tuberosa Perr.

A rare species with mealy-white stems and leaves. Leaves dentate, wavy margins about 25 mm long. Flower deep pink or rose. Madagascar. (Sect. Kalanchoë)

Kalanchoë tubiflora (Harv.) Hamet

Tall-growing species with slender erect stems, rarely branched. Stems greenish-brown, glabrous. Leaves narrow and almost cylindrical, grooved on upper surface and plantlets forming at the apex, greyish-green with pinkish and purplish blotches. Flowers reddish to purple. A well-known species from Madagascar. (Sect. Bryophyllum)

Kalanchoë velutina Welw.

Fleshy stemmed species, somewhat creeping. Lower leaves ovate-lanceolate, upper leaves narrow and slightly rounded. All stems, branches, leaves and inflorescence short hairy, hence its name. Flower yellow to pink. From Tanzania, Angola and other parts of East Africa. (Sect. Kalanchoë)

MONANTHES—small shrubby plants with leaves crowded at ends of branches. Flowers inconspicuous, but a delicately attractive genus. All from Madeira and Canary Islands.

Monanthes brachycaulon (Webb et Berth.) Lowe

Small, shrubby, with lax rosettes. Leaves fleshy, spatulate, somewhat flat. Inflorescence minutely hairy giving the effect of a cobweb. Flowery white.

Monanthes polyphylla Haw.

Forms dense cushions of bluish-green rosettes, stems prostrate. Leaves small, club-shaped and flower red.

OROSTACHYS provides species from cooler areas,

but very attractive and unusual plants.

Orostachya chanetii (Lev.) Bgr.

Small, light green fleshy rosette. Leaves of two different lengths, greyish-green to brown and brownish, apex tipped with fine bristle. Flower in dense pyramidal panicle, white with reddish markings on sepals. China.

Orostachya spinosus (L.) Bgr.

A perennial species, grouping. Leaves form a strong rosette very similar to *Sempervivum*. Leaves obovate wedge-shaped with spiny apex, greyish-green. Long inflorescence with yellow flowers. East Asia.

SEDUM species seem numerous and are found in very many parts of the world including Britain and other parts of Europe, Africa, as well as the Americas, and these species are considered elsewhere. Many are relatively hardy, while others require certain protection from extreme cold and damp. For classification purposes the genus has been divided into sections and series, but these are not referred to in this record.

Sedum brevifolium D.C.

Low perennial forming cushions of minute ovate leaves, white pruinose, flushed red. White flowers on short stalks. Europe and Morocco.

Sedum dasyphyllum L.

Saxicolous—low perennial, not rosulate, small opposite rounded leaves, fleshy, bluish-green, with short hairs. Flowers white. North Africa and southern and western Europe. A number of varieties of the species are recorded which have only slight differences from the species.

Sedum sieboldii Sweet

A very graceful species with semi-pendent branches. Leaves sub-circular, set in whorls of three, glaucous blue, edged red. Flowers pink. Tends to lose all leaves and branches during resting season, then growing again from the base. There is also a beautiful variegated form whose green leaves have yellow, cream and pink markings. Endemic to Japan.

Sedum spurium Marsch. Bieb.

A rambling species, mat forming with thin reddish stems and many round green leaves, margins minutely hairy, rosulate. Flowers white, pink or red. Indigenous to Caucasus.

SEMPERVIVUM – rosette plants, forming cushions with colourful inflorescences of densely set flowers. Rosettes die after flowering. All are from mountainous regions of south and central Europe, Caucasus to Soviet Union, parts of Asia Minor and north Africa.

Sempervivum arachnoideum L.

Leaves forming small rosettes, covered with hairs creating a cobweb effect. Flowers pinkish or reddish.

Sempervivum ciliosum Craib.

Compact rosette, globose, with leaves ovate-lanceolate, greyish-green with margins and lower surface of the leaves ciliate. Flower yellowish.

Sempervivum tectorum L.

Many sub-species and varieties according to geographical distribution. The 'house-leek'. Ovate cuspidate leaves, grey-green, tipped red. Flowers reddish or green.

SINOCRASSULA are rosette forming species, minutely haired. Mostly perennial, some biennials. Endemic to the Himalayas through to China.

Sinocrassula yunnanensis (Franch.) Bgr.

Forming dense clusters of tight rosettes of many closely set fleshy pointed leaves, rounded on the back surface, dark green, finely papillose. Flowers whitish with red tips.

Others of the *Crassulaceae* are represented by rather obscure genera and/or isolated species, some are of consequence.

Afrovivella simensis (Hochst.) Bgr.

Small species with fleshy stem and many branches forming mats. Leaves in rosettes, oval and pointed with white spiny tip, and margins ciliate. Flower on long scape, in clusters, pink. Ethiopia.

Chiastophyllum oppositifolium (Ledeb.) Bgr.

A creeping succulent species very like *Umbilicus* – with roundish, oval leaves, somewhat dentate and narrowing at the base. Flower creamy-yellow. From high altitudes in the Caucasus.

Hypagophytum abyssinicum (Hochst.) Bgr.

An unusual and attractive species with slender cylindrical stems arising from tuberous base, jointed, glabrous. Fleshy oval leaves, red spotted margins. Flower whitish with reddish spots. Ethiopia.

Rochea coccinea (L.) D.C.

A much branched species with small pointed leaves on slender stems, closely set, green upper surface, red lower surface. Flowers numerous in cymes, scarlet. An attractive houseplant.

Rosularia glabra (Rgl. et Winkler) Bgr.

With elliptical or spoon-shaped leaves with pointed apex forming bright green rosette. Flowers on short stalks, yellowish red. Endemic to Turkestan.

There are several species of *Rosularia*; all are similar to Sempervivums and require similar culture but will not accept too much frost and snow.

Cucurbitaceae

The gourd family includes many fascinating and unusual genera, often with caudices, mostly creeping or climbing as vines, and often with very attractive fruits. While frequently the growth is of a succulent nature, it is generally considered the succulence lies in the root system – the tuber or caudex. There are exceptions where the succulent aspect is centred in the leaves. An uncommon family with a great number of rare and desirable species.

Acanthosicyos horrida Welw.

Has long fleshy taproot with a tall, erect, leafless stem. The name implies a thorny plant, and this species has long thorns in pairs along the stem. Flower yellowish green. Fruit spiny, edible. From coastal regions, South West Africa.

Corallocarpus tenuissimus Busc. et Musch.

A much-branched, erect plant often with angled stems, very succulent. Leaves palmate into lobes. Slender peduncle having several whitish-yellow flowers. Fruit smooth, fleshy and rounded. From arid areas of South Africa and Rhodesia.

Corallocarpus glomeruliflorus Schweinf.

With thick club-shaped caudex branching from apex. Elongated branches, upper branches hairy. Leaves broad and rounded with toothed margins and somewhat undulate. Flowers dioecious – small, yellowish-green. Orange fruits, small, egg-shaped and longitudinal lines. Endemic to the Yemen.

Dendrosicyos socotrana Balf. f.

Large tree-like species with swollen trunk and white bark. Thin, somewhat pendent spiny branches and thistle-shaped leaves, rather rounded and palmate, dentate margins, papillose both sides. Flowers yellowish and glandular hairy fruits. Island of Socotra. A very rare species.

Gerrardanthus macrorhizus Harv. l.c.

With urn-shaped almost round caudex to 30 cm diameter. Thin woody stems and branches, climbing. Leaves variable, triangular and lobed, sometimes rather rounded with pointed tip, thin but fleshy, darkish green. Flowers yellowish-brown. Fruit has obscure longitudinal angles, glabrous and smooth, becoming slender at the base. From arid regions of Kenya and Tanzania.

Kedostris africana (L.) Cogn.

Has become a well-known species. Large fleshy, whitish, tuberous root or caudex. Stems slender, climbing and branching. Leaves somewhat triangular in form, with lobes, fresh green, somewhat rough. Flower yellowish. Fruits deep orange, obscurely furrowed about 15 mm long, oval. Distributed throughout South and South West Africa and parts of East Africa.

Kedostris nana (Lam.) Cogn.

Tuberous rooted with long slender stems and branches, climbing or prostrate. Leaves heart-shaped, rounded apex, margins slightly undulate. Flowers yellowish, small. Fruit bright red, oval with rounded base, smooth, about 16 mm long. Endemic to South Africa.

Melothria punctata Cogn.

(syn. *Zehneria scabra* (L.f.) Sond.) With greenish-grey caudex branching from apex, somewhat woody, climbing with tendrils. Leaves ivy-shaped, rough and hairy. Flowers dioecious, yellowish. Small fruits, rounded and pointed at tip, crimson, 14 mm long. Widespread distribution in East and South Africa, parts of India, Malaysia and Philippines.

Momordica rostrata A. Zinn.

With fleshy succulent basal stem, irregularly ribbed. Branches thin, rambling, narrow palmate leaves. Flower deep yellow. Fruits somewhat spiny, pinkish-orange. Endemic to tropical East Africa.

Neoalsomitra podagrica Van Sten.

Beautiful vine-like succulent with stems spindle-shaped at the base-swellings have blunt thorns homologous to leaf bases. Branches also develop this characteristic, until leaves appear. Leaves simple, then 3 to 5-foliate. Flowers yellowish-green. Selabes.

Neoalsomitra sarcophylla (Roem.) Hutch.

A succulent vine with slender fleshy stems, much branched, cylindric and pendent. Leaves elliptic-ovate, three to each petiole, channelled, succulent. Flower rather insignificant, greenish-yellow, but they are numerous and attractive as such. Fruits smooth, obtusely 3-sided, sub-cylindric 5 cm long. A rare species of considerable merit from Philippines, Thailand and Burma.

Seyrigia humbertii Keraudr.

Vine-like slender stems, somewhat 4-angled, fleshy and covered with thick white wool arising from a rounded tuberous root. Has tendrils and very small pinkish-brown flowers. Fruits unknown. Madagascar.

Seyrigia gracilis Keraudr.

Tuberous root, rounded. Stems vine-like, slender and cylindrical, jointed branches with tendrils. Somewhat purplish-grey throughout. Flowers pale greenish-yellow. Fruits unknown. Madagascar.

Telfairia occidentalis Hook. f.

Stout caudex and fleshy roots. Climbing vine with rounded branches. Leaves 5-foliate, elliptic-ovate, many veins, margins dentate, bright green. Flowers small, whitish flushed purplish-red at throat. Fruits large and ovoid-oblong to about 60 cm long, deeply channeled or furrowed, greenish-yellow. A distinctive species from deserts of West Africa.

Telfairia pedata (Smith) Hook.

A thick tuberous, fleshy root. Stems woody, perennial, branching freely. Leaves 3 to 7-foliate, ovate-oblong tapering at tips, margins usually very dentate – upper surface smooth, lower surface rough. Flowers purplish. Fruit green, very large, furrowed. From the deserts of South and East Africa, Madagascar.

Xerosicyos danguyi Humb.

A climbing succulent with tendrils branching from the base, cylindrical stems. Leaves almost round, fleshy, margins entire. Flower small, whitish. Madagascar. Called the 'penny plant'.

Xerosicyos perrieri Humb.

A climbing species, smaller than *X. danguyi*, having cylindrical stems with alternate rounded, somewhat

Hoya multiflora (courtesy of Professor Rauh)

Old World

ABOVE *Trichocaulon cactiforme*

ABOVE *Edithcolea grandis* (courtesy of Professor Rauh)

BELOW *Pachypodium baronni* v. *windsori* (courtesy of Professor Rauh)

BELOW *Muiria leortenseae* (courtesy of Professor Rauh)

pointed greyish-green flat leaves, margins entire. Tendrils opposite leaves. Flowers small, white. Madagascar.

The family has become increasingly popular and undoubtedly many more species will become cultivated as greenhouse plants, if for no other reason on account of the beautiful fruits which frequently compensate for the insignificance of the flowers.

Didiereaceae

Contains a number of unusual succulents, all endemic to Madagascar. Some are now becoming available in cultivation, while others will remain comparatively rare for many years to come.

Alluaudia adscendens Drake

A spectacular species, tree-like to 12 m high. Thick, fleshy, becoming woody stem and few branches which are furnished with long conical thorns. Leaves rounded, somewhat heart-shaped. Long flower stalk with small insignificant flowers. Madagascar.

Alluaudia dumosa Drake

Large species with elongated stem, tree-like to 6 m high. Branches freely. Usually without leaves, but with few solitary fleshy thorns. Flower insignificant, male flower globose, female oblong. Madagascar.

Alluaudiopsis fiherenensis H. Humb. et P. Choux.

A tall graceful species rarely seen in cultivation. Elongated branches with solitary thorns. Leaves oblong-elliptical, sometimes more ovate, dark green. Inflorescence dichotomous with small flowers. Dioecious. Endemic to Madagascar.

Alluaudia procera Drake

The best-known of this genus, tree-like species up to 12 m or more high. Erect, few branches armed with longish thorns which widen towards the base. Leaves obovate, succulent—new leaves turned firstly horizontal, later vertical. Madagascar.

Other species of *Alluaudia* recorded are, *A. comosa* and *A. humbertii* which have many similar characteristics to those mentioned with individual peculiarities.

Decaryia madagascarensis Choux.

A tree with an erect trunk to 8 m high. Branches spreading with many thorny twigs, zig-zag, succulent and leaves rather small, sparse, fleshy, heart-shaped set under a pair of thorns, solitary. Flower small on short inflorescence. Endemic to Madagascar.

Didierea madagascarensis H. Baill.

An erect, tree-like species to 6 or 7 m high. Branches only few with thorns which are sometimes solitary, often dense from leaf cushions and basal tufts of obovate leaves. Flower small, on short stalks from the thorny leaf cushions. A peculiar species of a distinctive genus. Endemic to Madagascar.

Didierea mirabilis H. Baill.

Tree-like to 4 m high having very swollen trunk, resembling a caudex, often 60 cm wide. Erect and many branches spreading horizontally. Has dense leaf cushions, with long, sometimes curved, black thorns, linear leaves and male or female flowers. An extraordinary plant with apparently close relationship with *D. madagascarensis*. Madagascar.

Dioscoreaceae

Have one outstanding feature–the large caudex covered with corky-bark, irregularly distributed or in large raised wart-like protruberances. The caudex is fleshy and with age can grow to well over 1 m thick. The genus *Testudinaria* is sometimes considered synonymous with that of *Dioscorea*–and for this record they are being kept separate.

Testudinaria elephantipes (l'Her.) Lindl.

A popular and important species with large caudex and angled protruberances. Long vine-like growth, very branched with small green leaves, somewhat triangular or often 3-lobed. Flowers insignificant. A South African plant from near Kl. Kommaggas. Commonly known as 'The Elephant's Foot'.

Testudinaria sylvatica (Eckl.) Kunth

Caudex much flatter than *T. elephantipes*–often completely flat and having the appearance of being just dead wood. Stems tend to be deciduous, these are thin and elongated, branching freely with pronounced triangular leaves, and insignificant flowers. Endemic to many parts of South Africa.

Euphorbia horrida—one of the species often grown for house or office decoration.

Euphorbiaceae

Comprise one of the largest of all plant families, many of which are succulent. Very few families have so wide a distribution; 'spurges' are to be found the world over! Many diverse and unusual forms abound within the succulent species, all possessing the complicated flower structure typical of the Euphorbia, known as the cyanthium. While some species are bi-sexual, others are either male or female—and plants of both sexes are required to produce seeds. The fruit develops as a woody capsule containing three seeds, which when ripe are ejected with force. All species have milky sap; in some instances this can be exceedingly poisonous. Therefore great care must always be exercised in the handling of plants to ensure that the sap does not get into the eyes or open wounds. Other species are entirely harmless and in fact are used for animal fodder.

EUPHORBIA – the largest genus, has been divided into groups or sections for suitable classification, the main consideration being the peculiarities of the plant growth, not the flower. Extreme characteristics can be observed, from thorny bushes to giant columns resembling some cactus species– pencil-shaped stems to completely globular plants. Many species are armed with strong thorns, others are totally thornless.

Euphorbia abdelkuri Balf. f.

A very rare species with dark grey-green stems

A typical succulent Euphorbia showing the similarity of some species in this genus with true cacti.

Euphorbia altrispina—fairly typical of the thorny succulent Euphorbias.

A very dwarf succulent Euphorbia.

and many branches. These are generally cylindrical with no thorns and possibly leafless. Young plants tend to develop with rather different growth, with wrinkled grey-green stems somewhat ribbed with pronounced angles and marginal protuberances. Abd al Kuri, Socotra.

Euphorbia aeruginosa Schweick.
Branches bluish-grey or brownish-green with many brownish spines. Rounded stems, somewhat spirally twisted. A rare species from Transvaal.

Euphorbia bupleurifolia Jacq.
Usually with simple caudex, sometimes branching from the base with terminal leaves. Generally deciduous. Inflorescence on long stalk with greenish-yellow flowers. Cape Province and Natal.

Euphorbia cap-saintemariensis Rauh
A dwarf species growing from a large tuberous root system. Branches freely from the crown of the tuber, nearly 1 cm thick, rounded or slightly angled and with scars from deciduous leaves, greyish-white. Leaves from the terminal forming a rosette –narrow, undulate and curved inwards along the margins. Inflorescences bear 2 to 4 cyathia. From **limestone rock at Cap Sainte Marie, Madagascar.**

Euphorbia crispa (Haw.) Sweet
A rare perennial species with caudex root system, branching from the base. Leaves on long stalks, narrow, tapering, minutely haired. Margins undulate. A rare species from Van Rhynsdorp and Calvinia Div., Cape Province.

Euphorbia decidua Bally & Leach

An unusual species with top-shaped caudex branching from the apex. Branches short, usually 3-angled and very spiny–and deciduous. Little known in cultivation, but of easy culture and attractively miniature. Endemic to Rhodesia and possibly Malawi formerly Nyasaland.

Euphorbia delphinensis Ursch et Leandri.

A thorny shrub, much branched, ovate leaves with pronounced veins and undulated margins. An easily cultivated species with green flowers. Fort Dauphin, Madagascar.

Euphorbia francoisi J. Leandri

A low species with large tuberous root. Stems from the base, cylindrical with small spines. Leaves at terminal ends, undulate, tapering. Fort Dauphin, Madagascar.

Euphorbia genoudiana Ursch et Leandri

An interesting thorny bush with cylindrical stem and branching freely. Leaves pale green, small and elongated, usually in groups. Inflorescence with long peduncle with greenish-yellow cyathia. Mahafaly, Madagascar.

Euphorbia grandicornis Goebel.

An outstanding species, large growing with spiny 3-angled stems, wing-like, with deep constrictions forming 'waists'. Angles curved and wavy with hard marginal edge. Stout spines, usually in pairs. A spectacular plant. Natal.

Euphorbia lophogona Lam.

Shrubby species with many terminal leaves. Stem and branches tend to thicken towards the apex, very angled with attractive pink flowers. Fort Dauphin, Madagascar.

Euphorbia milii de Moulin. (syn. *Euphorbia splendens*)

One of the best-known of the Euphorbias, some times called 'Crown of Thorns' and used as a house-plant. Shrubby plant, very spiny and leafy–with red flowers in profusion. Of easy culture. West and Madagascar. There are other forms and varieties of this species with slightly varying growth and different coloured flowers.

Euphorbia obesa Hook. f.

A popular and well-known species–spherical in shape with broad ribs creating shallow furrows. Beautifully marked with many reddish-brown and dark green lines running transverse and longitudin-ally–almost plaid-like. Plants dioecious. Graaff Reinet Div. Cape Province.

Euphorbia oncoclada Drake

A totally spineless species, erect cylindrical stems, frequently divided into small joints or constrictions. Stems covered with leaf scars slightly indented.

Euphorbia milii (syn. *E. splendens*)

Euphorbia obesa

Small leaves, quickly deciduous. An uncommon species from Ejeda and Saint Augustin, Madagascar.

Euphorbia opuntioides N. E. Br.

Resembling an Opuntia. Branches from the base with fleshy flattened and somewhat elongated joints with slightly crenate margins and few insignificant slender spines. Pungo Andongo, near Candumba, Lower Guinea. Very rare in cultivation.

Euphorbia pachypodioides Boit.

Resembling a Pachypodium, erect with fleshy club-shaped stems and terminal leaves and inflorescence with deep red flowers. Little known in cultivation, lime-hills in Ankarana, West Madagascar.

Euphorbia poissoni Pax

A branching species, very succulent with cylindrical stems and branches, 3–5 cm thick, somewhat tubercled, without thorns and greyish-green. Leaves at apex of branches, long and narrow. An unusual and rare species from the area of Jose, northern Nigeria and other West African countries.

Euphorbia squarrosa Haw.

A low and very spiny succulent species with caudex. Has many spreading and procumbent stems, usually 3-angled, dark green – frequently twisted, with greyish spines from the tubercles along margins. Kingswilliamstown Div. Cape Province.

Euphorbia trigona Haw.

An attractive tree-like erect plant, 3 or 4-angled, wing-like, dark green with white mottling. Margins with spines. Branches freely from the main stem. South West Africa.

Euphorbia turbiniformis Chiov.

One of the most unique species, a miniature with a top-shaped root and flat-rounded stem about 4 cm diameter. Has central growing point with very small cyathium on short peduncles. Not an easy plant in cultivation. Migiurtinia Province of Somalia.

Euphorbia unispina N. E. Br.

Somewhat similar in many respects of *E. poissoni*, with cylindrical stems and branching freely, with few thick leathery leaves crenate and notched at the apex, spreading at branch terminals. Stems with solitary spines. Generally distributed in West Africa – northern Nigeria and the Congo.

Euphorbia xylophylloides Ad. Brogn. ex Lem.

An arborescent species with roundish stem, branching with compressed, almost flattened erect branches and joints, rounded at the apex. Small leaves develop but are quickly deciduous. Endemic to Madagascar.

MONADENIUM have many similarities to Euphorbia and are well represented throughout East and South Africa, many central territories and coastal regions.

Monadenium coccineum Pax

An erect species, usually branching with 5-angled stems, greenish-purple. Leaves glabrous and pos-

Monadenium coccineam

sibly deciduous. Flower bright red. From Tanzania north of Lake Eyassi in North Province, Masai Dist. on stony slopes.

Monadenium lugardae N. E. Br.

Fleshy, cylindrical stems, glabrous and spineless, somewhat tessellated. Leaves form loose rosette at terminal ends, fleshy, obovate and serrated on marginal tips. Greenish flower.

Monadenium stapelioides Pax

Stems usually erect or semi-erect, cylindrical and generally unbranched. All stems have spirally arranged tubercles and leaf scar. Leaves near to apex, obovate and tapering towards the base. Flower greenish and pinkish-white. From many parts of tropical East Africa.

Monadenium stellatum Bally

A most unusual species, with single erect stems, cylindrical with many longitudinal grooves and pronounced tubercles, resembling stalks, horizontal from the stem. These are tipped with leaf scars and a few short spines. Leaves glabrous, deciduous, tapering towards the base, undulate towards the apex. Greenish-white flowers.

SYNADENIUM – a small group of tree-like succulents, very much branched with many large leaves, evergreen in habitat, but sometimes deciduous in cultivation.

Synadenium capulare (Boiss.) L. C. Wheeler

A large shrub up to 2 m high with many succulent branches having numerous leaf scars. Wide wedge-shaped leaves, somewhat ovate, bright green. The inflorescence is branched with yellowish-green flowers. A very poisonous plant from Sheba Valley in the Transvaal, also Natal and Swaziland.

Synadenium grantii Hook. f.

The best known of this genus, tall and erect with many branches. Large bright green leaves, ovate-spatulate, margins finely dentate. Flower brownish-red. Uganda, Tanzania and Rhodesia.

There is a most beautiful variety, *S. grantii* v. *rubra*, with all the characteristics of the species, but with maroon-red leaves.

Geraniaceae

Has representation with two genera – of reasonably easy culture, often deciduous, but having very succulent stems and branches.

Pelargonium echinatum Curt.

Small growing species with erect fleshy branches, having many prominent stipules. Leaves 3 to 5-lobed somewhat rounded with crenate margins, greyish and rather hairy, on long stalk. Flowers on long peduncle, purple. Endemic to many parts of South Africa.

Pelargonium juttae Dtr.

Small growing species developing large caudex base. Branches freely on short stems with leaves on long stalks, dissected, semi-pinnate with hairy surface. A rare species from South West Africa in Otavi region.

Pelargonium paradoxum Dtr.

A very succulent species with thickened rounded fleshy stems with many leaf scars, light green or yellowish. Leaves develop near the tips of the branches, narrow and fleshy with curled and deeply crenate margins, grey-green and having short hairs. Flowers whitish in umbels. Gr. Namaland in South West Africa.

Pelargonium sidifolium (Thumb.) Knuth

Similar to *P. echinatum*, but having no stipules. An easily grown species which branches freely with 3 to 5-lobed leaves, margins crenate. Flowers small, reddish-purple in clusters. Transvaal.

Pelargonium tetragonum (L.f.) l'Her.

A well-known succulent species, erect with thin angled stems, fleshy, pale green. Leaves 5-lobed, heart-shaped and crenate margins. Deciduous. Flowers pink and purple on long stalks. South Africa.

Sarcocaulon burmannii (D.C.) Sweet emend. Rehm.

Miniature bushy plant with many thick, somewhat spiny, greyish-green branches, small irregularly indentated leaves and pinkish white flowers. Bushmanland, South Africa.

Sarcocaulon l'heritieri (D.C.) Sweet.

Slender-stemmed dwarf shrub having many thin white spiny branches. Leaves are elongated heart-shaped, bright green. Small yellowish-white flowers. From the border of the Namib, South West Africa.

Sarcocaulon multifidum R. Knuth

A beautiful miniature plant with thick branches growing horizontally. Stem without spines, leaves developing in small tufts, hairy, greyish-green. Flowers on long stalk, pink – much larger than the leaves. South West Africa in mountainous country.

Sarcocaulon rigidum Schinz.

Several varieties of this species, with differing characteristics dependent upon habitat conditions. The species is a spreading miniature shrub, very succulent stem and very spiny branches. Leaves all along the stems, 2-lobed, deciduous. Flower scarlet with narrow petals. From the coastal region east of Luederitzbay, S.W. Africa.

Gesneriaceae

Streptocarpus saxorum Engl.

Stems very succulent with dark rich green fleshy leaves and large purplish flowers, Tanzania. Less succulent species include *S. kirkii* Hook. f. and

S. hirsutissimus E. A. Bruce both endemic to tropical Africa.

Gnetaceae

Includes one of the most extraordinary plants known.

Welwitschia bainesii (Hook. f.) Carr.

This legendary plant is from the desert areas of South West Africa and Angola. Endemic to coastal regions where its main sustenance is derived from the surface dew which settles daily, the result of hot days and cold nights. Has huge thick woody caudex and long tap-root with two thick and fleshy succulent leaves, strap-like to 6 m long, glaucous, and waxy-green, with parallel veins, growing from the base, not the apex. Inflorescence cone-like on stalk, female green, male reddish-brown.

Icacinaceae

Includes two genera of curious plants, the species of which have a large caudex with only small flowers of little consequence.

Pyrenacantha malvifolia Engl.

A species with very large caudex, often deformed, sometimes over 1 m diameter. Thickish stems develop from the apex of the caudex having only few leaves, flowers very small. Dioecious – fruits on female plants orange-red. Tanzania.

Pyrenacantha vitifolia Engl.

A rare species having very large thickened, caudex-like rhizomes. Many branches, clambering, with brownish-green skin. Leaves somewhat round, deeply lobed, dark green, deciduous. Flowers small from branch terminals. This species is also dioecious – female plants have orange fruits. Kenya.

Trematosperma cordatum Urb.

A succulent caudiciform, caudex up to 25 cm diameter, greyish. Few cylindrical fleshy branches with many small hairs. Leaves heart-shaped, elongated and prominent veins. Flowers insignificant. Somalia.

Labiatae

A large family of herbaceous plants embracing the mints. A few can be included as succulents and these are mainly found in Africa, but have their counterparts elsewhere.

Aeolanthus repens Oliv.

Of creeping habit, sometimes becoming semi-erect, stems somewhat angled and hairy. Small elongated fleshy leaves and purple flowers. Fairly well distributed in tropical Africa.

Plectranthus prostratus Gurke

Low growing pubescent species with many soft branches. Leaves thick, soft and crenate about 14 mm long. Flowers in raceme, purple. Tanzania. Many others of this genus are borderline succulents, perhaps *P. fischeri* Gurke is the only species deserving mention as truly succulent.

Leguminosae

Is one of the larger plant families with genera represented the world over. It is remarkable that one genus only contains a succulent species.

Dolichos seineri Harms.

A plant almost unknown in cultivation. Has very large caudex, very fleshy. Stems form a bushy habit to about 1 m high. Leaves in triplets, minutely hairy, soft. Flowers in racemes, very beautiful, bluish, like butterflies. North Hereroland and other regions of South West Africa.

Neorautenenia ficifolia (Benth.) C. A. Smith

Has large fleshy caudex, somewhat elongated with rough bark-like surface. Pale green leaves, tripartite, soft with prominent veins. Flowers small, pale yellow. Transvaal, South Africa. This is representative of just a few of the same genus which have been introduced into cultivation in recent years, and all have similar characteristics and are possibly synonymous.

Liliaceae

Is represented by several genera – species are indigenous to many parts of Africa and Madagascar, also some of the off-shore islands. *Aloes* in many species abound, some growing to 4 m or more, yet at the other extreme several are constant miniatures. Many are found on rock-faces in arid conditions, others where rainfall is high – some are climbers

A collection of mainly Arabian Aloes.

A strikingly marked but as yet unnamed Aloe species.

while others have almost pendent habit, so diverse is this genus. Species of Liliaceae provide considerable interest – and with very few exceptions all are of easy culture.

Aloe albiflora Guill.
(syn. *Guillauminia albiflora*.)
Small clumping species with compact rosettes. Long narrow leaves, tapering at apex, grey-green with many small white spots, margins with many closely set soft whitish teeth. Inflorescence simple with delicate white flowers, scented. An outstanding species from Fort Dauphin Div. Madagascar.

Aloe aristata Haw.
Small grouping species with dense rosette of dark green leaves with scattered white spots. Inflorescence usually branched with lax reddish flowers. A well-known attractive species from South Africa.

Aloe cooperi Bak.
Plants usually solitary, but often clumping with grass-like leaves, long slender, fresh-green with

sometimes few spots near base. Leaves usually deciduous. Inflorescence simple, with conical raceme and pinkish and green flowers. Widely distributed in South Africa, Cape Province to Natal.

Aloe distans Haw.

A popular, well-known creeping species with many base offsets. Forms fleshy rosette, leaves bluish-green with whitish spots on both surfaces, and usually 3 teeth near apex on lower surface, margins with yellowish teeth. Inflorescence dichotomously branched, densely flowering with reddish blooms. West Cape Province.

Aloe doei Lavr.

Plants usually solitary. Rosette medium with dull green leaves with occasional white markings, margins with reddish-brown teeth. Inflorescence usually 3-branched with conical raceme and flowers, yellow covered with white hairs–a feature of many of the South Arabian species. This is from arid foothills in the Subhaihi country.

Aloe ferox Mill.

Tall growing species with stem simple, often to 5 m high. Thick sword-shaped leaves with somewhat spiny upper surface and more so on the back–margins with reddish or brown teeth. Single inflorescence with branches–large reddish-orange flower, dense, cylindrical. Widely distributed throughout South Africa.

Aloe haemanthifolia Berg.

So named on account of its resemblance to Haemanthus. A very rare species, stemless, with wide thick bluish-green leaves, rounded at apex. Grows at high altitudes on steep slopes. Inflorescence simple with red flowers. From high mountains near Frenchhoek, Cape Province.

Aloe haworthioides Bak.

Small stemless species to about 5 cm wide. Thin tapering leaves form dense rosette, leaves with prominent white markings on upper and lower surfaces and small white marginal spines. One of the most attractive of the genus but with somewhat insignificant orange-red flower from simple inflorescence. Central Madagascar.

Aloe humilis (L.) Mill.

Small-growing species forming clusters. Rosettes about 7 cm, leaves glaucous-green, tubercled with irregular white prickles, margins with soft white teeth. Inflorescence simple, scarlet flowers. East Cape Province.

Aloe longistyla Bak.

Stemless compact rosette about 22 cm wide. Leaves glaucous, lanceolate, both surfaces with whitish spines, margins with white teeth. Short inflorescence, simple, dense raceme with pinkish-red flowers. Central and south-eastern regions of Cape Province, South Africa.

Aloe parvula Berg.

Stemless rosette with blackish-green leaves with darkish spots, margins with softish white teeth. Inflorescence simple, lax raceme with reddish flowers. A beautiful species from central Madagascar.

Aloe polyphylla Schonl. ex Pill.

A very rare and unusual species. Short stem forming spirally ascending rosette. Leaves grey-green, back surface with keel, margins with pale teeth. Inflorescence branched with greenish flowers having purplish tip. Basutoland.

Aloe rauhii Reyn.

Another miniature species with grey-green leaves and numerous H-shaped spots. An open rosette with spreading leaves, margins with minute white teeth. Inflorescence simple with loose cylindrical raceme, flower rose-scarlet. On sandstone rock in south-west region of Madagascar.

Aloe suzannae D. Dec.

Tall growing species of particular charm with leathery dark greyish-green leaves, slightly roughened, margins with brownish teeth. Inflorescence simple with cylindrical raceme, very elongated, with dense yellowish-rose flowers. As a young plant it is exceptionally attractive. Southwest Madagascar.

Aloe tenuior Haw.

A 'climbing' species in bushes with branches to 3 m long. Thin stems, losing its leaves near the base, and forming loose terminal rosette. Leaves glaucous-green with no markings, margins with white edge and teeth. Raceme cylindrical and tapering towards apex, flowers yellow. Eastern Cape Province.

Aloe variegata L.

Stemless species with many offsets and forming

Aloe polyphylla—the example below shows the typical spiral arrangement of the rosette—a character it seldom develops in cultivation (above).

clumps. Leaves in three ranks, lanceolate, lower surface keeled, dark green with whitish spots and markings, usually in transverse bands. Margins with small white teeth. Inflorescence simple, sometimes branched, loose cylindrical raceme. The 'partridge breasted aloe'. Cape Province.

CHAMAEALOE is a monotypic genus of consequence, closely related to Aloe.
Chamaealoe africana (Haw.) Bgr.
Small rosette, grouping freely. Long slender pale green leaves with whitish spots on lower surface and margins with soft white teeth. Inflorescence simple, flowers greenish-white. Southern Cape Province.

169

GASTERIA contains many and varied species, many of which are most difficult to determine, to a degree due to the remarkable differences which occur between young plants and mature ones. Gasterias very easy cross-pollinate, and in consequence many of the plants in cultivation are very likely hybrids and there is little opportunity to know the parentage. All are very attractive and suitable as house-plants. Care must be taken not to presume correct naming. Only few can be easily recognized.

Gasteria armstrongii Schoenl.

A striking and sought-after species of character. Usually stemless, with thick glabrous leaves, sometimes almost as wide as long, mostly prostrate forming a rosette about 10 cm diameter. Leaves blackish-green or brownish, with whitish or green

Gasteria batesiana Rowl.

One of the most outstanding and readily recognized species. Somewhat spiral rosette of triangulate-lanceolate leaves, very stiff and 3-angled, with keel on back surface. Leaves darkish or olive-green with numerous greenish-white dots creating a roughened surface. Inflorescence reddish. Zululand.

Gasteria liliputana Poelln.

A usually stemless species with rosette spirally arranged. A charming miniature plant, forming groups. Narrow oblong-lanceolate leaves of dark green, with a definite keel on the under-side, greenish-white irregular spots on the upper surface, margins serrate, whitish. Inflorescence red. From Peddie Road, near Grahamstown, Cape Province. tubercles, margins with sharp keel towards the apex. Flower pinkish-red. Cape Province.

There are several others which merit reference and can be considered distinctive species – *G. poellnitziana* Jacobs., *G. maculata* (Thunbg.) Haw., *G. verrucosa* (Mill.) Duv. can be recommended.

HAWORTHIA consists of a great number of species and varieties with varying forms and peculiarities, usually of clustering habit, but few remain solitary. The genus has been divided into many sections to enable better grouping of these complex species. All are of mainly miniature growth. Flower rather insignificant, usually whitish, rarely yellow.

Haworthia blackburniae Bark.

Has loose rosette of narrow leaves, almost grass-like but firm, dark green and slightly grooved on the upper surface. Lower surface with blunt keel and margins with hard teeth. A desirable and sought-after species, but rarity makes it uncommon in cultivation. Oudtschoorn Div. Cape Province.

Haworthia bolusii Bak.

A very beautiful species with dense rosette of numerous incurved pale green leaves with terminal bristles. Upper surface with numerous lines, back surface keeled – margins and keel with long soft teeth and white bristles. Other species have similar characteristics, *H. setata* and its varieties in particular. Western parts of the Karoo, Cape Province.

Haworthia cooperi Bak.

A well-known and quickly grouping species. Pale green leaves, fleshy, oblong-lanceolate, with transparent green lines on both surfaces, margins very minutely toothed, keeled on back surface. From Somerset East, Cape Province.

Haworthia limifolia Marl.

Another very distinctive species together with the several varieties and forms which have their own peculiar characteristics. Firm rosette with shortish triangular leaves abruptly taper towards the apex. Leaves are greyish-green with many longitudinal lines and tubercles in transverse lines, keeled on the back surface. Still a rare species of great attraction. Cape Province and Transvaal.

Haworthia marumiana Uit.

Leaves dark-green obovate to oblong lanceolate, tapering to terminal bristle. Upper surface with transparent lines and pellucid spots, usually oblong in shape, between the lines. Back surface with two keels. Leaf margins and keels have transparent teeth. From Ladysmith, Cape Province.

Haworthia maughanii v. Poelln.

A fitting partner to *H. truncata* – leaves form a rosette with the tips flattened, greyish-green, roughened by minute tubercles. L. Karroo, Cape Province.

Haworthia obtusa v. pilifera forma truncata Jacobs.

There are several forms and varieties of *H. obtusa*, and this is one of particular note equalled only by *H. obtusa v. dielsiana*. Leaves form tight rosette, are abruptly truncate, no keel, rounded with smooth margins or only minute teeth and no bristle at apex. From Kingswilliamstown, Cape Province.

Haworthia reinwardtii (S.D.) Haw.

An outstanding species with several varietal forms. With spirally arranged leaves forming an elongated rosette, leaves darkish-green with many white or greenish tubercles. Well-known in cultivation–all varieties are of decided interest. Cape Province.

Much space would be required to record all members of this genus; those quoted are only a very small cross-section and omit many deserving of mention. An excellent group of plants for the amateur collector.

Certain other genera closely allied to *Haworthia* require to be mentioned here:

POELLNITZIA is separated from Haworthia and Astroloba because of the flower characteristics– only one species is included, but there is also a variety on record.

Poellnitzia rubiflora (L. Bol.) Uitew.

Dense-leafed rosette with elongated stems, offsetting from the base. Thick triangular leaves, blue-green or greyish, lower surface keeled, margins and keel with minute teeth. Long flower spike with orange-red flowers more similar to an Aloe. Southern Cape Province.

Haworthia truncata Schoenl.

Has a number of recognized forms, all with distichously arranged leaves, erect but sometimes curved inwards, darkish or greyish-green, both surfaces tubercled. The tips of the leaves appear as if they have been cut off and are completely flat. A desirable and rare species from Oudtshoorn Div. Cape Province.

Haworthia uitewaaliana Poell.

With dark-green or greyish-green leaves, elongated and incurved towards the tip. Back surface with keel from near the base, keel and margins set with thick whitish tubercles. Cape Province, Namaqualand.

BOWIEA, a bulbous group of succulents usually with very thin or threadlike stems, trailing or climbing. The onion-like bulb which remains exposed on the surface is a feature of the genus.

Bowiea volubilis Harv. ex Hook.

Very large bulbs, dividing and developing groups, almost round and light green. Has long thin trailing stems with insignificant thin leaves and small greenish-white flowers. Rampant growing from early spring until late summer, then stems tend to wither and dry back. Endemic to South Africa.

BULBINE, an interesting genus of fleshy and very succulent plants generally having bright yellow flowers, rarely orange-red. In cultivation some are winter growing and flowering.

Bulbine frutescens L.

Has thin, cylindrical, soft, grass-green leaves from elongated stems, forming lax clusters. Flower bright yellow, but there are other forms, one with white flowers and another with orange-red flowers described *B. frutescens* 'Hallmark' Rowl. n. cv. Ashingtonia I:8 (1973) whose origin is still undecided. From East London, Cape Province.

Bulbine mesembryanthoides Haw.

A real miniature with small caudex–deciduous in winter. Leaves only to 15mm long, bright green and thickish, almost mimicking some of the stemless mesembryanthemums. Flower on slender stem, golden-yellow. Namaqualand, Cape Province.

BULBINOPSIS

An Australian group very similar to the *Bulbines* of Africa, originally included in *Bulbine*.

Bulbinopsis semibarbata Haw.

A supposed annual species, but continuity can sometimes be obtained by rooting of cuttings. Loose inflorescence with yellow flowers. Easily grown from seeds. Endemic to Australia.

LOMATOPHYLLUM are closely related to the genus *Aloe*, usually forming branches with rosettes. All known species are from Madagascar and the island of Mauritius.

Lomatophyllum citreum Guill.

Stemless plants with dark green leaves recurved and forming loose rosette. Margins with triangular shaped teeth. Very attractive yellowish flowers.

Lomatophyllum macrum (Haw.) Salm. ex Roem, et Schult.

Large-growing species with sword-like leaves,

tapering at the apex, bright green, margins with small red teeth. Flower reddish.

Lomatophllum orientale Perr.
Short-stemmed species with few leaves, elongated with marginal spines. Inflorescence simple with yellowish-red flowers.

Lomatophyllum sociale Perr.
Species with many branches and loose rosette. Leaves elongated, narrowing at the base, dull green or reddish. Flowers carmine-red, fruits form berry-like in clusters.

SCILLA includes many bulbous species, some of which are very well-known in cultivation and are indeed considered hardy plants. Certain species have become recognised as succulents.

Scilla pauciflora
Small bulbous plant, suckering freely. Leaves fleshy, pale green with deeper green markings. Flowers greenish. South Africa.

Scilla socialis
Large bulb, very swollen base, suckering from the base with wide, short dark green fleshy leaves with many pale blotches and markings. Flower greenish-blue. South Africa.

Scilla violacea
Small bulbous species with swollen base, suckering freely. With slender fleshy leaves, upper surface, olive-green with silver markings. Under surface, brownish-red. Flowers small, greenish-blue. South Africa.

Other bulbous or semi-bulbous succulents could well be included—the problem exists as to when to distinguish between a bulb, as such, and a succulent. The genera *Chortolirion, Litanthus* and *Drimia* are possibly border-line cases. Only one is worthy of particular note.

DRIMIA Jacq. with dense fleshy leaves from the base, forming a somewhat scaly bulb.

Drimia haworthioides Bak.
Species with elongated succulent leaves from the base about 20 mm long and 2 mm thick, dark green on upper surface, purplish grey on back surface. Leaves deciduous in resting period. Flowers from long stem, greenish-yellow or greenish-white. Endemic to South Africa.

Mesembryanthemaceae

Provides one of the outstanding representations of African flora—sometimes referred to as *Aizoaceae*, and *Ficoidaceae*. Whichever record is accepted, the designation, *Mesembryanthemum*, will always be respected. Distribution widespread. From north eastern Africa, through tropical East Africa and down to Cape Province and from tropical West Africa to South West Africa, and Australia and elsewhere. A great number of genera are involved, far too many to detail, but certain representative genera and species will receive attention and brief descriptions given. Mesembryanthemums have many forms—the leaves are always very succulent whether they are shrubby species or stemless. Flowers are 'daisy-like' and generally of easy culture.

ALOINOPSIS—dwarf species, with tuberous roots. Many leaf forms, but with few exceptions all are tuberculate. Includes about 17 species.

Aloinopsis malherbei (L. Bol.) L. Bol.
Leaves erect, fan-shape, truncate at tip, upper surface flat and back surface convex, margins and surfaces tuberculate. Flower brownish. Cape Province.

Aloinopsis peersii (L. Bol.) L. Bol.
Thick fleshy roots. Leaves 2 or 4 together, upper surface flat, back surface rounded, bluish-green. Flower yellow. Cape Province.

ARGYRODERMA—stemless plants, caespitose, rarely only one growth. Leaves ovate or semi-cylindrical, smooth and glabrous. Well over 50 species are recorded, but many of these have close resemblances to one another.

Argyroderma framessi L. Bol.
Caespitose, growths with 2 leaves, upper surface oval, back surface roundish, smooth, blue-green. Flower pinkish-purple. Cape Province.

Argyroderma roseum (Haw.) Scheant.
Species with 1 or 2 growths. Leaves together at base and united half-way up, upper surface flat, lower surface convex, smooth, blue-green. Flower deep rose. Cape Province.

BERGERANTHUS—stemless plants forming clusters,

leaves semi-cylindrical with keel, smooth. Includes about 12 species.

Bergeranthus scapiger (Haw.) N. E. Br.
Freely suckering, leaves forming loose rosette, 12 cm long, pronounced edges, smooth, dark green. Flower golden-yellow. Cape Province.

Bergeranthus jamesii L. Bol.
More compact and low growing with thick fleshy leaves, sword-like, upper surface flat, back surface has sharp keel, greenish-blue. Flower yellowish. Cape Province.

BROWNANTHUS – an interesting and unusual genus, rather rare in cultivation. Much branched, erect often with nodes along the stems; only about 6 species are known.

Brownanthus ciliatus (Ait.) Schwant.
Dwarf species, with many internodes giving the effect of being segmented. Leaves short and narrow. Flowers small, white. Cape Province.

Brownanthus pubescens (N. E. Br.) Bull.
Low-branching plant with spreading stems and internodes, leaves slender, erect, sub-cylindrical covered with small papillae. Flower white. South West Africa.

CARPOBROTUS a well-known genus, many species of which are semi-hardy in Britain, and completely hardy in southern Europe. Much used for ground cover. Usually 2-angled, branches prostrate and very stout leaves, 3-angled. About 20 species.

Carpobrotus acinaciformis (L.) L. Bol.
Two-angled stems with short branches. Leaves fleshy, thick, sword-shaped, edges slightly rough, pale greyish-green. Flower large, carmine. Cape Province.

Carpobrotus edulis (L.) N. E. Br.
Leaves 3-angled on elongated branches, spreading. This species is known as the 'Hottentot Fig', the fruits of which are eaten in South Africa. Widely distributed throughout the world as a naturalized plant, flowers large in a number of colours, reddish, yellow, pinkish and purple. Cape Province.

CEPHALOPHYLLUM are mostly prostrate plants, often caespitose, leaves in tufts, mostly elongated and angled and includes over 70 species.

Carpobrotus edulis

Cephalophyllum alstonii Marl.
Prostrate species, leaves in tufts, erect, generally sub-cylindrical with somewhat flattened upper surface to about 7 cm long, grey-green. Flowers very beautiful, deep red. Cape Province.

Cephalophyllum cupreum L. Bol.
Prostrate creeping species, strong and fleshy. Leaves short, narrow and thick, tapering sharply with obscure keel, pale green. Very large flower, brownish-red and yellow. Cape Province.

Cephalophyllum serrulatum L. Bol.
Prostrate growing. Leaves 75 mm long, flat on upper surface, keeled on back surface, becoming rounded, margins serrulate, bright green. Flower small, purplish-pink. Cape Province.

CHEIRIDOPSIS species have many forms, from elongated leaf-pairs to small obovate pairs, which dry back during resting period and form a sleeve for the following leaf-pairs. Includes over 90 species.

Cheiridopsis candidissima (Haw.) N. E. Br.
Much spreading species forming cushions. Growths with 1 to 2 pairs of leaves, boat-shaped, flat upper surface, back surface rounded at lower end, then keeled, silver-grey. Flowers pale pink. Cape Province.

Cheiridopsis meyeri N. E. Br.
Short-stemmed, much-branched miniature species with small obovate leaves, light greyish-green, and numerous dark dots. Upper surface nearly flat, back surface semi-cylindrical, keel towards the apex. Flowers yellowish. Cape Province.

Cheirdopsis peculiaris N. E. Br.
A distinctive species usually with one growth and 1–2 leaf pairs. Lower pair usually prostrate, to 5 cm long and 3 cm wide, grey-green. Succeeding growth at first erect with flat upper surface, rounded, keeled on back surface, thick, smooth. Flower yellow. Cape Province.

Cheiridopsis tuberculata (Mill.) N. E. Br.
Stemless with long narrow leaves, united at the base into a sheath or sleeve. Upper surface flat, back surface rounded and keeled towards the blunted tip, bluish-green. Flower yellow. Cape Province.

CONICOSIA have many stems and branches, spreading or ascending, often with a caudex-like root. Ten species are recorded.

Conicosia muirii N. E. Br.
Large fleshy caudex to 40 cm diameter. Stems prostrate, creeping, leaves long and narrow with a grooved surface, purplish-green. Flowers lemon-yellow. Cape Province.

Conicosia communis (Edwards) N. E. Br.
With fibrous roots developing woody stem with age. Leaves 3-angled, long and narrow, and shorter on flowering branches. Flower very beautiful, pure yellow. Cape Province.

CONOPHYLLUM an interesting group allied to Mitrophyllum. Have only a short growing season. First pair of leaves form the 'cone' and in dormant stage they very much resemble this – 'cono' means cone-like. Includes about 25 species.

Conophyllum grande (N. E. Br.) L. Bol.
With opposite 2-angled keeled sterile leaves, about 8 cm long, upper surface flat, back surface rounded with blunted tip, light green. Flower pure shining white. Cape Province.

Conophyllum latibracteatum L. Bol.
Very tall species to nearly 70 cm high. Leaves about 11 cm long, narrow, upper surface somewhat flattened, back surface rounded with blunt apex, deep green. Flower yellow. Cape Province.

CONOPHYTUM consists of dwarf plants, caespitose with shortened axis and branches. Body shape takes many forms – all consisting, however, of two united leaves. The new bodies are always formed within the old; they take sustenance from the older leaves until only the skin remains; this protects the new growth during resting period. In cultivation rest from January to June. Flowers solitary on a short stalk, many colours. Nearly 300 species recorded. For classification purposes the genus has been divided into sub-genera, and again into series and sub-series, but these are not being included here.

Conophytum bilobum (Marl.) N. E. Br.
Stemless, forming mats. Bodies somewhat heart-shaped, free only at the tips which are blunt and rounded, light green or whitish-green, edges red. Flower red. Cape Province.

Conophytum calculus v. *calculus* (Bgr.) N. E. Br.
An unusual caespitose species, bodies globose, fresh green to grey-green with no markings, often mostly enclosed in the brownish skins of older bodies. Flower yellow with brownish tips. Cape Province.

Conophytum concavum L. Bol.
Caespitose forming mats of several small bodies, rounded with flattish top, soft, minutely hairy, whitish with fissure compressed and hairy. Flower small, white. Cape Province.

Conophytum elishae (N. E. Br.) N. E. Br.
Caespitose forming cushions. Bodies thick, club-like, two-lobed with many small dots, bluish-green. Flowers yellow. Cape Province.

Conophytum gratum (N. E. Br.) N. E. Br.
Caespitose forming cushions. Bodies somewhat pear-shaped with top slightly convex, fissure 1 mm deep, smooth, bluish-green with many minute greyish dots. Flower deep red. Cape Province.

Conophytum leuteum N. E. Br.
Clustering, forming cushions. Bodies small, somewhat pear-shaped, top flattish or convex with impressed fissure, greenish-grey and many dark green dots on upper surface with fewer on sides. Flower bright yellow. Cape Province.

Conophytum ovigerum Schwant.
Small species forming thick cushions. Bodies ovate

Ceropegia radicans

Pterodiscus speciosus

Epiphyllum alba 'Superbous'

A collection of Conophytum species.

Dactylopsis digitata

and tapering towards the base, top rounded and indented towards the fissure, with dark dots, green. Flowers yellow. Cape Province.

DACTYLOPSIS consists of only one known species, rare in cultivation.
Dactylopsis digitata (Ait.) N. E.. Br.
Very succulent plant forming dense mats in habitat where it grows near salt pans. Leaves alternate to about 12 cm long, thick, blunt, digitate, unevenly cylindrical, greyish-green. Flower small, white. Cape Province. A much higher temperature is required for this species as flowering season is November to January–a complete rest must be maintained throughout the summer months.

DELOSPERMA are generally shrubby plants, often thickly branched, spreading and prostrate forming mats. Of easy culture. Contains well over 100 species some of which are rare in cultivation.
Delosperma aberdeenense (L. Bol.) L. Bol.
A compact-growing species forming dense clusters. Many branches with small acute leaves rounded on

the back surface and flat on the upper surface. Flowers purplish. Cape Province.

Delosperma echinatum (Ait.) Schwant.
Dense bushy plants, with many branches. Leaves ovate-hemispherical covered with bristly papillae. Flowers solitary, yellow or creamy-white. Cape Province.

DIDYMAOTUS recognizes only one species, rather rare in cultivation.

Didymaotus lapidiformis (Marl.) N. E. Br.
Stemless and very succulent. Leaves two together, thick about 2 cm long 3 cm wide, triangular with rounded apex, upper surface flat, back surface with distinct keel, white-greyish-green. Flowers solitary from either side of the base of the growth, white with pinkish centre. Karroo, Cape Province.

DINTERANTHUS – stemless plants forming mats, stems with 1–3 pairs of leaves which are united at the base, whitish with large yellow flowers. Includes 6 species.

Dinteranthus pole-evansii (N. E. Br.) Schwant.
Species with usually one growth. Leaf pairs united for half their length, upper surface flat, back surface rounded with keel, greyish-white, no dots. Flower deep yellow. Cape Province.

Dinteranthus wilmotianus L. Bol.
Usually with one growth and 2-leaves. Leaves small, upper surface somewhat flat and tapering,

Dinteranthus wilmotianus in flower.

back surface rounded with 1 or 2 keels, smooth, greyish-pink. Flower golden-yellow. Cape Province.

DIPLOSOMA consists of only two known species. Both are rare, interesting and uncommon in cultivation.

Diplosoma leopoldtii L. Bol.
With unequal leaves, connate along part of one edge, semi-circular, upper surface somewhat flattened or convex with bluntly rounded angles and tip, fleshy, smooth, darkish green marked also transparent dots and lines. Flower purple. Cape Province.

DOROTHEANTHUS are annuals, beautiful flowers of easy culture. Includes 11 species and a few varieties.

Dorotheanthus bellidiformis (Burm.) N. E. Br.
Small-growing species branching from the base with leaves usually basal, long, narrow, papillose, fleshy. Flowers on stalks, many colours – white, pink, red, orange, etc. Cape Province.

DRACOPHILUS includes 4 species, all with fleshy leaves, forming cushions. Allied to the genus *Juttadinteria*.

Dracophilus montis-draconis (Dtr.) Dtr.
Growths with 2 or 3 pairs of leaves, united at the base. Leaves 3-angled with blunted edges and top about 4 cm long. Surface slightly rough, bluish-green. Flowers solitary, white, sometimes pinkish. South West Africa.

DROSANTHEMUM includes over 100 species of shrubby plants, mostly prostrate, occasionally erect, leaves covered with small papillae resembling the genus *Drosera*, the sun-dew. Of easy culture-free flowering.

Drosanthemum dejagerae L. Bol.
An erect species to 15 cm high, many branches, younger ones with papillose hairs. Leaves small, thick, flat on the upper surface, somewhat keeled – wider at apex and papillose. Flowers purple. Cape Province.

Drosanthemum floribundum (Haw.) Schwant.
Cushion-forming species, creeping and branching.

Leaves cylindrical and thicker towards the apex, light green. Flowers pale pink. Cape Province.

EREPSIA are shrubby plants with fleshy, later woody stems, 2-angled. Leaves 3-angled, with broad sides and prominent keel. Includes 36 species.

Erepsia aperta L. Bol.
Prostrate species forming compact shrub, elongated branches with internodes. Leaves falcate with sharp keel, sides flattened or convex and few dots. Flowers solitary, small, pink. Cape Province.

Erepsia gracilis (Haw.) L. Bol.
A tall erect plant to 60 cm high, branches slender, reddish becoming grey. Leaves 3-angled with short shoots at the axils, 2 cm long, slightly incurved, narrowing towards the apex, recurving and producing a hook-like tip, fresh green with transparent dots. Flowers purple-rose. Cape Province.

FAUCARIA—mostly compact, fleshy plants and leaves furnished with marginal teeth. Flowers quite large, yellow, rarely white. Plants of good appearance and easy culture. Includes about 30 species.

Faucaria candida L. Bol.
Leaves tapering, rounded in the upper part and more bluntly square in the lower. Back surface with keel, distinctly white and whitish lines on the lower surface, tip somewhat blunted. Margins with white teeth densely crowded. Flower white. Cape Province.

Faucaria felina (Haw.) Schwant.
Leaves rhomboidal, somewhat elongated, tapering gradually, keeled with whitish-grey dots and margins with curved pink teeth. Flowers yellow to orange. Cape Province.

Faucaria tigrina (Haw.) Schwant.
A very popular species often called 'Tiger's Jaws'. Leaves about 5 cm long, rhomboidal-ovate, upper surface flat, under surface rounded, tapering and keeled towards the apex, the tip forming a little 'chin', greyish-green with many white dots. Margins furnished with pronounced teeth, recurved and tapering to points. Flower golden-yellow. Cape Province.

FENESTRARIA includes only two species with windows at the tips of the leaves—in habitat most of the leaves are buried.

Fenestraria aurantiaca N. E. Br.
Caespitose forming cushions. Leaves somewhat clavate, upper side slightly flat, back surface rounded and rounded tip, 3 cm long, smooth, fleshy, greyish-green. The leaf tip is almost transparent. Flower bright yellow. Cape Province.

FRITHIA is very similar to *Fenestraria*, particularly in form of growth. Includes only 1 species.

Frithia pulchra N. E. Br.
Small species, erect leaves, somewhat clavate, truncate at tip, translucent, window-like, greyish-green. Beautiful flowers, carmine-purple with white centre. Transvaal.

GIBBAEUM consists of about 20 species of considerable interest as cultivated plants. Caespitose with shortened stems. Bodies have two fleshy leaves united together at the base, often very unequal lobes with cleft at the apex or lower down the side. Occasionally leaves are spreading.

Gibbaeum album N. E. Br.
Forms clumps. Leaves variously long, fleshy, ovoid with fissure slightly open, leaves to nearly 3 cm long, keeled apex covered with minute hairs. Flowers white. Cape Province.

Gibbaeum dispar N. E. Br.
Cluster forming. Bodies of 2 unequal-sized leaves, oval, somewhat keeled, grey-green with velvety hairs. Fissure very deep. Flower lilac-pink. Cape Province.

Gibbaeum heathii (N. E. Br.) L. Bol.
Forming clumps. Leaves whitish-green, obovoid to 3 cm high. Leaves compressed with fissure reaching centre of body. Flowers white, turning pink. Cape Province.

GLOTTIPHYLLUM has over 60 species, many have close resemblance to one another. Fleshy plants of easy culture. Too much watering tends to produce elongated unnatural growth. They should be grown fairly 'hard' when the most normal characteristics will be seen.

Glottiphyllum album L. Bol. ms.
A branching species of unusual significance on

A Glottiphyllum species in flower.

Glottiphyllum album

account of the white flowers. Fleshy leaves, somewhat keeled, often of unequal length, tapering towards apex. Cape Province.

Glottiphyllum linguiforme (L.) N. E. Br.

Leaves distichous, lingulate, fleshy, glossy, green. Flower on short stalk, golden yellow. This species particularly requires fairly dry conditions, otherwise it can become exceedingly flabby and uninteresting. South Africa.

HEREROA are easily grown species forming clusters or sometimes small shrubs. Includes 36 known species.

Hereroa aspera L. Bol.

Shrubby plant to 8 cm high, branches freely. Leaves semi-cylindrical, upper surface flat, under side rounded with blunted tip, with many pronounced dots, dark green. Flower yellow with reddish tips. Cape Province.

Hereroa nelii Schwant.

Growths with 1 to 3 pairs of leaves. Leaves falcate curved, 3 cm long. Upper surface flat, back surface keeled at tip, covered with tubercles. Flower yellow. Cape Province.

LAMPRANTHUS – shrubby plants, erect, prostrate or spreading. Of easy culture and very free-flowering. Embraces over 130 species.

Lampranthus conspicuus (Haw.) N. E. Br.

Shrubby with thick creeping branches. Leaves incurved at branch terminals, about 6 cm long, bright green often dotted, reddish tip. Flowers reddish-purple with cream centre. Cape Province.

Lampranthus roseus (Willd.) Schwant.

Erect spreading shrub to 60 cm high. Linear leaves 3 cm long covered with translucent spots. Flowers in profusion, large, soft pink with yellow centre. Cape Province.

LITHOPS – pebble-like plants, often called 'living stones'. A very large genus of over 80 species and varieties from very dry desert regions where often they are almost buried or indiscernible in rock crevices. All species have a window-like top surface, so even when the plant is partially buried the light can still penetrate into the plant for its survival. New growth develops at the axils of the old growth which withers and acts as a protective sheath for the new leaves, finally as only a skin. Not difficult to cultivate, but a very light position is essential for greatest success. Resting period – December to May. For classification purposes the genus has been divided into two sub-genera: *Xantholithops* for those with principally yellow flowers and where the fissure does not extend over the whole body: *Leucolithops* to include white flowering species and with a fissure which divides the two leaves completely.

Lithops bella (Dtr.) N. E. Br.
Forming clusters, bodies about 30 mm high with rather convex top surface. Has the colour of granite mimicking the environment from which it originates. Flower yellow. South West Africa.

Lithops dorotheae Nel
Forming clusters, bodies obconical, dove-grey, with flat top, having translucent windows with many reddish and greyish markings. Flower yellow. Cape Province.

Lithops comptonii L. Bol.
Clustering freely, bodies greyish-green up to 4 cm with deep fissure making the leaves 'gape'. Top with window, amethyst with brownish and purplish markings and white spots in the 'islands'. Flower yellow. Cape Province.

Lithops julii (Dtr. et Schwant.) N. E. Br.
There are also two varietal forms of this species. Caespitose, somewhat conical with convex top surface, the fissure extending right across, pearl-grey. The margins of the fissure have dots each side. Flower white. South West Africa.

Lithops opalina Dtr.
Somewhat constricted oval bodies with fissure extending right across, 3 cm high, bluish-white, top surface with purplish tint. Flower white. S.W. Africa.

Lithops optica (Marl.) N. E. Br.
Caespitose forming largish clump. Bodies greyish-white with pronounced fissure making cleft, leaf tips convex, spreading with whitish transparent windows. Flower white. There is a beautiful and rare form, *L. optica forma rubra* (Tisch.) Rowl. which is almost identical to the species, but the body is reddish-purple and the windows more apparent, flower white. South West Africa.

Lithops salicola L. Bol.
Forming clusters, sometimes solitary. Bodies silvery-grey, oval with top surface convex and having large translucent greenish-grey or reddish windows, and numerous little greyish islands. Flowers white. Orange Free State.

MITROPHYLLUM closely allied to Conophyllum but differing in the structure of the fruits. Most species are rare in cultivation. Plant has similar leaf structure to the Conophyllums one leaf pair rising from the lower pair, some which are united the whole length and others part way only, the former serving as a kind of 'sheath' for the latter. Includes only few species, possibly no more than 6 and some are in doubt.

Mitrophyllum mitratum (Marl.) Schwant.
Caespitose. Stems thick, fleshy, later becoming woody. Leaves very succulent, 8 cm long, rather triangular, and those spreading are slightly convex on the upper surface forming a deep furrow, back surface rounded and keeled. Flowers white with red tips to petals. L. Namaqualand, Cape Province.

MONILARIA are an interesting genus of semi-shrubby, low-growing plants, often jointed into small segments, leaves small, fleshy and generally sub-cylindrical. Closely related to Mitrophyllum and Conophyllum.

Monilaria peersii L. Bol.
Shrubby to about 12 cm high with several short branches and internodes. Leaves short, narrow with obscure keel near tip which is round at apex, covered with papillae, fresh green. Flowers white. Cape Province.

MUIRIA includes just one rare species which is extremely succulent with short fibrous root system. Considered difficult in cultivation.

Muiria hortenseae N. E. Br.
Growths consist of two completely united fresh green leaves forming what appears to be a globular body. Fissure hardly apparent until the flower is produced – this is solitary, pinkish-white. L. Karroo, Cape Province.

NANANTHUS consists of about 10 known species, all with very tuberous roots and tufted growth.

Leaves distinctive with usually many white dots.
Nananthus aloides (Haw.) Schwant.
Clumping from the base with many leaves which are lanceolate with a grooved upper surface, keeled towards apex, dark green with numerous white dots. Edges rather rough also with dots. Flower on short stalk, yellow. Cape Province.

OPHTHALMOPHYLLUM – an interesting genus of about 18 species, stemless and very succulent with fibrous roots. Bodies fleshy consisting of two leaves almost totally united, the tips sometimes 'spreading' with windows.
Ophthalmophyllum lydiae Jacobs.
Usually solitary with small obconical bodies about 2 cm high with fissure forming a complete cleft at the top, olive-green and many transparent dots. Flower white, pink tips. Cape Province.
Opthalmophyllum schlechteri Schwant.
Usually solitary, bodies cylindrical, somewhat flat top with pronounced fissure. Tops of lobes with transparent windows, fresh green to reddish. Flower white. Cape Province.

PLEIOSPILOS are popular plants with varying leaf shapes, clumping freely with large flowers, often scented. Includes over 30 species – all of easy culture, free-flowering.
Pleiospilos bolusii (Hook. f.) N. E. Br.
Very succulent species, stemless with pairs of thick, stone-like keeled leaves 4 cm long and nearly as broad. Leaves flattened on upper surface, light grey-green, with many darkish green dots. Flowers deep yellow. Cape Province.
Pleiospilos leipoldtii L. Bol.
Leaves of various shapes, generally obovate to about 7 cm long, keeled at the bottom, pointed at apex, dullish green with numerous prominent dots. Flowers yellow, white centre. Cape Province.
Pleiospilos optatus (N. E. Br.) Schwant.
Much branched from base, forming clumps. Leaves 2–4 in one growth to 4 cm long, flattened on upper surface, rounded and keeled below tip, reddish-green with tinges of purple and numerous green dots. Flower yellow. Cape Province.
Pleiospilos willowmorensis L. Bol.
A popular and well-known species with 2–4 leaved

growth, flattened upper surface somewhat sickle-like and keeled. Leaves of unequal lengths, purplish-green and covered with many dots. Flower yellow, white centre. Cape Province.

PSAMMOPHORA includes only 4 species, low-growing, tufted with dense woody stems, branches often buried so only leaves are seen. Leaves sticky, bluish-green and in habitat are invariably covered with sand.
Psammophora longifolia L. Bol.
Small species, tufted, growths with 4–6 leaves to over 4 cm long and 12 mm wide, upper surface linear, flat and somewhat tapering, lower surface rounded with keel which is drawn forward over the upper surface, olive-green to brownish, surface rough, sticky and often sand-encrusted, a protection from undue transpiration. Flower white. South West Africa.

RABIEA – a species with fleshy roots and crowded branchlets. Leaves spreading, very dissimilar in appearance one leaf to another. Sharply tapering and keeled, usually with many wart-like white or brown dots. Flowers solitary. Includes only 6 species and a few varietal forms.
Rabiea albinota (Hae.) N. E. Br.
Forming a dwarf succulent rosette consisting of 6–8 triangled leaves, somewhat sabre-like, to about 10 cm long, flattened on upper surface and covered with many whitish warts. Flowers yellow. Cape Province.

RHOMBOPHYLLUM recognizes only 3 species, shrubby or caespitose with tuberous roots, leaves somewhat rhomboidal, margins often with 1 or 2 teeth, otherwise entire.
Rhombophyllum dolabriforme (L.) Schwant.
With 'stag's-horn'-like leaves, wedge shaped, spreading, upper surface flat and tapering, lower side semi-cylindrical with keel, green and translucent dots. Large flowers, golden-yellow. Cape Province.

RUSCHIA is one of the largest genera of Mesembryanthemums with about 350 species. Shrubby, somewhat erect but sometimes more prostrate and forming tufts. Branches often covered with dead leaf remains. Leaves of various shapes, elongated or rounded with pronounced keel, amplexicaul, very long sheath.

Ruschia dualis (N. E. Br.) L. Bol.

Forming clusters up to 5 cm high with mature branchlets covered by dry leaves. Leaves 2 together, united near to base, upper surface flattened, back surface semi-circular and keeled with firm margins, greyish-green. Flowers small, deep pink. Cape Province.

Ruschia pygmaea (Haw.) Schwant.

A very miniature species forming compact mats with short branchlets, 1–2 pairs of leaves, each pair different, the upper pair united at tip, the skin of which dries and covers the succeeding pair which have spreading leaves, rounded on upper surface and keeled below. Flowers small. Cape Province.

SCELETIUM consists of 22 species and few minor forms – somewhat unusual, often giving the effect of a papery skeleton-like structure caused by leaves persisting after withering. Spreading plants with prostrate stems and elongated rounded leaves, somewhat papillose when young. Species contain mesembrine, a poisonous drug.

Sceletium archeri L. Bol.

Plant with short stems and elongated prostrate branches, slender with internodes. Leaves very succulent, erect, lanceolate, tapering towards apex, papillose, dull green, 15 mm long sheath about 2 mm. Flower solitary, pale yellow. Cape Province.

SCHWANTESIA are compact plants, low growing with leaves of various shapes and peculiarities. Plants have internodes encased in leaf-sheaths. Leaves of unequal pairs. Flower solitary. Includes 10 known species.

Schwantesia acutipetala L. Bol.

Leaves short, narrow and fleshy, tapering sharply. Upper surface flat, lower surface rounded near base and sharply tapering towards apex, pronounced edges, smooth, bluish-green, sometimes reddish edges. Flowers yellow. Found in Namaqualand, Cape Province.

Schwantesia ruedebuschii Dtr.

A rare species forming clumps to 10 cm high. Leaves boat-shape, upper surface almost flat or convex, back surface rounded near base with rounded margins, mottled white with the tips expanding and furnished with thick blue teeth, brownish tip. A very attractive species, pale yellow flowers. South West Africa.

STOMATIUM comprises about 40 species of easily grown, attractive leafed plants, fragrant, nocturnal flowers. Forming clusters, short stemmed with two pairs of leaves often of unequal length, keeled towards the apex, somewhat tuberculate.

Stomatium agninum (Haw.) Schwant.

A branching species with soft, boat-shaped, grey-green leaves, upper surface flat, lower surface convex and keeled, 3-angled, margins, few teeth. Flowers yellow. Cape Province.

Stomatium fulleri L. Bol.

Stemless, clustering to about 50 cm high. Leaves somewhat 3-angled, flat on upper surface, the tip recurved, back surface convex and keeled at apex, edges with few teeth, both surfaces rough, the lower has many whitish warts. Flowers yellow. Cape Province.

TITANOPSIS includes about 6 extremely attractive species with unusual leaf markings. All are dwarf growing, clumping freely with terminal flowers on long stalk and bracted.

Titanopsis calcarea (Marl.) Schwant.

Forming clustering rosettes of spreading leaves with fleshy roots. Leaves, greyish, spatulate, resembling pieces of limestone, to 25 mm long, covered with greyish-white tubercles. Flowers yellow. Cape Province.

Titanopsis schwantesii (Dtr.) Schwant.

Dwarf clustering species forming mats. Leaves light bluish-grey, somewhat inclined to 3 cm long. Wide at base, tri-cornered near apex, most of the upper part and sides covered with roundish yellow-brown warts. Flowers yellow. South West Africa.

TRICHODIADEMA has 31 species of shrubby plants having peculiar leaves covered with papillae on the surface and with spreading glistening bristles at the tip, forming a 'diadem'. Of easy culture with many small flowers of different colours.

Trichodiadema barbatum (L.) Schwant.

Turnip-shaped roots with many prostrate branches. Leaves small, slightly recurved, grey-green and wart-like papillae. Leaf tip with black bristles. Flowers about 3 cm vivid red. Cape Province.

Trichodiadema densum (Haw.) Schwant.

A popular, well-known species with very fleshy rootstock, almost a caudex. Short stems forming tufts with leaves crowded together 20 mm long and 4 mm thick, dark green with numerous papillae, the tip with long radiating white bristles. Flowers about 3 cm, violet-red. Cape Province.

VANHEERDEA are clump forming with extremely succulent leaves similar to those of many of the genus Gibbaeum, always symmetrical, keel and margins finely dentate, bodies sub-globose. Includes 4 species.

Vanheerdea roodiae (N. E. Br.) L. Bol.

Bodies to about 25 mm high, semi-globose, fleshy leaves partially united. Inner surface flat, outer surface rounded and distinctly keeled at tip, pale green with minute whitish hairs. Flowers orange-yellow. Bushmanland, Cape Province.

Much more could be said of this important family and other genera could well deserve mention, but this cross-section is certainly representative of one of the foremost of succulent plant families.

Moraceae

Includes plants from the Old World and the New. With few exceptions the flowers are small and of little consequence. The one genus mentioned here embraces a number of curious plants, not all of which are succulents. The true succulents are of great interest, and the flowers, although far from beautiful, are most fascinating.

Dorstenia crispa Engl.

Cylindrical stem to over 30 cm high, swollen at base, dark green or blackish-green, glossy, with numerous papillose leaf bases. Branching from apex, leaves at terminal ends, oblong, with margins slightly dentate and curled. Inflorescence on longish stalk, 'heads' oval with 8 or 10 spreading bracts. Kenya.

Dorstenia hildebrandtii Engl.

A well-known species with compact fleshy caudex, sub-globose and succulent stem and few branches, olive-green. Leaves, elongated with undulate margins somewhat fleshy. Inflorescence solitary from leaf axils, 'heads' ovate 5 mm, set within 8 bracts, 5 mm long and several smaller bracts. Endemic to Kenya.

Dorstenia gigas Schweinf.

Thick fleshy stem, cylindrical, narrowing towards the apex to about 2 m high. Short smooth branches develop towards the top with leaves only at the ends. Leaves in whorls, oblanceolate, dark green on upper surface, lower surface slightly pubescent. Flower yellowish-green. Found on rock-faces in Socotra. A rare and desirable species.

Dorstenia gypsophila Lavr.

A recent discovery. About 120 cm high. Stem somewhat thickened with greyish-white bark. Numerous branches, leaves in rosettes at terminal ends. Leaves ovate, cordate or cuneate, pubescent with margins undulate and dentate. Flower, heads small with 7 to 8 bracts to 8 mm long. Somalia.

Other species of *Dorstenia* are recorded, *D. foetida* (Forst.) Lam. is close to *D. gypsophila* and originates from Kenya.

Passifloraceae

Includes many species of the genus *Adenia*, some of which are non-succulent vines and have no attractive flower. A few are considered succulent and come within the category of caudiciform plants, and it is primarily the unusual characteristics of the plant growth which accounts for its popularity as a cultivated plant.

Adenia digitata (Harv.) Engl.

Large rounded caudex, sometimes malformed, having greyish skin. Erect fleshy stem from the caudex, slightly branching with digitate leaves in groups towards the terminal ends. This species is considered poisonous. Transvaal.

Adenia fruticosa Burtt-Davy

Has very large, somewhat elongated caudex, usually deformed, brownish-green. Branches freely, rambling and climbing, fleshy, greenish to greyish-brown. Leaves globose-ovate, deciduous. Flowers yellowish and insignificant. Transvaal, S. Africa.

Adenia globosa Engl.

Possibly the best-known of this remarkable genus. Has massive swollen caudex to about 1 m thick, with the appearance of a large grey-green stone. Short branches, twig-like, develop from the top of the caudex, but sometimes to about 2 m length or more, furnished with stout and long thorns, all greenish-grey. Rarely with leaf, but sometimes, immediately following the rains, small narrow lanceolate leaves appear but soon fall. Grouped inflorescence with bright red, star-like, scented flowers. Tanzania.

Adenia pechuelii (Engl.) Harms

Usually with large fleshy caudex, rounded and long tap roots. Sometimes the thick base is more elongated, almost bottle-shaped–greenish-grey. Many stems and branches, somewhat spiny. Leaves lanceolate, deciduous. Small inflorescence with 3 flowers. Fruit palish pink. South West Africa.

Adenia spinosa Burtt-Davy

Massive swollen succulent trunk, partly subterranean, dull greyish-green to about 2 m high. Branches freely, usually from the upper part of the stem, but occasionally also from the lower parts. Branches armed with sharp straight spines. Leaves rather small, deciduous. Flower creamy-yellow which appears before the leaves. Transvaal.

Adenia venenata Forsk.

Thick, somewhat elongated fleshy stem to about 2 m high, with smooth greenish bark. Branches freely, greenish, rope-like and many tendrils. Leaves small and deciduous. Flowers yellowish-green. Endemic to Nigeria.

Pedaliaceae

Includes some interesting succulents, many with caudex. Certain are annuals such as *Pedalium murex* L. from Madagascar and East Africa. Few genera contain species of consequence.

Pterodiscus angustifolia Engl.

An interesting species having very fleshy base with many succulent branches, almost shrubby, purplish-green, to about 25 cm high. Leaves very succulent, narrow oblanceolate, deep green, margins usually undulate and dentate at apex.

Flower deep yellow with purplish markings in the tube, scented. Tanzania.

Pterodiscus aurantiacus Welw.

Irregularly shaped caudex to about 25 cm high and at the end short thickish branches, somewhat fleshy. Leaves elongate-lanceolate, wavy-edged with slight indentations, bluish-green. Flower yellow. Namaland, South West Africa.

Pterodiscus procumbens

(syn. *Harpagophytum procumbens* (Burch.) DC.) A trailing plant with fleshy tuberous roots and opposite leaves, pale greyish-green, lobed. Flowers from the leaf axils, red or purplish. Fruits brownish, barbed with recurved spines. South Africa.

Pterodiscus luridus Hook.

Similar in many parts to *P. aurabtiacus*. Thickish-fleshy stem to about 40 cm high. Branches freely with oblong leaves, upper surface dark green, lower surface bluish. Flower yellowish with many red dots. Stem, branches, leaves, flowers somewhat pruinose. Cape Province.

Pterodiscus speciosus Hook.

A small fleshy-stemmed succulent with enlarged base, about 15 cm high. Leaves develop in the upper part, linear-oblong, dentate, dull green. Flowers purplish-pink. Cape Province.

Sesamothamnus guerichii (Engl.) Bruce

Very succulent caudex, compact with papery skin, greyish-green. Many spiny branches, somewhat woody. Leaves small, spatulate, quickly diciduous. Flowers small, bright yellow. South West Africa.

Sesamothamnus lugardii N. E. Br.

Low caudex with many semi-erect branches from base and sides forming a tree-like plant to about 2 m high. Branches succulent and tapering with few spines, leaves from the axils of the spines, small, somewhat oblong, greyish-green. Flowers whitish. Transvaal, Rhodesia and other parts of tropical Africa.

Piperaceae

Contains the very popular genus *Peperomia*. While the majority of the species are endemic to the Americas, and often epiphytic, there are those from Asia, Africa and Madagascar. The majority of species are true succulents.

Peperomia crassifolia

An erect species, fleshy, stiff with bright green stems. Leaves succulent, alternate, usually obovate to about 6 cm long, fresh-green, paler green on lower surface and pale midrib. Tropical Africa.

Vitaceae

Includes two genera of note–at one time united, now divided on account of varying characteristics.

Cissus quadrangularis L.

Climbing species with tendrils, stems fleshy, 4-angled, constricted at the nodes, almost leafless, but sometimes few leaves at constrictions, 3 lobed. Flowers green, followed by reddish-black berries. Tropical Africa, Arabia, South Africa, eastern India.

Cissus rotundifolia (Forsk.) Vahl.

A climbing species with 4-angled stems and somewhat rough, uneven corky edges. Leaves perennial, fleshy, rounded, greyish-green having serrate margins. Flowers very small, greenish, followed by red berries. From coastal regions of Tanzania.

Cissus cactiformis Gilg.

Climbing species with tendrils. Has large tuberous root, almost caudex and 4-angled stems, sharply winged with pronounced constrictions and rough thorny edges, rather wavy. Leaves occasionally at inernodes, deciduous. Fruits black. This is very similar to *C. quadrangularis,* and very likely a variety or perhaps synonymous. From savannah country, East Africa.

Cyphostemma bainesii (Gilg. et Brandt) Desc.

With bottle-shaped trunk to 25 cm thick and 60 cm high or more, few stout branches, all very fleshy and covered with papery yellowish-green skin which peels readily on matured plants. Leaves green, coarsely serrate. Fruits red. Endemic to South West Africa.

Cyphostemma juttae (Dtr. et Gilg) Desc.

Long, thick and fleshy trunk up to 2 m high, smooth and yellowish-grey paper-like skin which peels with age. Divides into few branches at apex and has coarsely serrated irregular leaves, upper surface waxy green, under side with translucent hairs. Fruits yellow or red. Gt. Namaland.

Cyphostemma seitziana (Gilg et Brandt) Desc.

Very swollen and often mis-shapen caudex-like stem up to nearly 2 m high. Few branches from near the apex. Trunk and branches with yellowish smooth skin. Leaves fleshy, long-ovate with pronounced serrate margins, grey-green, deciduous. South West Africa.

Several other species of Cissus and Cyphostemma are recorded, but in general most have many characteristics similar to those mentioned. All are of easy culture but a minimum temperature of 50°F is advised for success.

Part 2
The Cultivation of Succulents

Epiphyllum hybrid 'King Midas'

6 Succulents as Indoor and House Plants

In an age when plants have become an integral ingredient of interior decoration – in fact, accepted as a most essential factor in home ornamentation – succulent plants in general have an important function, with so many pertinent qualities to recommend them.

For years succulents have been used as houseplants – sometimes, perhaps, without the owner really being aware of this. *Sansevieria trifasciata* v. *laurentii* (mother-in-law's tongue), *Aloe variegata* (The partridge breasted Aloe), *Hoya carnosa* (The 'wax plant'), Christmas cactus – *Schlumbergera* and *Zygocactus* species and cultivars, remembering also the Easter cactus; these are just a few selected at random which can be found in many homes, and very worthy attractions they prove to be.

There is also the fact that in more recent times, when a high percentage of the population are compelled to become city or town dwellers – often living in flats or in limited accommodation where there is no garden – the need for houseplants becomes even greater.

No real problems are likely to be encountered in caring for succulent plants in the home. The modern house is generally well equipped with ample lighting and also has the advantage of a warm, dry atmosphere – and these factors play a great part in ensuring successful culture. It is true that frequently succulents grown indoors can achieve equally successful results as with any other houseplant – in fact better than many – both as regard growth and flowering. Yes, it is well to remember that all succulents flower, and, what is even more important, many of the finest flowering succulents are readily adaptable as houseplants.

For over 100 years, cottage windows have been brightened by the lovely blooms of *Epiphyllum ackermannii*. To be precise, this is a cultivar produced in the early 1800s and without question one of the finest outcomes of man's endeavour in the realm of cross-pollination. This same remarkable houseplant is still seen adorning countless window-sills, continuing to be most floriferous, producing, year after year, on a matured plant, up to 100 large scarlet flowers during the spring and early summer. During the last two decades the sphere of Epiphyllum cultivars – erstwhile *Phyllocactus* sometimes referred to as 'Orchid Cactus', this being due to their truly exotic flowers – has developed and expanded. Where for years there seemingly were only the beautiful *Epiphyllum ackermannii* and perhaps the small flowering *Epiphyllum* 'Deutsche Kaiserin', with its masses of delicate shell-pink flowers, today these exotics are obtainable in almost every colour – excepting green and blue – highly scented, white or cream, sweetly performed yellows (still considered something of a rarity), pink varieties from pastel shades to deepish rose, peach and pale orange ranging to even deeper reddish-orange, crimson, scarlet, cultivars with purple, mauve or lilac blooms and many choice multicoloured varieties. With only trifling exceptions they are proving to be ideal houseplants.

Perhaps it is appropriate to discuss these a little further. Many people have made a practice of putting these Epiphyllums out-of-doors, in a shady position from July to October. This is a very commendable arrangement – but it must be remembered they will require regular watering and attention – also protection from garden pests such as slugs, snails, woodlice etc. Before the frosts

Epiphyllum hybrid 'Queen Anne'.

commence, place the plant in a light position indoors and buds should begin to form from early December, and subsequently from March onwards – possibly until well into July. They should provide a succession of beautiful flowers.

Some cultivars can be particularly recommended:

EPIPHYLLUM 'ACKERMANNII HYBRIDUS' – the old-fashioned cultivar . . . scarlet.

'Alba superbus' – large white and scented.
'Bliss' – large flower, pastel orange.
'Carnation' – a choice variety, carnation pink with rose centre.
'Cooperii' – large perfumed white.
'Dante' – multicoloured, orange, red and magenta.
'Deutsche Kaiserin' – shades of pink – smallish flower.
'Fiesta' – rich flame orange.
'Glamour Girl' – buttercup-yellow, exceptionally fine.
'Guatemala' – deepest red and purple, large flower.
'Impello' – open flower, lilac and mauve.
'King Midas' – one of the finest. Golden yellow with deep orange stripe.
'Maharajah' – deep purple.
'Princess Grace' – even deep pink – symmetrical cup-shaped flower.
'Queen Anne' – yellow and cream, scented.

'Regency' – very large scented cream.
'Sun Goddess' – beautiful dust-orange.
'Thalia – multi-coloured, red, purple and magenta.
'Zoe' – begonia pink, very choice.

There are nurseries which specialize in Epiphyllums and who offer those mentioned above, together with a great many more beautiful varieties, all as easy as one another in cultivation, and each having equally lovely flowers.

Mention has already been made of Christmas cactus. Here again considerable developments have been made to perfect new coloured varieties. The original is the outstanding 'rich magenta', and it would prove extremely difficult to procure a more rewarding houseplant than this well-loved plant. We live in days when the demand is for 'something different' – and so with the Christmas cacti a good colour range of these late autumn and winter flowering plants can now be obtained. Some are not so readily available, but a thorough search of a specialist nurseryman's catalogue will probably be an aid to locating some of them. Confusion still exists as to the correct nomenclature of these cacti. For years they have been known as *Zygocactus*. *Zygocactus truncatus* was wrongfully considered to be the magenta flowering plant so popularly grown. It was then found to be a hybrid of *Zygocactus truncatus* and *Schlumbergera russelianum,* and the name of *Schlumbergera* × *'Bridgesii'* became associated with the plant. Since then further complications have stalked it – insofar as suggestions being put forward purporting different origins – true to say, 'its had a rough ride'. However, whatever the name or parentage, it still holds right of place as the accepted and popular Christmas Cactus. These require much the same treatment as Epiphyllums. A period out-of-doors can be advantageous and an encouragement to flower production, but by late September they should be set in a position indoors in readiness for flowering. A word of warning, and this is very important. Buds will begin to appear in late autumn – from that time it is unwise to reposition the plants as far as light is concerned. Great disappointment has been expressed when the buds have fallen off – and turning the pot around can possibly be one of the main causes. The best plan is to place a marker–a label is suitable–in a given position in the pot and thus you have the means of determining that the plant always faces the same direction in relation to the light, wherever it is placed. The situation as regards natural light should remain the same throughout the flowering period. This may not be the only cause of bud-drop– under-watering or over-watering can also cause problems–likewise a draughty position can create havoc. Watch for these dangers and remember it is possible for a whole season's flowering to be lost on any of these accounts.

The following selection of Christmas cacti can be recommended:

ZYGOCACTUS TRUNCACTUS–a parent of the original Christmas Cactus–magenta.

× 'Lilac Beauty'–lilac petals with white throat.

× 'Frankenstoltz'–deep rose-pink with whitish throat.

× 'Weihnachtsreude'–pastel orange with tinges of magenta.

× 'Noris'–a robust variety with magenta and red-orange flowers.

× 'Wintermärchen'–almost white–slightly shaded pink.

delicatus–a species–small flower on small plant– white.

× 'Bridgesii'–the typical Christmas Cactus– magenta.

Present-day botanists have united the genus *Zygocactus* with that of *Schlumbergera*, therefore any or all of the above species and cultivars may be offered as Schlumbergera and not as Zygocactus– but it is all the same thing. All are winter flowering excepting *Schlumbergera gaertneri*, better known as the 'Easter cactus', which is, of course, a spring-flowering species. Another spring flower is *Rhipsalidopsis rosea*; this and hybrids between the two species require much the same treatment as Epiphyllum and Zygocactus. The ancestors of all those mentioned were rain-forest plants, enjoying conditions which left no room for long periods of drought. Equally so in the home: never let the roots become completely dry–it is dangerous and can cause withering. The best way to retain moisture is to stand the pot in a saucer containing peat or vermiculite, and take care to keep this constantly moist. During the growing and flowering seasons plants should be watered moderately, and in very warm weather an over-head spray can be a great asset but be careful of incessant wetness which can be disastrous. Fertilizing is very helpful especially when the flower buds form. Many proprietary brands can be used for this purpose, but it would appear that any fertilizer prepared for tomato crops is beneficial to these cacti and encourages both growth and blooms.

It must not be presumed that any cactus or succulent is automatically a suitable subject for house culture. This is far from true. There are numerous exceptions, and guidance from an expert should be sought. Some plants are temperamental and require a great deal of understanding coupled at times with very peculiar and rigid cultural demands such as could not be provided in ordinary house conditions–in other words, they are not readily adaptable. Nevertheless, the urge can sometimes be too strong, and the challenge too great! In which case, be sure to select the brightest position possible, coupled with facilities to give higher temperatures, and success may be achieved –but be prepared for disappointments. One word of encouragement, however. Many excellent collections of succulents have been maintained in bay-windows, where maximum light is guaranteed.

A built-in window-box might well be contemplated for succulents–but here we are veering towards greenhouse culture, and much that applies to greenhouses would equally refer to a glazed window-box–and this is dealt with elsewhere.

Certain rules should be constantly observed if successful culture of cacti and succulents as house-plants is to be achieved:

(i) All plants prefer a reasonably light position; remember light is a major essential; without it plants can become etiolated and 'soft'. It is an even greater necessity than warmth.

(ii) Correct watering is all-important. If a minimum room temperature of $60°F$ is maintained, then water freely throughout the growing season, and, out-of-season, just keep the root system moist, not wet. It is not necessary to dry succulents out completely. *Never* apply water when the compost is already moist. Give the plants the opportunity of using up the moisture you've given already–after all, they are succulents able to store water against possible drought–that is their nature and this must always be accepted and encouraged.

If a much lower temperature applies, say down to 45°F, then a complete rest is necessary; only Epiphyllums, Zygocactus and Schlumbergera and similar species should remain just moist.

It has become almost a creed to presume that water must be given from below; in other words, the pots stood in water and allowed to absorb their fill. This is all right, but not essential. There is no reason why watering should not be effected by overhead spraying, and this method helps to keep the plants clean and free from dust.

When watering, water well–not a teaspoonful every day or so; this only tends to give the plant 'indigestion', and is really one of the speediest ways of encouraging root rot and plant destruction. Learn the difference between so-called *regular* watering and *necessary* watering. There can be no stipulated time lag in this respect–more plants have been lost through wrong watering and over-watering than were ever lost by underwatering. If in doubt–*don't*. As an aid to correct watering, the use of a hydrometer can be recommended–purchasable from many garden shops and centres–and a convenient 'do or don't' implement. Rain water? Read what has been said about this elsewhere.

(iii) Fertilizing is important for all houseplants; succulents are no exception. Applications every three or four weeks during the growing season are advisable and only apply when the soil is already moist. This enables the fertilizer to percolate freely throughout the container and be readily assimilated.

(iv) When repotting is necessary–and this can be a frequent occurrence–it is best attended to in spring. If it is advisable to transfer into a larger container, then carefully up-turn the pot, tap gently so that the whole ball of soil is loosened and can be easily removed, inspect for root decay and cut away any damaged roots. Check also for pests, which can be equally dangerous. Then place into new container filling in around with fresh compost. It is sometimes wiser to remove much of the old surface soil and replace with new. If the same-sized pot is to be used, then it is imperative to remove some of the old soil from sides and surface; inspect thoroughly, and treat as above.

Another popular method for growing plants indoors is the use of a trough or bowl–where several plants are grown together. Miniature gardens have become exceedingly popular in recent years, and so often succulents are the acceptable choice of plants for this purpose. One important thing must be borne in mind–the plants selected must be capable of growing happily together–or have a kinship. A specialist nurseryman could advise on this. For example, it would be most unwise to include a Christmas cactus with *Aloe variegata*–they have distinctly different requirements. Zygocactus, Epiphyllums, species of Rhipsalis and Peperomia would make good companions. Likewise *Aloe variegata* would live ideally with species of Notocactus, Echinocereus, Parodia and Crassula. If in doubt, seek the help of an expert.

Preparation of the bowl or trough must have careful thought and planning. Firstly, choose the right container. Anything less than 4″ depth is not really serviceable.

Most containers of this sort have no drainage holes as this might make them impracticable in other respects. Therefore the base should be freely spread with crocking, e.g. broken pieces of clay pots or $\frac{1}{2}$″ washed gravel–all to a depth of not less than $1\frac{1}{2}$″. This crocking, together with charcoal chippings to keep the soil sweet, can act as a reservoir and very often the roots will go down into the crocking for surplus moisture which may have accumulated. This also calls for extremely careful watering–it's so easy to give too much–and the crocked area must not become a constant 'pool'. When the plants are resting, the container will require very little water at all. This is another instance when a hydrometer would be very useful.

No succulent plant should ever be used in Bottle Gardens. This literally means the automatic extermination of the plant–it is certainly one of the quickest ways to kill–be it a cactus, epiphytic or otherwise, or any other variety of succulent, from jungle or from desert. Bottles weren't meant for cactus–or cactus for bottles!

7 Greenhouse Culture

There is much to say in favour of the greenhouse. If our natural surroundings do not provide the required climatic conditions for the successful growing of succulents, then the only alternative is to create them – and what better than a greenhouse?

It is true to say that it was never intended by nature that we should grow plants under glass – or, for that matter, in pots. However, these two go hand-in-hand to give to the plant enthusiast the scope to grow and enjoy such exotics as may capture his imagination. By this means success can be achieved if due attention is given to detail – an understanding of the plants and what they require, the use of personal initiative and enterprise.

First, the greenhouse. Make sure it is sound and strong, a well-built construction, leak-proof, with proper provision for ventilation, the roof not too low – or for that matter, not too high; a slightly raised floor is useful, enabling surplus moisture to seep away at, or below, floor level, and has a reliable heating system.

The question is asked, 'Which is best, wood or metal?' This is really a matter of choice. It is considered that wood might be warmer, but, of course, wood can rot, so take every care in treating all timbers. Likewise, metal tends to be cold – but perhaps more durable, and again, metal can rust, so be sure a rust-proof alloy is supplied: alternatively, satisfactory preservatives should be applied. Whichever is selected, it is wise to have the greenhouse erected on a concrete base so that neither wood nor metal bars have direct contact with the soil.

The glazing is very important – the use of wide panes of glass and narrow glazing bars ensures maximum light, and if the glass is taken to almost ground level, it serves to make 'under the bench' a very useful area.

Substitutes for glass are now finding a ready market – light polythene to provide double glazing has much to commend it – but to use the heavy plastic sheeting, which tends to become almost opaque in only a short time, is not advised as, above all, it can restrict the benefits derived from sunlight. The greenhouse is mainly an 'enclosure' to protect plants from excessive rain and extreme cold – that, and little else – and nothing should allow for the advantages of good sunshine to be lost.

Ventilation is a most important factor to consider. If correct attention is not given to this aspect, all manner of problems can arise. Condensation is one of the biggest difficulties to combat – and it is most frequent that drips, be it from condensation or from faulty construction, find their way onto the plant or plants which matter most. Drips are a menace and must be avoided at all costs. Correct ventilation serves to make such problems well-nigh non-existent. Very few greenhouses are supplied with sufficient vents. It might be argued that vents offer a welcome to leakages from outside elements – but good vents can be fitted and weatherproofed – and frankly you cannot have too many vents. Fresh air never killed plants.

We live in fortunate days of automation. Automatic temperature controlled 'openers' can be fitted to any vent, which will open and close according to the thermostatic setting. This is truly a labour saver and worthy of every consideration, especially when a greenhouse may have to be left all day; it might be chilly in the morning, and not advisable for vents to be opened or very little. Then, as the day warms up, and ventilation is really necessary, automatic vents open accordingly – then start closing when the thermostat instructs. Whether or not automatic methods are adopted, it cannot be stressed too greatly that any process which allows for an oppressive or stagnant air condition proves injurious to the plants. Remember we are considering the requirements for succulent plants – and it is well to recall that such plants or their forebears originated from wide open spaces. We cannot reproduce such vast expanses – but we should strive to get as near the bright, breezy conditions as possible. Brief mention has been made of leaky vents – and this equally applies to any fault in the structure which allows for rain seeping in. If you have such a greenhouse, there are suitable sealers produced commercially which will help to solve these difficulties – any good garden sundriesman would gladly advise and recommend suitable products for the purpose.

I have known of some constructions with doors at both ends. This is a good thing, and opens up another method of ventilation. What better could be expected on a sultry day than to have doors open at either end to allow for a through current of air? However, a danger does lurk here – in fact more than one danger. This can also be the cause of draughts under certain circumstances, so must not be considered a 100% alternative to window vents. Another danger is from animals or birds which might have easier access through a door than through a window – and they can effect a great deal of damage. Netting can be affixed to the window vent quite easily to keep out birds or insects, but this is not always so easily done with doorways, but not, of course, impossible. It is a thought to consider.

Heating is also a matter of paramount importance – a factor to consider seriously when trying to grow succulents successfully. There are so many forms available: some old-fashioned which have stood the test of time and experience; others which sound remarkably good, and perhaps are, but they still have no background of practical experience, and using new methods must throw the onus very much on to the shoulders of the greenhouse owner. Well, what is best to use? It is a matter of taking your choice.

Pipe heating has been tested for generations and, undoubtedly, if carefully installed and maintained (that goes for the boiler and the pipes) it would take a great deal of effort to find better – and this form of heating can be fuelled by coal, coke, gas or oil, coupled with thermostatic control. Air heating has become increasingly popular both with commercial growers and amateurs; it is clean, efficient and, if everything has been done correctly – the right capacity air heater, ducting and any other detail carefully checked – possibly one of the finest foolproof methods of heating yet invented; hot air reaches to every corner of the house in a matter of seconds from when the heater commences operating. Convector heaters, portable ones, are ideal for the small greenhouse – oil or electric, it does not matter, but do be certain the capacity of the heater is sufficient to do the job required. The heater cannot be blamed if it was not guaranteed for the area of greenhouse in which it finds itself.

Beware of stoves which were not intended for greenhouse heating! There is no true economy in using an old electric fire or oil stove which is no longer wanted for any other purpose. Dangers lurk in such equipment. I have seen beautiful collections of well-kept succulents become completely blackened overnight due to a faulty oil stove, not intended for the purpose, which has blown out black smoke for hours until soot has covered everything. If you want to get the full benefit from heating, then use the right equipment and have the work installed correctly.

It is easy to talk about heating and almost at once the impression is given that succulents must have constant heat. This is not so. There are exceptions, of course, but such exceptions are nearly always in the minority and can be catered for separately without undue expense caused by keeping all-round high temperatures. During the rest periods – that is, November to March or thereabouts – the majority of plants will be quite content with $45°F$ – or a lift to say $50°$ would assuredly be welcome. Such is the necessary maximum. More tender plants, requiring higher temperatures, can have a small section segregated from the rest of the greenhouse, using polythene or glass, and can have supplementary heating easily installed. A small electric bulb, say 15 or perhaps 25 watts, in a waterproofed holder, with a clay flower-pot set over it as a cover, will radiate sufficient additional heating for a small area at little expense.

To summarize as regards heating – it cannot be stressed too often that any equipment used must be without fault, kept clean and checked regularly. Oil, gas, electric, coke – all are excellent commodities to use – but without due care of the apparatus they can prove dangerous to the users and disastrous to the plants.

If you are going to grow cacti and succulents in your greenhouse do not mix them up with tomatoes, ferns or grape-vines. Useful and decorative as these might be, they are not the most suitable companions for cacti and succulents, even though it has been known for certain succulent plants apparently to flourish mixed in with cucumbers and chrysanthemums, plus the tomatoes. This is really 'one up' for the poor succulents which try to tolerate any conditions and suffer many discomforts to survive. Keep a succulent house for succulents. These warnings are possibly unnecessary, as most collectors find their greenhouses so often over-full with succulents that other things would not have a chance.

Cultivation of succulents under glass is reasonably simple if common sense and very obvious guide-lines are followed. If the purpose is to grow a mixed collection of cacti and other succulent plants, then this should not present undue problems, but one great factor must be recommended, that the selection of plants is such that all the species will grow well together, requiring or accepting the same conditions – temperature, watering, resting and environment. This means: (a) What surroundings would the plants have enjoyed in nature? (b) Are they 'desert' plants, used to full light for most of the year? (c) Would they accept the same resting period? (Obviously this would be our winter months.) Alternatively, there are plants which would flourish better in shade or partial shade, and this particularly applies to rain forest and jungle plants, and then a different approach to 'resting' must be adopted. It is not wise to mix the two groups in one greenhouse unless suitable prepara-

A rare Echinocactus species—the sort of plant that may well become the pride of a collector.

tions have been made to accommodate them in varying conditions. Partitioning is easy to erect and this can be in any durable material; possibly plastic sheeting is to be preferred above all else. It is a matter of trying to understand what you are growing. Lack of attention in these respects can cause many disappointments and frustrations.

A passing mention has been made earlier regarding shading. This is an important matter when it comes to successful growing. The conditions developed in the greenhouse, well ventilated as it may be, can sometimes, in very hot oppressive

weather, be totally foreign to what would occur in habitat even in the hottest and driest season. Scorch cannot be overlooked, and while ventilation goes two-thirds of the way to offsetting this, good shading provides the other third safeguard. To set minds at rest, shading will not be detrimental to flower producing! It is customary for greenhouses to be erected facing east and west. This is considered the best situation to gain the benefit of full light and, of course, maximum light is an essential requirement. However, sunshine, as opposed to light, will have every opportunity of pervading the greenhouse, and, as it has to travel through glass, this can, at times, be much magnified, hence sorching, and nothing disfigures a plant more quickly and more permanently. Therefore, shading is a *must* and can be done easily and effectively. It is possible to make or purchase blinds which are undoubtedly the best of all methods – hessian is a very suitable material and fairly cheap, also slatted blinds offer another splendid system. The process usually resorted to is painting the glass with a special compound which can be purchased from garden sundriesmen. If this is used, then follow the directions for mixing and applying – but wait until the necessity arises before doing the job – it becomes a rather semi-permanent method and so often the need for removing it, when duller and colder weather descends, is overlooked. Don't leave it to wash off on its own accord – it might not happen. It is easier to give shade than to give sunshine; too much shade can damage plants, or make them grow 'soft', and surplus moisture tends to hang around just a little too long if shading remains unnecessarily.

When the collection is a mixed one, it is advisable to apply some method of shading throughout the brighter months to protect the area set aside for 'shade-lovers'. Such plants can accept a measure of surplus moisture, but not too much – they are used to a high humidity and moist conditions, and if these are not made available it will mean the plants can wither, or, to say the least, look very unhappy. On the other hand, if the whole collection is for

A fine collection of mixed cacti showing several rare cristate forms.

these varieties, then the question of shading is simplified and the only time it will not be needed are the months when sunshine and light are least available – late autumn, winter and just the very beginning of spring.

Successful growing does demand certain chores. Automation has not supplied a totally foolproof method of dealing with these. It is a manual effort, one which must be systematically undertaken. Watering is of great consequence. Haphazard watering is dangerous; you must know what you are doing. The question arises, 'When and how often do plants need watering?' It is totally impossible to determine this by any system of prior-planning. We are not able to foresee weather conditions and changes – a period of heatwave can dry out pots in a few hours, while even in so-called summer, a pot may remain moist for many days. So water when the soil is dry, then water well. A little, whether it wants it or not, is a dangerous practice and ultimately spells disaster.

From early November until March it is advisable to restrict watering almost entirely, and if a very low temperature of under $45°F$ is maintained, total dryness must be effected. By the end of the rest period the soil may have become hard, as well as dry, and if soil-less composts have been used, a problem may be presented in getting the soil moist again, more so when dealing with a peat-based compost. However, wetting agents can be obtained. These are mixed with the water for the first application, so the soil will more readily absorb moisture. It is known that certain washing-up liquids make excellent wetting agents and do no harm to the plants. It is not essential to use rain water; in fact, if it is impossible to guarantee the cleanliness of rain water, then much better to use tap water at all times. While there may be a certain amount of lime in it, this can be easily offset, and it is certain that no direct infection by undesirable bacteria, algae and the like, is encouraged. The idea that tepid water must be used in colder weather is yet another fallacy. Water direct from the tap can be used without fear. One final word on this subject. Light overhead spraying is very beneficial in hot weather; this should be given in the evenings, after the sun has gone down, and will have the effect of creating humidity similar to dew, which is an encouragement to growth and flowering.

A very different method of watering is required in the case of shade-loving plants, including epiphytes and Epiphyllum hybrids. The resting period does not occur as with desert plants. Lack of water spells impeding danger. If the root system dries out, then the tendency is for it to dehydrate and rot. This rotting can even be encouraged by the renewal of watering. Therefore, such plants must be kept moist—*not* wet—at the roots throughout the year. Root rot is one of the most prevalent difficulties encountered, and while this might be due to other conditions, it is undoubtedly true that the main cause is allowing the plant to dry out. The roots seem to shrivel almost immediately, so that when watering is renewed they have lost the capacity of taking up moisture—and so rot sets in.

One aspect has not yet been mentioned. There are certain South African and South West African plants which are winter growers; they stay dormant all the summer months, then come into leaf from September onwards and subsequently into bloom. Here is an instance where an understanding of the plant is tremendously important. If it is growing, then it must be watered. Unfortunately it has not been possible to change the habits of these plants in cultivation so that they forget their seasons. This factor will call for higher temperatures and winter watering—in other words what is done for succulents in the summer must be provided for these winter growers during the colder weather. If such provision cannot be made, it is better not to indulge in such luxury plants.

The subject of potting and soils can be made a very complex matter, and this is certainly not the intention here. However, a very practical and sensible approach is essential. No subject has encouraged more arguments among gardening addicts than the question of compost. What satisfies one is totally unacceptable to another. When it comes to succulents, some gardeners endeavour to relate their growing media to that which applies in nature, and really this just cannot make sense. To emulate nature precisely would require the use of many varying soil formulas. In addition there would be a demand for extremely varying growing conditions

—varying from one species to another. No plants grow in sheer sandy deserts where rainfall is non-existent, but they often survive in impoverished soil, on stony wastes, on cliff faces and mountain ridges—frequently where water is at a premium and where they are often kept waiting months or even years for rain.

On the other hand, some succulents enjoy a comparatively comfortable existence, where conditions are conducive to the production of handsome plants with magnificent growth. So back to the compost formula. How can you produce a compost which on the one hand is a 'survival' mixture, and on the other hand is one which is to encourage fantastic growth and development? Frankly, a survival growing mix is not sufficient; here it is possible to improve on nature, and the plants will readily respond. It should be the pride and ambition of any grower to do something better than would occur in habitat. So use a compost which grows plants and grows them well. In these days it is possible to purchase many branded composts ideally suited to the majority of cacti and succulents.

The age of soil-less composts is very much with us. With very few exceptions, succulents relish these. Nevertheless, certain factors must be borne in mind. A porous mixture is a 'must'. Therefore, any soil-less compost must have a good proportion of very sharp-washed sand, preferably 1/8th washed coarse gravel, as much as 30% or more of the bulk. If the compost is commercially prepared without this ingredient it need be no problem to add, but the mixing must be done thoroughly. Soil-less composts are prepared with nutrients which last only for a matter of weeks, but excellent results can be achieved in that short period. Therefore, additional fertilizing must be undertaken at regular intervals, otherwise the plant will eventually succumb. It is usually considered wise and necessary to fertilize every three or four weeks throughout the growing season—a thriving plant needs plenty of food. One aspect of major importance must be remembered before leaving the subject of soil-less composts, and that is watering. Great care must be given to this, especially if plastic pots are in use. These require less water than clay pots, and it is so easy to over-water. Soil-less composts demand excellent drainage and more will be said about that later; otherwise excessive dampness can encourage sciara fly, one of the most dangerous pests to be avoided, as succulents have no natural immunity against this sort of problem.

Many other popular soil mixtures are commercially available, some of long standing repute with much to recommend them. These are usually prepared according to prescribed formulas supplied by eminent research establishments, and if the ingredients are correctly proportioned and no carelessness has been allowed in the preparation, they have the quality of growing excellent plants. An increasing difficulty today is that of getting good-quality loam, an ingredient in all such composts. The fields of Britain are still suffering the after effects of herbicides, fungicides, pesticides and so many other 'cides' which have built up in the soil and to a degree contaminated it – a fact which causes concern. Be certain the supplier of your compost is himself satisfied with the product he is selling and will stand by it. A good compost is excellent – a not-so-good is invariably bad and will not contribute to good growing.

To finalize the subject of greenhouse culture: just a few comment to summarize what has already been referred to, together with a few 'rules' which, if observed, can save many a heartache.

If you use plastic pots – they are cheap to buy, easily cleaned, and equal to any clay pots in successful growing – be sure to crock the pot well. It is not a matter of covering the hole to stop the soil falling out – the hole wasn't put there for that purpose. Crocking should be of sufficient depth to allow surplus moisture to percolate freely and escape through the drainage hole. Too shallow crocking means the compost is liable to press too heavily and harden, which will tend to create a complete 'seal' at the bottom of the container. Stagnation can then set in, and succulents cannot tolerate 'wet feet'.

Be sure you use the right fertilizers, prepared correctly for the greatest benefit to the plants. Too much nitrogen certainly promotes growth but does not influence flowering. Don't feed a scraggy plant or a dehydrated one – it will probably want a lot of

'hospital' treatment before it can receive nutrients again. Ascertain why it is in this condition. Examine the roots; they may be rotten and therefore incapable of taking up moisture at all. Only a plant growing well will take nutrients – the response will be rapid.

Cacti and succulents are sometimes said to flourish on neglect. This is not so. They may survive, but not flourish. One only has to leave a plant unattended or uncared for over a period of a few months, or even weeks, and the result will be only too apparent. Furthermore, it is unlikely ever be the same again, however much kindness may be showered upon it afterwards. On the other hand, when due attention is given to its needs, the reward justifies the effort. Remember, once a plant is placed in a container its success or failure is in the hands of the grower; it cannot water, feed or do much to help its own survival; the thinking and effort must be ours.

There is an increasing interest in the propagation of succulents. This is by no means a difficult task, and there are various methods whereby plants can be increased at relatively little cost.

Very few plants can compete with succulents for easy, almost 'do-it-yourself' propagation. So often it is heard 'You just break a piece off and it will grow.' That is almost correct if not taken too literally. Several cacti species – Opuntias probably offer the finest example – provide endless scope for increase by removing the pads which root so easily. This equally applies to Epiphyllums or Euphorbias – and hosts of other species – when, for the purpose of propagating, a small section can be removed, allowed to callus, then set in a light and very porous compost and stood in a semi-shady position until a root system has developed. If such cuttings are taken in warm weather they will require no other form of heating, but if the operation takes place during periods of inclement conditions then the use of a propagating frame, with some sort of under heat, is recommended. Watering must not be overlooked during the rooting period, but extreme care must always be exercised. Too much water will rot the cutting, while too little will encourage dehydration. Many species of globular cacti will develop offsets naturally. While it is not a wise thing

Cephalocereus senelis growing happily beside a large Agave species.

to take them off indiscriminately for the purpose of propagation, it is nevertheless a fact that such offsets from Echinopsis, Lobivia, Mammillaria, Rebutia and others with similar habit will quickly root if treated as suggested for Opuntias, etc. With Echinopsis and some other genera, the 'pups' come away from the parent very easily and mostly have their roots already. If, however, the need arises literally to sever the offset, then treat this operation with due care. Using a very sharp knife, let the

wound be as small as possible. Dusting the cut surfaces with sulphur powder is one way to safeguard against infection. Remember, the need to allow the wound to callus is very important. Incidentally, most succulents have a watery sap which very soon heals. There are some Euphorbias, Ceropegias and Hoyas which have milky sap–latex –and this can ooze for some while after the cut has been made, often to the detriment of both plant and cutting. It is best to dip the cutting in cold water immediately. This will have the rapid effect of stopping the flow of sap. It is not always so easy to deal with the parent plant, but a can of water can be used to spray over the cut section which will quickly staunch the 'bleeding'.

Another method of propagation is grafting. This should not be done for the sake of grafting. If a plant grows well on its own roots why bother to graft? Grafting is mainly used for propagating plants which are themselves inclined to be temperamental or very slow growing on their own roots, or are most effective-looking when grafted; in the latter category is the Christmas cactus, when a stately 'standard' has much to commend it! Recent years have seen the introduction and development of seedlings minus chlorophyll. Chlorophyll is what produces the green colouring – or perhaps it should be said the *correct* colouring – in plants, mainly as it applies to the plant body. When a few thousand seeds are sown, some species have a tendency to develop a few 'freaks' – little red, yellow or white plant bodies which feed on the cotyledon; then normally, when the cotyledon dies, the little seedling dies too; it hasn't the means of looking after itself. The idea of trying to save these little seedlings originated in Japan, so that now we have 'red-knobs' (they are even termed 'strawberry knobs'), yellow, orange or white knobs. There is an elusive attraction about them. When they were first introduced there was rare excitement. A new sort of plant had been developed by man's skill, but it was also rumoured that it was a result of radiation, the after-effects of the atom bombs dropped on Japan. Whether we like them or not is immaterial – the fact is simply that such subjects can *only* survive by grafting. Another new venture into the realm of grafting has been undertaken by a leading German university where annual and biennial species of succulents have been grafted on perennial stock, the result being a perennial 'annual'. Let grafting be undertaken only when there is a worthwhile end product.

Care must be taken in the selection of suitable stock. Most globular cacti, species of Trichocereus or Harrisia are very satisfactory. In such grafts the union is effected by a horizontal cut, with provision made for the scion to be held in position

securely until the union is complete – usually a matter of only a few days. The use of an elastic band is ideal. When dealing with Christmas cacti and similarly epiphytic plants, the best stock is Hylocereus, Selenicereus, Pereskiopsis or Pereskia – or even Opuntia. A young but strong and erect stock should be selected about 25 cm or more in length dependent upon the height required for the 'standard'. Here the method of grafting is by a slit or 'V' shaped cut; the scion should have the skin of the section to be inserted carefully removed and then be immediately set in the cleft and held in position by a cactus spine. The sap of the scion and that of the stock will encourage a quicker and more satisfactory union.

The correct time for grafting is late spring and early summer months. Possibly May and June are best. Stand the grafts in a warm, shady and airy place, keep moist, and the results should be satisfactory.

The other method of propagation is, of course, by seed. This, after all, is the most natural and most satisfying. It can prove an exciting experience and nothing is more stimulating than to look at fully matured flowering plants and have the great satisfaction of realizing they were grown by you from seed.

Packets of mixed seed are frequently offered commercially. This might not be the best way to go about the job. Seeds can vary tremendously in size: from particles like dust to seeds as large as peas. They may have different periods of germination and these factors can produce difficulties. Most specialist nurseries now offer named varieties of cacti and succulent seed; this is the better way, and in any case you will know what you are growing. As long as moisture and warmth are provided, together with a somewhat close atmospheric environment, seeds will germinate quite quickly. A shady position is recommended at first, and once the seedlings are through they should be given more light, but not too much at one time – carrying through the process gradually. Prepared seed composts are obtainable and can be thoroughly recommended; this is easier and safer than trying to prepare your own. Very small seeds should be lightly scattered and left uncovered, but with larger

It is quite possible to raise a collection of cacti as fine as these from a packet of mixed seed.

seeds the usual policy is to cover to the approximate size of the seed – the larger the seed the deeper the covering. After sowing, soak the container thoroughly, preferably by immersion in water, but not too much or the top layer of soil, with the seeds, may float away. Then cover with a sheet of glass and paper, place either in a propagator or in a place away from direct sunlight where a temperature of 70°F can be maintained throughout the period of germination. Never let the soil dry out, but discriminate between the soil being moist and being wet.

Following germination, the main concern is to see that the seedlings do not rot. Once they are given further light there is the great fear of damping off – and as with most things, prevention is better than cure. It is no problem to purchase, either from a garden sundriesman or chemist, such items as Chinosol (Potassium oxyquinoline sulphate) or Chestnut Compound, both of which are well-established and well-recommended preventatives. They should be mixed with water and lightly sprayed over the tray of seedlings at the first watering after germination. It is then a matter of getting the seedlings accustomed to more light, but again a gradual process is best. Together with light, give more ventilation and reduce the temperature little by little so they learn to accept the normal conditions which would apply to mature plants.

Seedlings should be encouraged to grow all the time – that is for at least nine months continuously so as to enable them to be of sufficient size to accept the resting period requirements associated with the particular species. If adequately high temperatures can be maintained throughout the succeeding winter, there is no reason why the seedlings should not be allowed to continue growing right through to the following winter. Don't be too anxious to prick out the seedlings; wait until they can be handled easily and have taken on the appearance of the parent plant. While it is best to sow seeds thinly, the fact remains that even if the small plants appear to be overcrowded they will come to no harm if left untouched for quite a long while – at least to the stage when they can be readily pricked out into trays or individual pots.

After all this, when is the best time to sow? If you have the means to maintain sufficient warmth, then January is a good month. By the time they have germinated and are able to accept full light and ventilation, the spring months will have come and from then on, with correct attention, they should

not look back. If, on the other hand, it is not possible to make this provision for heat, then it is certainly wiser to wait until early spring before sowing. We hear about growing them in an airing cupboard. This is all very well if you remember they are there; they can easily be forgotten – 'out of sight, out of mind'. However, if you do use this method, place the whole tray, after it has been thoroughly moistened, into a plastic bag and seal it. This will at least conserve the moisture, but be sure to watch carefully, and when the seeds have germinated place the tray in a lighter position and so continue as with seeds grown in a propagator.

Yes, the greenhouse can prove a wonderful asset. Look after it and use it to its fullest capacity, but remember the snags which may develop if due care is not given to detail, and have the necessary remedies on hand in emergency.

8 Pests and Diseases

It is unfortunate that no form of plant-life is totally immune from pest and disease problems, and while succulents are relatively secure from many aspects of infestation, there are difficulties which may be encountered and must be resolved.

Diseases as such are few, and these are likely to affect only certain families or species. Frequently these disorders can be avoided altogether if due consideration is given to cultural requirements. So often the conditions which encourage disease are due to carelessness on the part of the grower.

The wisest policy is prevention. With the introduction of modern-day techniques it is reasonably simple to reduce pest penetration to a minimum and to a great degree provide the plant with efficient resistance to the more common diseases. Systemic insecticides and fungicides are assets to the grower, and if used wisely and in strict accordance with the producer's instructions, excellent results can be achieved. Systemics become operative soon after they are applied, and remain potent for a considerable period afterwards. If the plants are clean and healthy to start with, the use of systemics is undoubtedly the easiest and most effective method to keep them that way.

With only few exceptions, succulents are not marked or damaged by the application of insecticides or fungicides, systemic or otherwise, so long as the manufacturer's recommendations are observed. The more sensitive plants are invariably mentioned by the manufacturer, who advises against the use of the pesticide in such cases. Species of Crassula, Kalanchoe, Echeveria and certain other leaf-succulents can be blemished if due care is not maintained. This must be kept uppermost in mind when considering the use of malathion or any proprietary brand of insecticide containing this chemical.

It is not proposed to mention any particular brand by name, only the chemical involved. In certain instances, non-chemical remedies are preferable and due regard is given to this.

Pests

MEALY-BUG. Has the appearance of a very small woodlice about 2mm long, covered with a white mealy substance. The eggs are contained within the white tufts which are usually in close proximity. When only a small infestation is apparent apply methylated spirit (or better still, 1 part nicotine to 30 parts methylated spirit) to the affected area by means of small camel-hair brush. This will immediately remove the white coating and kill the pest. Alternatively, (a) *Nicotine* as a spray using 1 fl.oz. to 10 galls of water; (b) *Malathion* diluted as prescribed on container, or Malathion as an areosol; (c) *Systemic* preparations whereby the plant absorbs the poison and the pest dies in consequence.

RED SPIDER. This is not a spider at all, and not really red. More appropriately called 'spider mite'. Orange in colour, minute, almost too small for the naked eye to see, colonizing and becoming surrounded with very fine webs. The pest sucks the sap, resulting in disfigurement of plant body or reddening of the leaves.

Problem usually caused by too-dry conditions, bad ventilation; spider mites can only thrive in a hot and close environment. *Prevention* can be achieved by a more humid atmosphere and good ventilation, or at least these will act as deterrents. Systemics are effective and can provide a means of prevention.

ROOT MEALY BUG. A white dusty-looking substance around the root system and frequently noticeable on the inside of the container. A dangerous pest requiring urgent attention – will eat the roots and work its way into the base of the plant, particularly young fleshy plants. Can be washed off completely by fierce jets of water. It is wise to wash the roots totally clear of soil, then dip into a malathion solution before repotting. Systemic pesticides can immunize the plant if applied before infestation, and dosed periodically thereafter. Repeated dosages can also effect a cure.

EEL WORM. Or nematodes. Do not often affect small collections. The roots are contaminated and become swollen, developing small nodules. Drastic action is necessary. Cut away all infected roots, or take cuttings from the plant and re-root, destroying the original plant entirely. Chemical treatment is dangerous, protective clothing necessary.

SCALE INSECT. Resembles a minute 'limpet' – this is the female form which sucks the sap, lays her eggs. In due course the grubs move around until the females take the form of 'limpets' – and so the process continues. This pest can cause tremendous disfigurement to the plant. Systemics provide long-term protection. Oil-emulsion based spray will give rapid clearance of the pest – but this can remove the 'bloom' from leaf and stem surfaces in certain species.

SCIARA FLY. Most frequently associated with peat-based preparations – one of the few drawbacks to soil-less composts. Minute black flies – sometimes called 'Mushroom Flies' – which lay their eggs and when hatched the little white grubs eat the roots of seedlings and fleshy plants and into the base of the plant. Commercial treatments are available.

SLUGS AND SNAILS. Night prowlers causing great damage and disfigurement. Many killing compounds on the market – either in liquid form or pellets – all equally efficient.

WOODLICE are more of a nuisance than a pest – although the young are known to eat seedlings and young growth. There are many commercial preparations to deal with them.

APHIDS. Green-fly and Black-fly can do immeasurable harm to young growth and flower buds. Systemic insecticides are effective and can afford long-lasting protection.

WHITE FLY. A dangerous and persistent pest which attacks leaf succulents in particular, usually on the back of leaves. When the plant is 'brushed' they fly off in clouds, only to return again. Difficult to eradicate. Smokes are most effective, but should be used **STRICTLY** in accordance with the manufacturer's instructions. Dangerous if misused.

ANTS. While they do no real harm of themselves, they are a nuisance and considered to encourage aphids. mealy-bugs, etc. There are many products available to deal with ants.

Other pests are met with occasionally; caterpillars, earthworms, mice, etc. These are best dealt with by more manual means.

Diseases

Very few diseases and disorders affect healthy plants: the use of fungicides usually offers protection or cure, but good cultivation is the best remedy.

BLACK ROT. Appears to be most prevalent with Stapelias and epiphytic cacti. The blackening of the stem generally occurs at or just below soil level. The cause is not too certain but is considered to have an association with a high nitrogen content in the soil. The remedy also is not definite but a copper-based fungicide will possibly help. The best solution is to take clean cuttings, allow to callus and re-root, experimenting with a somewhat different soil media.

BASAL-STEM ROT. Closely akin to Black rot. The rot seems to arise from foot damage or disorders—sometimes due to being too cold, or excessive watering, and no fungicide can offset this condition. Take clean cuttings, dust with sulphur powder, and allow to callus before setting for re-rooting.

ROOT DISORDERS. These problems can be quickly appreciated when the plant fails to grow and shows signs of shrivelling. This can be due to wrong watering, too much or too little; under-potting; or a general souring of the soil. The use of charcoal chippings with the crocking will help to avert the last difficulty. Re-potting is necessary, examining the roots, trimming where required, and re-potting into good compost, and remember to crock and crock well.

Other aspects of damage to succulents have been considered in previous chapters—bud-drop with Christmas Cacti, scorching because of bad ventilation, damping off of seedlings—these and other headaches can be avoided if due regard is given to cultural requirements for greenhouse subjects.

WARNING

In conclusion it is well to remember that the chemicals used are toxic—be careful how they are handled—that the dosage is correct—and generally it is wise to wear some form of protective clothing. Care should be exercised as to where chemicals are stored—well away from children and pets. The dosage should comply with the instructions—also the time and the method. In this way damage to plants and humans will be avoided—there is no wisdom in trying to solve one problem and creating another!

Part 3
Directory

Directory of Families and Genera

This Directory lists genera and sub-genera which are currently accepted in botanical nomenclature and have been validly published, or are generally recognized in horticulture. *Those listed in italics* are considered obsolete names and are usually no longer applicable. In such instances indication is usually given of current generic title.

This record is undoubtedly far from complete, but an endeavour has been made to provide a reasonably comprehensive guide to those Plant Families whose genera include succulent plants.

Entries include: FAMILY, GENERIC TITLE, AUTHORSHIP, DISTRIBUTION.

Cactaceae

Acanthocalycium Backeb. ARGENTINA.
Acanthocereus (A. Bgr.) Br. & Rose MEXICO, COLOMBIA, GUATEMALA, BRAZIL.
Acantholobivia Backeb. PERU.
Acanthorhipsalis (K. Schum.) Br. & Rose ARGENTINA, BOLIVIA, PERU.
Akersia Buin. PERU.
Ancistrocactus (K. Schum.) Br. & Rose MEXICO, U.S.A.
Andenea Kreuz. (see Lobivia)
Anhalonium Lem. (see Ariocarpus)
Anisocereus Backeb. MEXICO, GUATEMALA.
Aporocactus Lem. MEXICO.
Aporocereus Fric & Kreuz. (see Aporocactus)
Archiebnerella F. Buxb. (see Mammillaria)
Arequipa Br. & Rose CHILE, PERU.
Arequipiopsis Kreuz. & Buin. (see Arequipa)
Ariocarpus Scheidw. MEXICO.
Armatocereus Backeb. PERU, ECUADOR, COLOMBIA.
Arrojadoa Br. & Rose BRAZIL.
Arthrocereus A. Bgr. BRAZIL.
Astrophytum Lem. MEXICO, U.S.A.
Austrocactus Br. & R. ARGENTINA, CHILE.
Austrocephalocereus (Backeb.) BRAZIL.

Austrocylindropuntia Backeb. ARGENTINA, ECUADOR, BOLIVIA, PERU, CHILE.
Aylostera Speg. BOLIVIA, ARGENTINA.
Aztekium Boed. MEXICO.
Azureocereus Akers & Johns PERU.
Backebergia H. Bravo MEXICO.
Bartschella Br. & Rose MEXICO.
Bergerocactus Br. & Rose MEXICO, U.S.A.
Binghamia Br. & Rose (see Haageocereus)
Blossfeldia Werd. BOLIVIA, ARGENTINA.
Bolivicereus Card. PERU, BOLIVIA.
Bonifazia Standl. & Steyern (see Disocactus)
Borzicactus Ricco. ECUADOR, PERU.
Brachycalycium Backeb. (see Gymnocalycium)
Brachycereus Br. & Rose GALAPAGOS ISLANDS.
Brasilicactus Backeb. BRAZIL, URUGUAY.
Brasilicereus Backeb. BRAZIL.
Brasiliopuntia (K. Schum.) A. Bgr. BRAZIL, PERU, ARGENTINA, BOLIVIA, PARAGUAY.
Bridgesia Backeb. (see Weingartia)
Brittonia Houghton ex. C. A. Armstr. (see Hamatocactus)
Browningia Br. & Rose PERU.
Buiningia Buxb. BRAZIL.
Cactus L. (see Melocactus etc.)
Calamorhipsalis K. Schum. (sub-genus)
Calymmanthium Ritter PERU.
Carnegia Br. & Rose non Perkins U.S.A., MEXICO.
Castellanosia Card. BOLIVIA, PERU.
Cephalocereus Pfeiff. MEXICO.
Cephalocleistocactus Ritt. BOLIVIA.
Cereus Mill. S. AMERICA.
Chamaecereus Br. & Rose ARGENTINA.
Chiapasia Br. & Rose (see Disocactus)
Chilenia Backeb. CHILE.
Chileorebutia Fric. (see Rebutia)
Chilita Orcutt (see Mammillaria)
Cipocereus Ritter BOLIVIA.
Cleistocactus Lem. BOLIVIA, ARGENTINA, PARAGUAY, URUGUAY.
Clistanthocereus Backeb. PERU.

Cochemiea (K. Brand.) Walton MEXICO.

Coleocephalocereus Backeb. BRAZIL.

Coloradoa Boiss. & Davids. U.S.A.

Consolea Lem. U.S.A., BAHAMAS, CUBA, JAMAICA.

Copiapoa Br. & Rose CHILE.

Corryocactus Br. & Rose PERU, BOLIVIA.

Corynopuntia F. M. Knuth U.S.A., MEXICO.

Coryphantha (Engelm.) Lem. MEXICO, U.S.A.

Cryptocereus Alex. MEXICO, COSTA RICA.

Cullmannia C. Distefano (see Wilcoxia)

Cumarinia (Knuth) Backeb. (see Coryphantha)

Cutakia Backeb. (see Arthrocereus)

Cylindropuntia (Engelm.) F. M. Knuth in Backeb.
  MEXICO, U.S.A.

Cylindrorebutia Fric. & Kreuz. (see Rebutia)

Deamia Br. & Rose MEXICO, HONDURAS.

Delaetia Backeb. CHILE.

Dendrocereus Br. & Rose CUBA.

Denmoza Br. & Rose ARGENTINA.

Digitorebutia Fric & Kreuz. ex Buin. (see Rebutia)

Disocactus Lindl. GUATEMALA, HONDURAS.

Discocactus Pfeiff. BRAZIL, BOLIVIA, PARAGUAY.

Dolichothele (K. Schum.) Br. & Rose MEXICO, U.S.A.
  MEXICO, U.S.A.

Ebnerella F. Buxb. (see Mammillaria)

Ebneria Backeb. (see Monvillea)

Eccremocactus Br. & Rose COSTA RICA.

Echinocactus (Link & Otto) Br. & Rose MEXICO, U.S.A.

Echinocereus Engelm. MEXICO, U.S.A.

Echinofossulocactus Lawr. MEXICO.

Echinomastus Br. & Rose MEXICO, U.S.A.

Echinopsis Zucc. BOLIVIA, BRAZIL, PARAGUAY,
  ARGENTINA.

Encephalocarpus A. Bgr. MEXICO.

Epiphyllanthus A. Bgr. BRAZIL.

Epiphyllopsis A. Bgr. BRAZIL.

Epiphyllum Haw. C. AND S. AMERICA, WEST INDIES,
  MEXICO.

Epithelantha (Web.) Br. & Rose MEXICO.

Erdisia Br. & Rose PERU, CHILE.

Eriocactus Backeb. BRAZIL, PARAGUAY.

Eriocereus (A. Bgr.) Ricco. ARGENTINA, BRAZIL.

Eriosyce Phil. CHILE.

Erythrorhipsalis A. Bgr. BRAZIL.

Escobaria Br. & Rose U.S.A., MEXICO.

Escontria Rose MEXICO.

Espostoa Br. & Rose PERU.

Euescobaria F. Buxb. (see Escobaria)

Eulychnia Phil. CHILE.

Eurhipsalis K. Schum. (sub-genus)

Facheiroa Br. & Rose BRAZIL.

Ferocactus Br. & Rose MEXICO, U.S.A.

Floresia Krainz & Ritter (see Weberbauerocereus)

Frailea Br. & Rose BRAZIL.

Glandulicactus Backeb. MEXICO.

Goniorhipsalis K. Schum. (sub-genus)

Grusonia F. Reichb. MEXICO.

Gymnanthocereus Backeb. PERU.

Gymnocactus Backeb. MEXICO.

Gymnocalycium Pfeiff. ARGENTINA, PARAGUAY,
  BOLIVIA, URUGUAY.

Gymnocereus Backeb. PERU.

Haageocereus Backeb. PERU.

Hamatocactus Br. & Rose MEXICO, U.S.A.

Harrisia Britt. U.S.A., JAMAICA, CUBA, HAITI.

Haseltonia Backeb. MEXICO.

Hatiora Br. & Rose BRAZIL.

Heliabravoa Backeb. MEXICO.

Helianthocereus Backeb. BOLIVIA, ARGENTINA.

Heliocereus (A. Bgr.) Br. & Rose MEXICO, GUATEMALA.

Hertrichocereus Backeb. MEXICO.

Heteropodium Backeb. (see Lepismium)

Hildewintera Ritt. BOLIVIA.

Homalocephala Br. & Rose U.S.A.

Horridocactus Backeb. CHILE.

Hummelia Backeb. (see Monvillea)

Hylocereus (A. BGR.) Br. & Rose WEST INDIES, VENE-
  ZUELA, MEXICO, PERU.

Hymenorebutia Fric ex Buin. (see Rebutia)

Islaya Backeb. PERU.

Isolatocereus (Backeb.) Backeb. MEXICO.

Jasminocereus Br. & Rose GALAPAGOS ISLANDS.

Krainzia Backeb. MEXICO.

Lasiocereus Ritt. PERU.

Lemaireocereus Br. & Rose MEXICO, HONDURAS,
  GUATEMALA.

Leocereus Br. & Rose BRAZIL.

Lepidocoryphantha Backeb. MEXICO, U.S.A.

Lepismium Pfeiff. BRAZIL, PARAGUAY, ARGENTINA.

Leptocereus (A. Bgr.) Br. & Rose CUBA.

Leuchtenbergia Hook. MEXICO.

Leucostele Backeb. BOLIVIA.

Lobeira Alex. (see Nopalxochia)

Lobivia Br. & Rose BOLIVIA, ARGENTINA, PERU.

Lophocereus (A. Bgr.) Br. & Rose MEXICO.

Lophophora Coulter MEXICO.

Loxanthocereus Backeb. PERU.

Machaerocereus Br. & Rose MEXICO.

Maihuenia Phil. ARGENTINA, CHILE.

Maihueniopsis Speg. ARGENTINA.

Malacocarpus Salm Dyck. non Fisch. & May BRAZIL,
  URUGUAY, ARGENTINA.

Mamillopsis (Morr.) Br. & Rose MEXICO.

Mammillaria Haw. MEXICO, U.S.A.

Mammilloydia F. Buxb. (see Mammillaria)

Marenopuntia Backeb. MEXICO.

Marginatocereus (Backeb.) Backeb. MEXICO.

Maritimocereus Akers & Buin. (see Loxanthocereus)

Marniera Backeb. (see Epiphyllum)

Marshallocereus Backeb. MEXICO.

Matucana Br. & Rose PERU.

Mediocactus Br. & Rose BOLIVIA, PARAGUAY, MARTINIQUE, PERU.

Mediolobivia Backeb. BOLIVIA, ARGENTINA.

Melocactus (Tourn.) Link & Otto MEXICO, WEST INDIES, BRAZIL, PERU, VENEZUELA.

Micranthocereus Backeb. BRAZIL.

Micropuntia Daston U.S.A.

Mila Br. & Rose PERU.

Mitrocereus (Backeb.) Backeb. MEXICO.

Monvillea Br. & Rose BRAZIL, PERU, BOLIVIA, PARAGUAY.

Morangaya Rowl. MEXICO.

Morawetzia Backeb. PERU.

Myrtillocactus Cons. MEXICO, GUATEMALA.

Navajoa Croiz. U.S.A.

Neoabbottia Br. & Rose HAITI, DOMINICAN REP.

Neobesseya Br & Rose MEXICO, U.S.A.

Neobinghamia Backeb. PERU.

Neobuxbaumia Backeb. MEXICO.

Neocardenasia Backeb. BOLIVIA.

Neochilenia Backeb. CHILE.

Neodawsonia Backeb. MEXICO.

Neoevansia W. T. Marsh MEXICO.

Neogomesia Cast. MEXICO.

Neolloydia Br. & Rose U.S.A., MEXICO, CUBA.

Neomammillaria Br. & Rose (see Mammillaria)

Neoporteria (Br. & Rose) Don. & Rowl. CHILE, PERU.

Neoraimondia Br. & Rose PERU.

Neowerdermannia Fric. CHILE.

Nichelia Bullock. (see Neochilenia)

Nopalea Salm. Dyck. MEXICO, HONDURAS, GUATEMALA, WEST INDIES.

Nopalxochia Br. & Rose MEXICO.

Normanbokea Klad. & Buxb. MEXICO.

Notocactus (K. Schum.) A. Bgr. BRAZIL, URUGUAY, ARGENTINA.

Nyctocereus (A. Bgr.) Br. & Rose MEXICO, NICARAGUA, GUATEMALA.

Obregonia Fric & A. Bgr. MEXICO.

Oehmea F. Buxb. MEXICO.

Ophiorhipsalis K. Schum. (sub-genus)

Opuntia Mill. N., C. AND S. AMERICA, WEST INDIES.

Oreocereus (A. Bgr.) Ricco. ARGENTINA, BOLIVIA, PERU.

Oroya Br. & Rose PERU.

Ortegocactus Alex. MEXICO.

Pachycereus (A. Bgr.) Br. & Rose MEXICO.

Parodia Speg. BRAZIL, ARGENTINA, BOLIVIA, PARAGUAY.

Pediocactus Br. & Rose U.S.A.

Pelecyphora Ehrenb. MEXICO.

Peniocereus (A. Bgr.) Br. & Rose U.S.A., MEXICO.

Pereskia (Plum.) Mill. BOLIVIA, PERU, MEXICO.

Pereskiopsis Br. & Rose MEXICO.

Peruvocereus Akers (see Haageocereus)

Pfeiffera Salm. Dyck. BOLIVIA, ARGENTINA.

Phellosperma Br. & Rose U.S.A.

Philippicereus Backeb. CHILE.

Phyllocactus Link. (see Epiphyllum)

Phyllorhipsalis K. Schum. (sub-genus)

Pilocanthus B. W. Bens. & Backeb. (see Pediocactus)

Pilocereus Lem. non K. Schum. (see Pilosocereus)

Pilocopiapoa Ritt. CHILE.

Pilosocereus Byl. & Rowl. BRAZIL, WEST INDIES, PERU, MEXICO, VENEZUELA.

Piptanthocereus (A. Bgr.) Ricco. (see Cereus)

Platyopuntia Weber (sub-genus)

Polaskia Backeb. MEXICO.

Porfiria Boed. (see Mammillaria)

Praecereus Buxb. BRAZIL.

Pseudocoryphantha F. Buxb. (see Coryphantha)

Pseudoespostoa Backeb. PERU.

Pseudolobivia (Backeb.) Backeb. BOLIVIA.

Pseudomammillaria F. Buxb. (see Mammillaria)

Pseudomitrocereus Bravo & F. Buxb. (see Mitrocereus)

Pseudonopalxochia Backeb. (see Nopalxochia)

Pseudorhipsalis Br. & Rose COSTA RICA, MEXICO.

Pseudozygocactus Backeb. BRAZIL.

Pterocactus K. Schum. ARGENTINA.

Pterocereus MacDoug. & Mir. MEXICO.

Pygmaeocereus Johns. & Backeb. PERU.

Pygmaeolobivia Backeb. (see Mediolobivia)

Pyrrhocactus (A. Bgr.) Backeb. ARGENTINA.

Quiabentia Br. & Rose ARGENTINA, BRAZIL, BOLIVIA.

Rapicactus F. Buxb. & H. Oehme (see Gymnocactus)

Rathbunia Br. & Rose MEXICO.

Rauhocereus Backeb. PERU.

Rebutia K. Schum. BOLIVIA, ARGENTINA.

Reicheocactus Backeb. CHILE.

Rhipsalidopsis Br. & Rose BRAZIL.

Rhipsalis Gaertn. S. AMERICA, WEST INDIES, MADAGASCAR, ETC.

Rhodocactus (A. Bgr.) F. M. Knuth BRAZIL, GUATEMALA, COSTA RICA. WEST INDIES, ETC.

Ritterocereus Backeb. MEXICO, GUATEMALA, WEST INDIES, CHILE.

Rodentiophyla Ritt. CHILE.

Rooksbya Backeb. MEXICO.

Roseocactus A. Bgr. MEXICO, U.S.A.

Roseocereus Backeb. BOLIVIA.

Samaipaticereus Card. BOLIVIA.

Schlumbergera Lem. BRAZIL.

Sclerocactus (Br. & Rose) Benson U.S.A.

Selenicereus (A. Bgr.) Br. & Rose MEXICO, ARGENTINA, CUBA, HAITI, COSTA RICA, ETC.
Seticereus Backeb. PERU, ECUADOR.
Seticleistocactus Backeb. BOLIVIA.
Setiechinopsis (Backeb.) de Haas ARGENTINA.
Soehrensia Backeb. ARGENTINA, CHILE.
Solisia Br. & Rose MEXICO.
Stenocactus (K. Schum.) A. Bgr. (see Echinofossulocactus)
Stenocereus (A. Bgr.) Ricco. MEXICO.
Stephanocereus A. Bgr. BRAZIL.
Stetsonia Br. & Rose ARGENTINA.
Strombocactus Br. & Rose MEXICO.
Strophocactus Br. & Rose BRAZIL.
Submatucana Backeb. PERU.
Subpilocereus Backeb. COLOMBIA, VENEZUELA, GRENADA, CURACAO.
Sulcorebutia Backeb. BOLIVIA.
Tacinga Br. & Rose BRAZIL.
Tephrocactus Lem. S. AMERICA.
Thelocactus (K. Schum.) Br. & Rose U.S.A., MEXICO.
Thrixanthocereus Backeb. PERU.
Toumeya Br. & Rose U.S.A.
Trichocereus (A. Bgr.) Ricco. BOLIVIA, ARGENTINA, PERU, ECUADOR.
Trigonorhipsalis A. Bgr. (sub-genus)
Turbiniformis (Backeb.) F. Buxb. & Backeb. MEXICO.
Uebelmannia Buin. BRAZIL.
Utahia Br. & Rose U.S.A.
Vatricania Backeb. BOLIVIA.
Weberbauerocereus Backeb. PERU.
Weberocereus Br. & Rose COSTA RICA, PANAMA.
Weingartia Werd. ARGENTINA, BOLIVIA.
Werckleocereus Br. & Rose GUATEMALA, COSTA RICA.
Wigginsia D. M. Porter (see Malacocarpus)
Wilcoxia Br. & Rose MEXICO, U.S.A.
Wilmattea Br. & Rose GUATEMALA, HONDURAS.
Winteria Ritt. (see Hildewintera)
Winterocereus Backeb. (see Hildewintera)
Wittia K. Schum. PERU, PANAMA.
Yungasocereus Ritt. (see Trichocereus)
Zehntnerella Br. & Rose BRAZIL.
Zygocactus K. Schum. BRAZIL.

Agavaceae
Agave L. U.S.A., MEXICO, C. AND S. AMERICA, WEST INDIES.
Beaucarnea Lam. MEXICO.
Beschorneria Knuth. MEXICO.
Calibanus Rose C. AND E. MEXICO.
Dasylirion Zucc. U.S.A. (SOUTHERN STATES), MEXICO.
Furcraea Vent. MEXICO, WEST INDIES.
Hesperaloe (see Liliaceae)
Littaea (Tagl.) Bak. MEXICO, C. AMERICA (sub-genus)

Manfreda (Salisb.) Bak. U.S.A., MEXICO. (sub-genus)
Nolina Machx. (see Beaucarnea)
Samuela Trel. MEXICO, U.S.A. (SOUTHERN STATES).
Sansevieria Thunbg. TROP. AFRICA, INDIA, WEST INDIES, MADAGASCAR, ETC.

Amaryllidaceae
Ammocharis Herb. S. AND S.W. AFRICA, ANGOLA.
Haemanthus L. TROP. AND S. AFRICA.

Anacardiaceae
Pachycormus Coville BAJA CALIFORNIA, MEXICO.

Apocynaceae
Adenium Roem. & Schult. ARABIA, TANZANIA, KENYA, SOCOTRA.
Pachypodium Lindl. S.W. AFRICA, ANGOLA, MADAGASCAR.
Plumiera L. TROP. AMERICA, MEXICO, WEST INDIES.

Araceae
Philodendron Schott. S. AMERICA, WEST INDIES.

Araliaceae
Cussonia Thunbg. MADAGASCAR, TROP. AFRICA

Asclepiadaceae
Asclepias L. S. AND C. AFRICA.
Brachystelma R. Br. S. AFRICA.
Caralluma R. Br. S.W. MEDITERRANEAN REGION, ARABIA, ETHIOPIA, SOCOTRA, INDIA, AND PARTS N.S. AND E. AFRICA.
Ceropegia L. C. AND S. AFRICA, INDIA, MADEIRA, CANARY ISLANDS.
Cynanchum L. C. AND S. AFRICA, MADAGASCAR.
Decabelone Decne. S.W. AFRICA.
Decanema Decne. MADAGASCAR.
Diplocyatha N. E. Br. S. AFRICA.
Dischidia R. Br. INDIA, AUSTRALIA, PHILIPPINES.
Drakebrockmania White & Sloane SOMALI.
Duvalia Haw. S. AND S.W. AFRICA.
Echidnopsis Hook. C. AND S. AFRICA, ARABIA, SOCOTRA.
Edithcolea N. E. Br. KENYA, SOCOTRA, SOMALI, TANZANIA.
Fockea Endl. KAROO DESERTS TO ANGOLA.
Folotsia Cost. & Bois. MADAGASCAR
Frerea Dalzell E. INDIA (see Caralluma)
Hoodia Sweet S. AND S.W. AFRICA, ANGOLA.
Hoodiopsis Luckh. S.W. AFRICA.
Hoya R. Br. MALAYASIA, CHINA, INDIA, AUSTRALIA.
Huernia R. Br. S. AND E. AFRICA, ETHIOPIA, ARABIA.
Huerniopsis N. E. Br. S. AND S.W. AFRICA.
Karimbolea Descoings. S. AFRICA.

Kinepetalum Schltr. S. AFRICA.
Lithocaulon Bally E. AFRICA. (see Pseudolithos)
Luckhoffia White & Sloane S. AFRICA.
Pectinaria Haw. S. AFRICA.
Piaranthus R. Br. S. AND S.W. AFRICA.
Pseudolithos (Bally) Bally SOMALI.
Pseudopectinaria Laur. SOMALIA
Quaqua N. E. Br. S. AFRICA. (see Caralluma)
Raphionacme Harv. E. AFRICA.
Rhodiola. C. and S. EUROPE
Rhytidocaulon Bally E. AFRICA.
Sarcostemma R. Br. TROP. ASIA AND AFRICA,
 S.W. AFRICA, AUSTRALIA.
Siphonostelma Schltr. S. AFRICA.
Stapelia L. TROP., S. AND S.W. AFRICA, KENYA,
 TANZANIA, INDIA.
Stapelianthus Choux. MADAGASCAR.
Stapeliopsis Pillans S. AFRICA.
Stultitia Phillips S. AFRICA.
Tavaresia Welw. C., S. AND S.W. AFRICA.
 (see Decabelone)
Trichocaulon N. E. Br. S. AND S.W. AFRICA, MADAGASCAR,
 SOMALI.
Whitesloanea Chiov. SOMALIA.

Balsaminaceae
Impatiens L. MALAYSIA.

Basellaceae
Ullucus Calas PERU, CHILE.

Batidaceae
Batis L. U.S.A.

Begoniaceae
Begonia L. BRAZIL, MEXICO.

Bombacaceae
Adansonia L. MADAGASCAR, S.W. AFRICA, AUSTRALIA.
Bombax L. MEXICO.
Cavanillesia Ruiz. & Pav. E. BRAZIL.
Chorisia H.B. & K. S. AMERICA, WEST INDIES.

Bromeliaceae
Abromeitiella Mez. ARGENTINA, BOLIVIA.
Bromelia L. WEST INDIES, MEXICO, S. AMERICA.
Dyckia Schult. S. AMERICA.
Hechtia Klotzsch. MEXICO, U.S.A.
Puya Mol. CHILE, ARGENTINA, COLOMBIA.

Burseraceae
Bursera Jacq. MEXICO, U.S.A.
Commiphora Jacq. S.W. AFRICA.

Campanulaceae
Brighamia A. Gray HAWAII
Campanula L. MADEIRA, CANARY ISLANDS.
Lobelia L. ETHIOPIA.

Chenopodiaceae
Allenrolfia O. Ktze. U.S.A., ARGENTINA
Arhtrocnemum Moq. INDIA, TROP. AFRICA.
Microcnemum Ung.-Sternb. SPAIN
Pachycornia Hook. f. AUSTRALIA
Salicornia L. S. EUROPE, N. AND S.W. AFRICA
Salsola L. S. EUROPE, AUSTRALIA, C. ASIA ETC.
Suaeda Dumort COASTAL REGIONS, EUROPE, AMERICA,
 S. AFRICA, CANARY ISLANDS, MADEIRA.

Commelinaceae
Cyanotis D. Don. ASIA, TROP. AFRICA
Tradescantia L. N. PERU.
Tripogandra Raff. GUATEMALA

Compositae
Baeriopsis J. T. Howell GUADALUPE
Cacalia Cass. (see Senecio, Othonna)
Coreopsis L. U.S.A. (CALIFORNIA).
Coulterella Vasey and Rose BAJA CALIFORNIA
Espeletia Mutis ex Humb. & Bonpl. PLATEAUX OF ANDES,
 VENEZUELA TO COLOMBIA.
Gynura Cass. KENYA AND TANZANIA.
Hertia Less. TUNISIA.
Kleinia L. (see Senecio)
Notonia DC. (see Senecio)
Othonna L. S. AND S.W. AFRICA.
Pteronia L. S. AND S.W. AFRICA.
Senecio (Tourn.) L. N. AND S. AFRICA, MALAYSIA,
 MEXICO, MADAGASCAR, CANARY ISLANDS, ETC.

Convolvulaceae
Ipomoea L. S. AND S.W. AFRICA.
Merremia Dennst. S. AND S.W. AFRICA, E. AFRICA.
Turbina Raff. E. AFRICA, S. AFRICA.

Crassulaceae
Adromischus Lem. S. AND S.W. AFRICA.
Aeonium Webb. & Berth. CANARY ISLANDS, MADEIRA,
 N. AFRICA.
Afrovivella Bgr. ETHIOPIA.
Aichryson Webb. & Berth. CANARY ISLANDS, MADEIRA,
 AZORES.
Bryophyllum Salisb. (see Kalanchoë)
Chiastophyllum (Ledeb.) Stapf. CAUCASUS.
Cotyledon L. ARABIA, ETHIOPIA, E.S. AND S.W. AFRICA.
Crassula L. S. AND TROPICAL AFRICA, MEDITERRANEAN
 COASTS, ETC.

Dasystemon DC. S. AFRICA. (see Crassula)
Diamorpha Nutt. U.S.A.
Diopogon (see Jovibarba)
Dinacria Harv. S. AFRICA.
Dudleya Br. & Rose S.W. STATES OF U.S.A.,
   BAJA CALIFORNIA AND SONORA, MEXICO.
Echeveria DC. MEXICO, TEXAS, U.S.A., C. AMERICA, ETC.
Gormania Britt. W. AND N. AMERICA (see Sedum).
Graptopetalum Rose MEXICO, U.S.A. (ARIZONA).
Greenovia Webb. & Berth. CANARY ISLANDS.
Hypagophytum Bgr. ETHIOPIA.
Jovibarba Opiz. EASTERN ALPS, BALKANS, ETC.
Kalanchoë Adans. S. AND S.W. AFRICA, TROP. W. AFRICA,
   INDIA, MADAGASCAR, MALAYSIA, TROP. AMERICA,
   WEST INDIES.
Kitchingia Bak. (see Kalanchoe)
Lenophyllum Rose MEXICO, U.S.A. (SOUTH).
Meterostachys Nakai JAPAN, KOREA.
Monanthes Haw. CANARY ISLANDS, MADEIRA.
Mucizonia (DC) Bgr. C. AND S. SPAIN,
   CANARY ISLANDS, MOROCCO.
Oliveranthus Rose (see Echeveria)
Orostachys Fischer N. ASIA, JAPAN, KOREA.
Pachyphytum Link, Klotzsch. & Otto MEXICO.
Pagella Schoenl. S. AFRICA.
Pistorinia DC. IBERIAN PENINSULA, N. AFRICA.
Pseudosedum (Bois.) Bgr. C. ASIA.
Rhodiola L. NORTH EUROPE TO ARCTIC
Rochea DC. S. AFRICA.
Rosularia (DC.) Stapf. ASIA MINOR, CAUCASUS,
   HIMALAYAS.
Sedum L. N. EUROPE, GT. BRITAIN, C. AFRICA,
   MADAGASCAR, PERU, BOLIVIA, MEXICO, N. AMERICA,
   E. ASIA, MEDITERRANEAN AREA.
Sempervivella Stapf. HIMALAYAS.
Sempervivum L. C. AND S. EUROPE, CAUCASUS TO U.S.S.R.,
   ASIA MINOR, N. AFRICA.
Sinocrassula Bgr. HIMALAYAS, CHINA.
Thompsonella Br. & R. MEXICO.
Umbilicus DC. S. EUROPE, W. ASIA, CANARY ISLANDS,
   W. AND E. AFRICA, EGYPT.
Urbinia Br. & R. (see Echeveria)
Vauanthes Haw. S. AFRICA.
Villadia Haw. MEXICO, PERU, GUATEMALA.

Cruciferae

Cucurbitaceae
Acanthosicyos Welw. S.W. AFRICA.
Alsomitra Roem. TROP. AFRICA.
Anisosperma Manso. BRAZIL
Apodanthera Arn. U.S.A., MEXICO
Cephalopentandra Chiov. ETHIOPIA.

Ceratosanthes Burm. S. AMERICA, W. INDIES
Corallocarpus Hook. ARABIA, S. AFRICA, E. AFRICA,
   MADAGASCAR
Cucurbita L. U.S.A., MEXICO.
Dendrosicyos Balf. SOCOTRA.
Echinocystis Torr. & Gray U.S.A., MEXICO.
Gerrardanthus Harv. KENYA AND TANZANIA.
Ibervillea Greene MEXICO.
Kedostris Medic. E. AND S. AFRICA.
Melothria L. S. AND E. AFRICA, MADAGASCAR.
Momordica L. KENYA AND TANZANIA.
Neoalsomitra Hutchins. PHILIPPINES, BURMA,
   THAILAND.
Pisosperma Sond. E. AFRICA, S. AFRICA
Seyrigia Kerauda. MADAGASCAR.
Telfairia Hook. W. AFRICA, S. AND E. AFRICA,
   MADAGASCAR.
Trochomeria Hook. TROP. AND S. AFRICA.
Trochomeriopsis Cogn. TROP. AFRICA.
Tumamoca Rose U.S.A. (ARIZONA).
Xerosicyos Humbert MADAGASCAR.
Zehneria Endl. S. AFRICA

Didiereaceae
Alluaudia Drake S.W. MADAGASCAR.
Alluaudianopsis H. Humb. & P. Choux MADAGASCAR.
Decaryia Choux MADAGASCAR.
Didierea H. Baill. MADAGASCAR.

Dioscoreaceae
Dioscorea L. S. AFRICA, MEXICO.
Testudinaria Salisb. S. AFRICA.

Euphorbiaceae
Dactylanthes Haw. (see Euphorbia)
Elaeophorbia O. Stapf. W. TROP. AFRICA, ANGOLA,
   SIERRE LEONE.
Euphorbia L. AFRICA, CANARY ISLANDS, CEYLON,
   MEXICO, BRAZIL, ETC.
Jatropha L. TROP. AFRICA, MADAGASCAR,
   TROP. C. AND S. AMERICA, WEST INDIES, ETC.
Monadenium Pax. E. AND S. TROP. AFRICA, ETHIOPIA,
   KENYA, RHODESIA.
Pedilanthus Neck. WEST INDIES, BAJA CALIFORNIA,
   MEXICO.
Stenadenium Pax. TANZANIA. (see Monadenium)
Synadenium Boiss. E. AFRICA.

Fouquieraceae
Fouquiera H.B. & K. MEXICO, S. CALIFORNIA, U.S.A.
Idria Kellog BAJA CALIFORNIA.

Geraniaceae
Pelargonium L'Her. S. AND S.W. AFRICA, MADAGASCAR.
Sarcocaulon (DC.) Sweet. S. AND S.W. AFRICA.

Gesneriaceae
Rechsteineria Hoehne BRAZIL.
Streptocarpus Lindl. TROP. AFRICA

Gnetaceae
Welwitschia Hook. S.W. AFRICA.

Icacinaceae
Pyrenacantha Wight. E. AFRICA.
Trematosperma Urb. SOMALI.

Labiatae
Aeolanthus Mart. TROP. AFRICA
Coleus Lour. ARABIA, TROP. AFRICA, E. INDIA,
    MALAYSIA, MADAGASCAR.
Plectranthus L'Her. E. AFRICA.

Leguminosae
Dolichos L. S.W. AFRICA.
Neorautenenia Schinz. S. AFRICA

Liliaceae
Aloe L. N. TO S. AFRICA INCL. KENYA, ETHIOPIA,
    TANZANIA, ETC., MADAGASCAR, ETC.
Aprica Wills. (see Haworthia)
Astroloba Uitew. S. AFRICA.
Bowiea Harv. ex. Hook. E. AND S. AFRICA.
Bulbine L. S. AFRICA, E. AUSTRALIA.
Bulbinopsis Borzi. E. AUSTRALIA
Chamaealoe Bgr. S. AFRICA.
Chortolirion Bgr. S. AND S.W. AFRICA.
Drimia Jacq. S. AFRICA.
Gasteria Duval. S. AND S.W. AFRICA.
Guillauminia A. Bertrand MADAGASCAR.
Haworthia Duval. S. AND S.W. AFRICA.
Hesperaloe Engelm. MEXICO, U.S.A. (TEXAS).
Litanthus Harvey S. AFRICA.
Lomatophyllum Willd. MADAGASCAR, MAURITIUS.
Poellnitzia Uitew. S. AFRICA.
Scilla L. S. AFRICA, MEDITERRANEAN REGIONS.
Xanthorrhoea Sm. AUSTRALIA.
Yucca L. MEXICO, U.S.A.

Melastomataceae
Monolena Triana. COLOMBIA.

Menispermaceae
Stephania Lour. TROP. W. AFRICA, ANGOLA, CONGO, ETC.

Molluginaceae
Hypertelis E. Mey. ex Fenzl. S. AFRICA, S.W. AFRICA.

Moraceae
Dorstenia Plum. KENYA, SOCOTRA.
Ficus L. BAJA CALIFORNIA, SONORA, MEXICO.

Moringaceae
Moringa Burm. S.W. AFRICA.

Oxalidaceae
Oxalis L. S. AMERICA.

Passifloraceae
Adenia Forsk. E. AFRICA, SOMALI, S.W. AFRICA,
    MADAGASCAR.
Modecca Lam. (see Adenia)

Pedaliaceae
Harpagophytum CD. ex Meissn. S. AFRICA.
Holubia Oliv. S. AFRICA
Pedaliodiscus Ihlenf. E. AFRICA.
Pedalium Royen KENYA, TANZANIA, ETHIOPIA,
    SOCOTRA, MADAGASCAR, ETC.
Pterodiscus Hook. SOMALI, KENYA, SUDAN,
    S. AND S.W. AFRICA.
Sesamothamnus Welw. KENYA, S.W. AFRICA,
    C. AND TROP. AFRICA.
Rogeria J. Gay ex Delice TROP. AFRICA, S.W. AFRICA
Uncarina Stapf. MADAGASCAR

Phytolaccaceae
Phytolacca L. S. AMERICA.

Piperaceae
Peperomia Ruiz. & Pav. WEST INDIES, S. AMERICA,
    MADAGASCAR, ETC.

Portulacaceae
Anacampseros L. C. AND S.W. AFRICA, KENYA,
    TANZANIA, S. AUSTRALIA.
Calandrinia H.B. & K. AUSTRALIA, U.S.A. TO CHILE.
Ceraria Pears. & E. L. Stephens S. AND S.W. AFRICA.
Lewisia Pursh. WESTERN U.S.A., C. AMERICA, BOLIVIA.
Portulaca L. S. AFRICA, S. AMERICA, AUSTRALIA,
    WEST INDIES.
Portulacaria Jacq. S. AFRICA.
Talinopsis A. Gray MEXICO, SOUTHERN U.S.A.
Talinum Adans. S.W. AFRICA, MEXICO, WEST INDIES.

Rubiaceae
Hydnophytum Jacq. NEW GUINEA.
Myrmecodia Jack. MALAYSIA, AUSTRALIA.

Scrophulariaceae
Castilleva Mutis ex L.f. MEXICO, GUADELUPE IS.
Chamaegigas Dtr. S.W. AFRICA.
Dermatobotrys H. Bolus S. AFRICA.

Umbelliferae
Crithmum L. MADEIRA, CANARY ISLANDS,
    MEDITERRANEAN COASTS OF SPAIN AND PORTUGAL.

Urticaceae
Pilea Lindl. PERU.

Violaceae
Hymenanthera R. Br. NEW ZEALAND, AUSTRALIA.

Vitaceae
Cissus D.C. S. AND S.W. AFRICA, TROP. AFRICA, MEXICO.
Cyphostemma B. Desc. MADAGASCAR.

Zygophyllaceae
Augea Thunbg. S. AND S.W. AFRICA.
Zygophyllum L. CANARY ISLANDS.

Ficoidaceae–Aizoaceae
Ficoidaceae has been superseded by Mesembryanthemum. Aizoaceae is partially retained and currently only the genera Aizoanthemum and Sesuvium are included.

For the purposes of this directory all are listed under Mesembryanthemum.

Mesembryanthemum L.
All genera are indigenous to Africa–from Egypt, Algeria, Arabia–Ethiopia and N.E. Africa generally–Rhodesia and tropical West Africa, to S.W. Africa, throughout South Africa including mainly Cape Province, Orange Free State and Transvaal. Only three genera are recorded elsewhere–in Australia, Tasmania, New Zealand, St Helena and Chile. Some species are to be found in other areas, but these have been transported and become naturalized.
Abbreviations:
CP (Cape Province). TR. (Transvaal). OFS (Orange Free State). SWA (South West Africa). SA (South Africa).

Abryanthemum Necker (see Carpobrotus)
Acaulon N. E. Br. (see Aloinopsis)
Acrodon N. E. Br. CP.
Aethephyllum N. E. Br. CP.
Agnirictus Schwant. (see Stomatium)
Aistocaulon v. Poelln. (see Aloinopsis)
Aizoanthemum Dtr. ex Friedr. S.W.A. ANGOLA
Aloinopsis Schwant. CP.
Amoebophyllum N. E. Br. CP. SWA.
Amphibolia L. Bol. CP.
Anisocalyx L. Bol. CP.
Antegibbaeum Schwant. CP.
Antimima N. E. Br. (see Ruschia)
Apatesia N. E. Br. CP.
Aptenia N. E. Br. SA. (arid coastal areas)
Arenifera Herre CP. SWA.
Argeta N. E. Br. (see Gibbaeum)
Argyroderma N. E. Br. CP.
Aridaria N. E. Br. (see Nycteranthus)
Aspazoma N. E. Br. CP.
Astridia Dtr. & Schwant. SWA. CP.
Bergeranthus Schwant. CP.
Berrisfordia L. Bol. CP.
Bijlia N. E. Br. CP.
Bolusanthemum Schwant. (see Hereroa)
Braunsia Schwant. (see Ruschia and Echinus)
Brownanthus Schwant. CP. SWA.
Calamophyllum Schwant. SA.
Callistigma Dtr. & Schwant. SWA.
Carpanthea N. E. Br. CP.
Carpobrotus N. E. Br. CP. (also Australia, Tasmania and Chile)
Carruanthus Schwant. CP.
Caryotophora Leistn. SA.
Cephalophyllum (Haw) N. E. Br. CP. SWA.
Cerochlamys N. E. Br. CP.
Chasmatophyllum Dtr. & Schwant. CP. SWA. OFS.
Cheiridopsis N. E. Br. CP. SWA.
Circandra N. E. Br. (see Erepsia)
Cleretum N. E. Br. (see Dorotheanthus)
Conicosia N. E. Br. CP.
Conophyllum Schwant. CP.
Conophytum N. E. Br. CP. SWA.
Corpuscularia Schwant. (see Ruschia & Delosperma)
Crocanthus L. Bol. (see Malephora)
Cryophytum N. E. Br. (see Mesembryanthemum, Micropterum & Eurystigma)
Cylindrophyllum Schwant. CP.
Dactylopsis N. E. Br. CP.
Deilanthe N. E. Br. (see Aloinopsis)
Delosperma N. E. Br. Ethiopia. CP. TR. OFS. Rhodesia. N.E. Africa.
Depacarpus N. E. Br. (see Meyerophytum)

Derenbergia Schwant. (see Conophytum, Gibbaeum, Ophthalmophyllum)
Derenbergiella Schwant. (see Mesembryanthemum)
Dicrocaulon N. E. Br. CP.
Didymaotus N. E. Br. CP.
Dinteranthus Schwant. SWA. CP.
Diplosoma Schwant. CP.
Disphyma N. E. Br. CP. (also Australia, New Zealand, Tasmania)
Dorotheanthus Schwant. CP.
Dracophilus Dtr. & Schwant. SWA. CP.
Drosanthemum Schwant. CP. SWA.
Eberlanzia Schwant. CP. SWA.
Ebracteola Dtr. & Schwant. SWA.
Echinus L. Bol. CP.
Ectotropis N. E. Br. CP.
Enarganthe N. E. Br. CP.
Erepsia N. E. Br. CP.
Esterhuysenia L. Bol. CP.
Eurystigma L. Bol. CP.
Faucaria Schwant. CP.
Fenestraria N. E. Br. SWA. CP.
Frithia N. E. Br. TR.
Gibbaeum Haw. CP.
Glottiphyllum Haw. CP.
Gymnopoma N. E. Br. (see Skiatophytum)
Halenbergia Dtr. SWA.
Henricia L. Bol. (see Neohenricia)
Hereroa Dtr. & Schwant. SWA. CP.
Herrea Schwant. CP.
Herreanthus Schwant. CP.
Hydrodea N. E. Br. SWA. St Helena.
Hymenocyclus Dtr. & Schwant. (see Malephora)
Hymenogyne (Haw.) N. E. Br. CP.
Imitaria N. E. Br. CP.
Jacobsenia L. Bol. & Schwant. CP.
Jensenobotrya Herre SWA.
Juttadinteria Schwant. SWA. CP.
Kensitia Fedde CP.
Khadia N. E. Br. TR.
Lampranthus N. E. Br. CP.
Lapidaria Schwant. SWA.
Leipoldtia L. Bol. CP. SWA.
Lithops N. E. Br. CP. SWA. TR.
Litocarpus L. Bol. (see Aptenia)
Machairophyllum L. Bol. CP.
Macrocaulon N. E. Br. (see Carpanthea)
Malephora N. E. Br. SWA. CP. OFS.
Marlothistell Schwant. CP (see Ruschia).
Maughania N. E. Br. CP.
Maughaniella L. Bol. CP.
Mentocalyx N. E. Br. (see Gibbaeum)
Mesembryanthemum L. emend L. Bol. CP. SWA.

Mestoklema N. E. Br. CP.
Meyerophytum Schwant. CP.
Micropterum Schwant. CP.
Mimetophytum L. Bol. CP.
Mitrophyllum Schwant. CP.
Monilaria Schwant. CP.
Mossia N. E. Br. TR.
Muiria N. E. Br. CP.
Muirio-Gibbaeum Jacobs. CP.
Namaquanthus L. Bol. CP.
Namibia Dtr. & Schwant. SWA.
Nananthus N. E. Br. CP. TR. OFS.
Nelia Schwant. CP.
Neoaridaria Schwant. (sub-genus, see Nycteranthus)
Neohenricia L. Bol. OFS.
Neorhine Schwant. CP.
Nycteranthus Necker CP. SWA.
Octopoma N. E. Br. CP.
Odontophorus N. E. Br. CP.
Oophytum N. E. Br. CP.
Ophthalmophyllum Dtr. & Schwant. CP. SWA.
Opophytum N. E. Br. Algeria, Egypt, Arabia, trop. W. Africa, CP.
Orthopterum L. Bol. CP.
Oscularia Schwant. CP.
Ottosonderia L. Bol. CP.
Peersia L. Bol. (see Rhinephyllum)
Pentacoilanthus Rappa & Camarrone (see Mesembryanthemum, Psilocaulon, Nycteranthus)
Perissolobus N. E. Br. (see Machairophyllum)
Pherolobus N. E. Br. CP.
Phyllobolus N. E. Br. CP.
Piquetia N. E. Br. (see Kensitia)
Platythyra N. E. Br. CP.
Pleiospilos N. E. Br. CP.
Polymita L. Bol. CP.
Prenia N. E. Br. CP.
Prepodesma N. E. Br. (see Aloinopsis, Hereroa)
Psammophora Dtr. & Schwant. CP. SWA.
Psilocaulon N. E. Br. CP. SWA.
Punctillaria N. E. Br. (see Pleiospilos)
Rabiea N. E. Br. CP. OFS.
Rhinephyllum N. E. Br. CP.
Rhombophyllum Schwant. CP.
Rhopalocyclus Schwant. (see Leipoldtia)
Rimaria N. E. Br. (see Vanheerdia)
Roodia N. E. Br. (see Argyroderma)
Ruschia Schwant. CP. SWA.
Ruschianthemum Friedr. CP.
Ruschianthus L. Bol. SWA.
Saphesia N. E. Br. CP.
Sceletium N. E. Br. CP.
Schlechteranthus Schwant. CP.

Schoenlandia L. Bol. (see Delosperma)
Schwantesia Dtr. CP. SWA.
Scopelogena L. Bol. CP.
Semnanthe N. E. Br. CP.
Sesuvium L. E. AFRICA.
Skiatophytum L. Bol. CP.
Smicrostigma N. E. Br. CP.
Sphalmanthus N. E. Br. (see Nycteranthus)
Stayneria L. Bol. CP.
Sterropetalum N. E. Br. (see Nelia)
Stigmatocarpum L. Bol. (see Dorotheanthus)
Stoeberia Dtr. & Schwant. SWA. CP.
Stomatium Schwant. CP. OFS.

Synaptophyllum N. E. Br. SWA.
Tetracoilanthus Rappa & Camarrone (see Aptenia)
Thyrasperma N. E. Br. (see Apatesia)
Tischleria Schwant. CP.
Titanopsis Schwant. CP. SWA.
Trichocyclus N. E. Br. (see Brownanthus)
Trichodiadema Schwant. CP. BFS. Ethiopia.
Vanheerdea L. Bol. CP.
Vanzijlia L. Bol. CP.
Verrucifera N. E. Br. (see Titanopsis)
Wooleya L. Bol. CP.
Zeuktophyllum N. E. Br. CP.

Societies and Publications

Throughout the world there are Societies and Establishments which function for the precise purpose of furthering the interest in cacti and other succulent plants. In most instances periodicals are offered which contain information for the particular benefit of the collector.

The English-speaking world is extremely fortunate in this respect. The bodies listed hereunder accept international membership. Each organization issues its own regular publication and distributes to its respective membership, or by subscription.

National Cactus & Succulent Society
(43 Dewar Drive, Sheffield 7)
Quarterly Journals–subscription £2·00 per annum.

African Succulent Plant Society
(54 Fishponds Rd. Hitchin, Herts SG5 1NS)
Bi-monthly Journals–subscription £1·50 per annum.
This organization specializes principally with succulents other than cacti, particularly those from Africa.

Cactus & Succulent Society of Gt. Britain
(26 Glenfield Road, Banstead, Surrey)
Quarterly Journal–subscription £1·50 per annum.

Holly Gate Reference Collection
(Ashington, Sussex RH20 3BA)
Bi-monthly periodical in full colour–£2·50 per annum.
Providing up-to-date information and photographs of cacti, succulents and bromeliads. 'Ashingtonia'– an excellent colour work.

Mammillaria Society
(26 Glenfield Road, Banstead, Surrey)
Bi-monthly Journal–£1·50 per annum.
Specialist publication for those interested in the genus Mammillaria and kindred genera.

Cactus & Succulent Society of America
(Available through Holly Gate Reference Collection or African Succulent Plant Society)
Bi-monthly Journal–$7·50 per annum.
An excellent publication often with colour.

South African Aloe and Succulent Society
(P.O. Box 1193, Pretoria, South Africa)
Quarterly Journals–subscription details upon enquiry.
An outstanding publication with some colour plates. Non-cacti only.

Aloe, Cactus & Succulent Society of Rhodesia
(P.O. Box 8514, Causeway, Salisbury, Rhodesia)
Annual publication *Excelsa*–subscription details upon enquiry.

'Ashingtonia' (Holly Gate Reference Collection, Ashington, Sussex) Bi-monthly Journal

Backeberg, Curt. 'Die Cactaceae' (6 vols.) Gustav Fischer, Jena (1958–62)

Benson, Lyman. 'Native Cacti of California'. Arizona Press, Tucson (1969)

Benson, Lymon. 'Native Cacti of California', Stanford Univ. Press, Calif. (1969)

Breitung, A. J. 'The Agaves', Cactus & Succ. Soc. America Handbook (1968)

Britton, N. L. & Rose J. N. 'The Cactaceae' (4 vols.) Carnegie Instit. Washington (1923)

Haage, Walther. 'Cacti & Succulents' (Translation) Vista Books (1963)

Jacobsen, Herman. 'Handbook of Succulent Plants', Blandford Press, London (1960)

Journal, Nat. Cactus & Succ. Soc. (vols. 1–28) Quarterly Journal

Journal, Cactus & Succ. Soc. of America (vols. XXXV–XLV) Abbey Garden, Calif. Bi-monthly Journal

Journal, African Succ. Plant Soc. (vols. 1–7) Hitchin, Herts. Bi-monthly Bulletin

Rauh, Prof. Dr. W. 'Bromelien' 2, Ulmer (1973)

Reynolds, G. W. 'Aloes of South Africa', Aloes of S.A. Book Fund (1950)

Reynolds, G. W. 'Aloes of Trop. Africa & Madagascar', Aloes of S.A. Book Fund (1966)

Schwantes, Dr. G. 'Flowering Stones & Midday Flowers', (Trans.) Benn, London (1957)

White, A. C., Dyer R. A., Sloane B. L. 'Succulent Euphorbiae', Abbey Garden Press (1941)

Werdermann, E. 'Brazil & its Columna Cacti', Abbey Garden Press (1942)

Appendix of Authors' names

Principal Authors of Succulent Plant Descriptions

ALEXANDER, E. J.   Alexander

BACKEBERG, Curt   Backeb.
BAEHNI, C.   Baehni
BAILEY, L. H.   L. H. Bailey
BAKER, J. G.   Baker
BALFOUR, Prof. Isaac Bayley   Balf. f.
BALLY, Peter R. O.   Bally
BEAUVERD, Gustave   Beauverd
BENSON, B. W.   B. W. Benson
BENSON, Lyman   L. Benson
BERGER, Alwin   A. Berger
BIGELOW, J.   Bigel
BOEDEKER, F.   Boedeker
BOISSEVAIN, C. H.   Boissev.
BOISSIER, E. P.   Boiss.
BOJER, W.   Bojer
BOLUS, Dr. Louisa   L. Bolus
BRANDEGEE, K.   K. Brandegee
BRAVO, Dr. Helia   H. Bravo
BRITTON, Dr. N. L.   Britton
BROWN, Dr. N. E.   N. E. Brown
BRUCE, E. A.   E. A. Bruce
BUINING, Albert F. H.   Buining
BULLOCK, A. A.   Bullock
BUXBAUM, F.   F. Buxb.
BYLES, R. S.   Byles

CANDOLLE, Aug. de   DC. Aug.
CARDENAS, Dr. Martin H.   Cardenas
CAVANILLES, A. J.   Cav.
CHOUX, P.   Choux
CLAUSEN, R. T.   Clausen
COMPTON, R. H.   Compton
COVILLE, F. V.   Coville
COWPER, Denis   Cowper
CROIZAT, Leon   Croizat
CULLMANN, Dr. W.   Cullm.
CUTAK, Ladislaus   Cutak

DALZELL, N. A.   Dalz.
DANGUY, P.   Danguy
DECKEN, C. C. von der   Decken
DESCOINGS, B.   Descoings
DIELS, E. L. E.   Diels
DON, G.   G. Don
DONALD, John D.   Donald
DRAKE, S. A.   S. A. Drake
DYER, R. A.   R. A. Dyer

ECKLON, Christian F.   Ecklon
EHRENBERG, C. G.   Ehrenb.
EICHLAM, F.   Eichlam
ENGELMANN, George   Engelm.
ENGLER, Dr. A.   Engl.

FÖRSTER, F.   Förster
FOSTER, Robert C.   R. C. Foster
FRIC, A. V.   Fric
FRIES, R. E.   R. E. Fries

GALEOTTI, H. G.   Galeotti

GARDNER, C. A.   C. A. Gardner
GILG, Ernest F.   Gilg
GILLIES, J.   Gillies
GOEBEL, Prof. K. von   Goebel
GRAY, Asa   A. Gray
GRIFFITHS, Dr. D.   Griffiths
GRISEBACH, A.   Griseb.
GUILLAUMIN, A.   Guillaumin
GURKE, Dr. A. R. L. M.   Gurke

HAAGE, F.   Haage
HAMET, Prof. Dr. R.   Hamet
HARMS, H.   Harms
HAWORTH, Adrian H.   Haw.
HILDMANN, H.   Hildm.
HOOKER, Sir Wm.   Hook.
HOPFFER, C.   Hopffer
HORTICULTURAL ITEM   Hort.
HOSSEUS, C. C.   Hosseus
HOWELL, J. T.   Howell
HUMBERT, H.   Humbert
HUMBOLDT, BONPLAND, KNUTH   H.B.K.
HUTCHISON, P. C.   P. C. Hutchison

JACOBSEN, H.   Jacobsen
JOHNSON, H. & Kimnach M.   Johns. & Kimn.
JOHNSTON, J. R.   J. R. Johnston

KARWINSKY, Baron Wilhelm von   Karw.
KESSELRING, W.   Kesslr.
KIMNACH, Myron   Kimnach
KLOTZSCH & OTTO   Klotzsch & Otto
KNUTH, F. M.   F. M. Knuth
KOCH, C.   C. Koch
KRAINZ, H.   Krainz
KRAUSE, K.   K. Krause
KUPPER, W.   Kupp.

LABOURET, J.   Labouret
LAGERHEIM, N. G. von   Lagerheim
LAMARCK, J.   Lam.
LAVRANOS, J.   Lavranos
LAUTERBACH, K.   Lauterb.
LEACH, L.   Leach
LEANDRI, Prof. Dr. J.   Leandri
LEMAIRE, C.   Lemaire
LINDLEY, Dr. J.   Lindl.
LINK, H. F. & OTTO, C. F.   Link & Otto
LINNE, CARL (LINNAEUS)   L.
LODDIGES, C.   Lodd.
LÖFGREN, Dr. A.   Loefgren
LUCKHOFF, Dr. J.   Luckhoff

MARLOTH, Dr. R.   Marloth
MARTIUS, C. F. von   Mart.
MILLER, Philip   Miller
MIQUEL, F.   Miq.
MONVILLE, de   Monv.
MOORE, T.   T. Moore
MORAN, Dr. Reid V.   Moran

ORCUTT, C. R.   Orcutt
OTTO, C. F.   Otto

PFEIFFER, Dr. L.   Pfeiffer
PHILIPPI, R. A.   Phil.
POELLNITZ, Dr. Karl von   Poelln.
POISSON, H.   H. Poisson
POSELGER, H.   Poselger
PURPUS, Dr. J. A.   J. A. Purpus

QUEHL, L.   Quehl

RAUH, Prof. Dr. W.   Rauh
RAUSCH, W.   Rausch
REYNOLDS, George   Reynolds
RITTER, F.   F. Ritter
ROSE, Dr. J. N.   Rose
ROWLEY, Gordon D.   Rowley

SALM-REIFFERSCHEID-DYCK- J.   Salm-Dyck
SCHINZ, H.   Schinz
SCHLECHTER, F. R.   Schlechter
SCHONLAND, S.   Schonl.
SCHUMANN, Prof. Karl   K. Schum
SCHWANTES, Dr. G.   Schwantes
SHURLY, E. W.   Shurly
SMITH, C. A.   C. A. Smith
SMITH, Lyman B.   L. B. Smith
SPEGAZZINI, Dr. Carlo   Speg.
STANDLEY, P. C.   Standley
STAPF, F. M. or O.   Stapf
STEARN, Wm. T.   Stearn
STEIN, B.   Stein
SWARTZ, P.   Swartz

THUNBERG, Carl Peter   Thunb.
TORREY, J.   Torrey
TOUMEY, Prof. J. W.   Toumey
TRELEASE, W.   Trelease
TURPIN, Dr. Francois J. P.   Turpin

UITEWAAL, A. J. A.   Uitew
URBAN, Dr. I.   Urban
URSCH et LEANDRI   Ursch et Leandri

VAUPEL, D.   Vaupel
VELLOSO, J. M. de C.   Vell.
VERDOORN, I. C.   Verdoorn

WALTHER, E.   E. Walther
WALTON, F. A.   Walton
WATSON, S.   S. Watson
WEBER, A.   A. Weber
WEINGART, W.   Weingart
WELWITSCH, F.   Welw.
WENIGER, H. L.   Weniger
WERDERMANN, E.   Werderm.
WHITE and SLOANE   White & Sloane
WIGHT and ARN   Wight & Arn
WILLDENOW, C. L. von   Willd.
WRIGHT, C.   C. Wright

ZUCCARINI, J. G.   Zucc.

Index